WHAT YOU FEEL IS NOT ALL THERE IS

free your choices and your life from
the default world of the emotional matrix

DR. APRILIA WEST

EN
MASSE
MEDIA

Praise for *What You Feel Is Not All There Is*

'This compelling and potent book not only illuminates exactly how emotions shape your choices for better and for worse, it also helps you tap the power of infinite games to play your way to being the best version of yourself in any moment. Dr. West takes the reader through a state-of-the-art evidence-based skills training to harness choice points by decoding emotions, overriding unhelpful defaults, rewiring unhelpful patterns and making values-based moves – even in the face of intense stress, challenge, and pain. Reflections and experiential learning opportunities throughout the book help you lock in the learning and level up. By increasing your emotional efficacy you'll learn to become the hero of your own story, transforming what's possible for you and the future you're living into.'

Jane McGonigal, PhD, #1NYT bestselling author of *SuperBetter, Reality Is Broken* and *Imaginable*, and Director of Games Research & Development at the Institute for the Future

'On a foundation of scientific evidence, Dr. Aprilia West delivers an engaging, practical, and powerful skills training based on a transformative idea: when people break the trance of emotional reactivity they become more resilient, psychologically flexible, and emotionally intelligent. This is an extremely well-considered, conceptualized, and accessible book. Highly recommended.'

Rick Hanson, PhD, NYT bestselling author of *Resilient* and *Buddha's Brain*

'Dr. West offers a brief, structured, highly practical emotion efficacy skills training, integrating the latest evidence-based practices of mindfulness, acceptance, and emotion-processing strategies in a masterful way. The examples, reflections, and client dialogues really make the concepts come alive. And the experiential practice will help people learn and retain these important skills for wellbeing and performance. This book is a must-read for anyone who wants a more powerful relationship with their emotions.'

Kirk Strosahl, PhD, cofounder of Acceptance and Commitment Therapy (ACT) and co-author, *Brief Interventions for Radical Change*

'Dr. West begins her book, *What You Feel Is Not All There Is*, with truly essential words: your life as moments of choice. The beauty of her work and dedication to making healthy change for all who explore this book unfolds from its opening. The reader is invited to take a journey of purpose, guided by providing fundamental elements for living well. The skills include tuning into the moment, cultivating curiosity, leaning into discomfort, and connecting to values – creating vitality. This is a must-read book for those wishing to find in every moment a choice linked to meaning. *What You Feel Is Not All There Is* will be a permanent fixture in my office and a wholly recommended book for clients and friends. Thank you, April, for writing this beautiful work to help others heal.'

Robyn D. Walser, PhD, licensed clinical psychologist and author of the *Heart of ACT*, co-author of the *Mindful Couple: How acceptance and mindfulness can lead you to the love you want, Learning ACT II*, and *ACT for Moral Injury*

'Regardless of whether you are well-versed in writings on emotional intelligence and agility, mindfulness, and coping with stress and adversity, you must understand how enjoyable and useful this book is. Aprilia isn't like other folks. She has a gift for illuminating complex evidence-based ideas through memorable examples and stories. She offers powerful questions and experiential exercises that will enhance your life. If everyone wrote with this level of clarity and poignancy the world would be a healthier place.'

Todd B. Kashdan, PhD, professor of psychology, director of the Well-being Lab at George Mason University, and author of *The Art of Insubordination: How to dissent and defy effectively*

'In *What You Feel Is Not All There Is*, Dr. Aprilia West offers a stimulating guide for how readers can achieve meaningful engagement in every aspect of our lives, simply by mastering our relationship with our emotions. In doing so, Dr. West brings to bear her expertise as a psychologist, a coach, and a consultant to make the most impactful technologies of several empirically-based behavioral treatments available in a series of straightforward lessons and powerful exercises. The "Learnings" and "Challenges" at the end of each chapter make the text easy to use as a reference, and even the most psychologically savvy reader will find themselves returning to the text to cultivate improved emotional efficacy. By the end of the book, what becomes possible is approaching life as a series of new and potentially valued choices, by playing "infinite games" in any moment.'

Emily K. Sandoz, PhD, Endowed Professor of Social Sciences, and director of the Louisiana Contextual Science Research Group at University of Louisiana at Lafayette

'Maladaptive default patterns are at the root of unnecessary emotional suffering. The powerful, research-based program in *What You Feel Is Not All There Is* offers psychoeducation and experiential training to help people learn to override unhelpful defaults using powerful skills, including: emotion acceptance, distress tolerance, emotion regulation, and values-based choices. Dr. West's book will help readers optimize their moments of choice to embrace what really matters. This is a book that will change lives.'

Matthew McKay, PhD, co-author of *ACT for Interpersonal Problems* and *The Dialectical Behavior Therapy Skills Workbook*

'Everything you ever wanted and needed to know about emotions and how to handle them like a boss is in this book. Rich metaphors, personal examples, and case studies bring the material to life in a compelling and easy-to-digest format. A great resource for anyone who wants to powerfully navigate their emotional life.'

Jill Stoddard, PhD, author of *Be Mighty* and *The Big Book of ACT Metaphors*, co-host of the Psychologists Off The Clock podcast

'This delightful and brilliant book is guaranteed to make you RETHINK what you know about emotions, your choices, and what's possible for your life. While we all tend to trust our gut and let feelings dictate our behavior, this instinct interferes with the essential "choice point" – that poignant moment where we can pause and align our actions with our deeper values. With her signature playfulness and eloquence, Dr. West artfully weaves together storytelling, examples, and evidence-based skills into a highly accessible format to help us unplug from unhelpful default reactions and bravely stretch for the best possible version of ourselves.'

Victoria Lemle Beckner, PhD, Associate Clinical Professor, University of California at San Francisco, and co-author of *Conquering Post-Traumatic Stress Disorder*

'In this indispensable guide on authentically choosing your emotional adventures, Dr. West distills decades of clinical experience into a compendium filled with wisdom. Using step-by-step experiential practices, you can move toward your innermost interests, desires, and yearnings in order to step fully into your power, freedom, hope, and selfhood. This book will be a treasured volume in my personal and professional library.'

Mavis Tsai, PhD, cofounder of Functional Analytic Psychotherapy, Research Scientist and Clinical Faculty, University of Washington

'Dr. Aprilia West writes in a way that seamlessly blends pop culture and evidence-based practice. She provides entertaining and informative case examples, applied exercises, and experiential scripts. In *What You Feel Is Not All There Is*, Dr. West guides readers on a journey that helps nurture flexible relationships with their emotions, empowering them to act upon what matters most. This book provides a trove of practical tips for regulation and resilience building; I highly recommend it.'

Amy R. Murrell, PhD, Affiliate Faculty, University of Memphis and author of the Becca Epps Series on Bending Your Thoughts, Feelings, and Behaviors

'In *What You Feel Is Not All There Is*, psychologist and executive coach Dr. Aprilia West delivers a pragmatic and powerful guide to helping people demystify emotional life and disrupt unhelpful behavior patterns to increase meaning, wellbeing, and performance. This book is not only essential reading for the general public, but also for behavior analysts, therapists, and health professionals who want to use evidence-based skills to optimize the choices they make, moment to moment.'

Luisa Canon, PsyD., BCBA-D, adjunct professor, University of Reno, Nevada

'This is the book for anyone who wants to better understand the relationship between their emotions, peak performance, and wellbeing. As a psychologist and executive coach, I've seen how emotional reactivity is often the reason people end up living smaller, less meaningful and more painful lives. This unfamiliar relationship with our emotional experience creates errors in the decision-making code and can lock people into rigid patterns of behavior which can destroy meaning and joy. In *What You Feel Is Not All There Is*, Aprilia West weaves together cutting-edge research with vivid examples and storytelling to help readers learn powerful skills to override unhelpful default patterns and to stretch for what's possible, even in the face of stress and distress.'

Rob Archer, PhD, Director, Cognacity and founder, The Career Psychologist

'This is the book that all of us – especially leaders – need to navigate the current and uncertain environment we all live in. Emotional efficacy training is a genuinely useful approach for developing a wise relationship with emotions and designing a more rich and meaningful life. In *What You Feel Is Not All There Is*, Dr. Aprilia West has made the training accessible for everyone by combining empirical research with compelling real-life examples and experiential practice, all delivered with her trademark warmth, humor, and honesty. Relevant, smart, and fun. Highly recommended.'

Rachel Collis, Executive Coach and author of *Applying ACT to Workplace Coaching*, Sessional Academic, Graduate School of Business, Queensland University of Technology, Brisbane, Australia

'Dr. West has compiled a practical guide for consumers who are trapped in ineffective coping patterns as a result of difficulties regulating their emotions. The many skills outlined here offer a framework of "choice points" to develop successful strategies for responding to environmental stressors and emotional triggers and promote values-based living.'

Rochelle I. Frank, PhD, Assistant Clinical Professor, University of California, Berkeley and co-author of *The Transdiagnostic Road Map to Case Formulation and Treatment Planning*

*This book is first dedicated to my 'fairy' goddaughters,
Estella and Marissa. I love you both madly.
May you use your powers for good and have fun.
This book is also dedicated to all my clients
with whom I've had the privilege of partnering
and ultimately discovering what's possible when
we are grounded in our power and
authentically connected to what matters most.*

Project management and text design by Publish Central
Cover design by Sej Saraiya and Aprilia West
Edited by Michael Hanrahan and Julia Furr

Disclaimer:

While the author has made every effort to provide accurate contact information at the time of publication, neither the publisher nor the author assumes any responsibility for errors or for changes that occur after publication.

The material in this publication is of the nature of general comment only, and does not represent professional advice. It is not intended to provide specific guidance for particular circumstances and it should not be relied on as the basis for any decision to take action or not take action on any matter which it covers. Readers should obtain professional advice where appropriate, before making any such decision. To the maximum extent permitted by law, the author and publisher disclaim all responsibility and liability to any person, arising directly or indirectly from any person taking or not taking action based on the information in this publication.

The guidance in this book is not a substitute for medical advice or treatment.

CONTENTS

ACKNOWLEDGMENTS

When someone translates research into application, it only happens by standing on the shoulders of the people who did the work of gathering the data and disseminating it. While I have conducted original research on the emotional efficacy protocol skills in this book, creating and testing that protocol was only possible through years of peer-reviewed research from contextual behavioral science (aka third wave cognitive behavioral research) by many brilliant colleagues who came before me. All this work provides the foundation for emotional efficacy training, which underlies the theory and skills adaptation in this book.

While I could fill pages and pages with acknowledgements, I'd especially like to appreciate several colleagues whose work has enriched my personal and professional life and my work: Todd Kashdan, PhD for his research related to Psychological Flexibility, Wellbeing, and Curiosity; Rick Hanson, PhD for his work translating research around neuroplasticity and emotion; Steven C. Hayes, PhD, Kelly Wilson, PhD, and Kirk Strosahl, PhD who first conceptualized psychological flexibility processes and behavioral applications through Acceptance and Commitment Therapy (ACT); Daniel Kahneman, PhD for his robust and prolific work on the impact of bias in experience and decision-making; Tara Brach, PhD for her leadership, skill, embodiment, and dissemination of heart-centered, compassionate practice; Michelle Craske, PhD for her research related to Exposure Therapy, which critically and significantly informs learning theory; and, Marsha Linehan, PhD for the powerful and practical applications of Dialectical Behavioral Therapy (DBT) for people struggling with self-harm behaviors and emotion dysregulation.

I am also eternally grateful to my grad school mentor, colleague, and friend Matthew McKay, PhD for his support and encouragement toward the development of both the construct of emotional efficacy and the original Emotion Efficacy Therapy (EET) protocol.

I could not have written this book without the help of several people who consistently encouraged and supported me. First, I'm grateful to my sister, Julie Furr – without her support this book would not have found its way into the world. Writing a book during a pandemic seemed like an obvious choice, and yet, it created its own unique challenges that I couldn't have navigated without her emotional support and expert editing. Also, to my colleague and coach extraordinaire, Rachel Collis, for her generous feedback throughout, and her willingness to push me to create the best possible version of this work.

To several brilliant friends and colleagues for all of their helpful feedback and continuous encouragement: Luisa Canon, PsyD, BCBA-D, Victoria Beckner, PhD, Robyn Walser, PhD, Steph Catella, PsyD, Emily Sandoz, PhD, Natasha Smolkin, PsyD, Dave Chrastka, Dee McLaughlin, Josh Cherin, Brent Giannotta and Tasha Oldham. And last but not least, I could not have completed this book without the support and project management of Michael Hanrahan at Publish Central.

I always want to extend a big heartfelt thanks to all my clinician and coach colleagues from the contextual behavioral science, cognitive behavioral science, positive psychology, and prosocial communities, whose often thankless and unseen work continues to advance the knowledge and the tools we all need to intentionally evolve humanity and create a better world for us all.

01

YOUR LIFE
AS MOMENTS
OF CHOICE

… designing something changes the future that is possible.

Bill Burnett and Dave Evans, *Designing Your Life*

MANY CLIENTS SHOW UP WITH an understandable but tragically unrealistic agenda: to get rid of their emotional pain.

It's then my job to explain that painful emotional experiences are the price we all pay for being alive. In the wise words of Prince Westley from *The Princess Bride*, 'Life is pain, Highness. Anyone who tells you differently is selling something.'

In fact, pain is as certain as death and taxes. You could spend your whole life trying to escape this inescapable reality – and many people do. Or, you could get curious about what is actually in your control and what else is possible.

As it turns out, humans have a more important and interesting dilemma than how to get rid of emotional pain: you can choose how you respond to it. In other words, pain is inevitable, but *suffering with pain* is optional.

Here's how it breaks down:

Option 1: You can try to avoid pain and paradoxically suffer a smaller, less meaningful, and even more painful version of life than is possible;

Or,

Option 2: You can learn to harness pain as a purposeful opportunity to do the hard things that lead to your best possible life.

Presented in this way, the second option may seem like the obvious choice.

But the plot thickens …

What if I told you that – through no fault of your own – you're not as free to choose how you show up in your life as you feel?

It's as if you're trapped in the simulated reality of the emotional matrix, where it *feels like* you are consciously making authentic choices? When in fact, an estimated 98% of your decisions are driven by default emotional reactions designed to help you survive, but not necessarily thrive.[1]

This means there's a glitch in your choice-making code. You're wired to avoid pain, even when that causes unnecessary suffering and moves you away from what matters most. If you don't realize this, you won't even know you have a choice. And, you can end up far from what really matters to you; sometimes at a very high cost.

Like Neo in *The Matrix*, you may already have an unshakeable suspicion that your most authentic self is not in the driver's seat: instead of you 'having' emotions, it may seem like your emotions 'have you.'

This is why unplugging from the emotional matrix is a play of epic proportions. It requires shattering your previous conceptions about your emotions – especially painful ones – and how you relate to them. It means coming face to face with a new reality, where you recognize that in each moment you can choose to be controlled by unhelpful emotional defaults or to act on what matters most.

> ... THERE'S A GLITCH IN YOUR CHOICE-MAKING CODE. YOU ARE WIRED TO AVOID PAIN, EVEN WHEN THAT MOVES YOU AWAY FROM WHAT MATTERS MOST. IF YOU DON'T REALIZE THIS, YOU WON'T EVEN KNOW YOU HAVE A CHOICE. AND YOU CAN END UP FAR FROM WHAT REALLY MATTERS TO YOU; SOMETIMES AT A VERY HIGH COST.

But what if I told you that you already have the technology within you to override this default programming to design your best life?

Would you take the emotional 'red pill' and shift out of living on autopilot?

From blindly reacting to intentionally choosing?

From default to design?

The invitation is yours. If you accept, your journey has already begun.

UNPLUGGING FROM THE EMOTIONAL MATRIX

Let me break down in more detail how this sometimes glitchy and complex emotional coding works:

One. Your life is made up of moments of choice. In every moment, you have an opportunity to choose how you'll show up. This gives you many possible futures. What you choose will tell you how the story of your life unfolds.

3

Two. Your emotions are the primary motivational system for your choices. This means your relationship with your emotions is at the heart of the actions you take, moving you toward or away from what matters most to you in a given moment. Inside the emotional matrix simulation, your choices can get hijacked by unhelpful default reactions because it seems like *what you feel is all there is*. Without a powerful relationship with what you feel, you can unwittingly choose an under-realized, under-fulfilled life fraught with more pain.

Three. You have the technology to unplug. But to completely free your choices and your life, you need the skills to decode your emotions, rewire unhelpful patterns, and act in ways that align with your innermost interests, desires, and yearnings – to unlock the best possible version of yourself and design your best life.

As you can see, unplugging from the emotional matrix is no small endeavor. But let's dive even deeper.

Whether you realize it or not, you make around 35,000 choices a day (yes, that's a lot of choosing).[2] You are always choosing in both imperceptible and noticeable ways: to shift in your seat, or sit still; to get out of bed, or hit the snooze button five times; to finish up an email, or squirrel over to a pinging text; to Netflix and pizza, or hit the gym; to work on your relationship, or get a divorce.

It might *feel like* you are authentically choosing. But in reality – outside the simulated world of your emotional experience – you can see the majority of your choices are shaped by fast or automatic hardwired or learned reactions. And they are not always aligned with what really matters to you in a given moment. Over time, they can become deeply ingrained unhelpful patterns of behavior that keep you from what's possible for you in your life.

> IT MIGHT *FEEL LIKE* YOU ARE AUTHENTICALLY CHOOSING. BUT IN REALITY - OUTSIDE THE SIMULATED WORLD OF YOUR EMOTIONAL EXPERIENCE - THE MAJORITY OF YOUR CHOICES ARE SHAPED BY FAST OR AUTOMATIC HARDWIRED OR LEARNED REACTIONS.

In this way you are always either operating by default or by design. You're running on autopilot or you're acting from your truest interests, desires, and yearnings. And because you can survive pretty well just on autopilot, it's easy to miss how many opportunities you have not just to survive, but to thrive.

With an estimated 98% of your choices (around a billion per life-time) shaped by potentially unhelpful default reactions, you can see how your choices are not nearly as effective as they could be.[3] This type of decision-making leads to errors in judgment and missed opportunities. You can unwittingly move in directions you don't want to go and land in places you don't want to be.

This also means that if you're like most people, you're not operating at your highest potential. There's no shame in this. Even the most brilliant, rational, and accomplished people succumb to errors in choice-making when they are trapped in an unconscious, less than powerful relationship with their emotions. You may not realize how much more capable you are, or that so much more is possible for you in your life. This means that in moments of choice, your relationship with your emotions could be your greatest liability – or your greatest asset.

> ... IN MOMENTS OF CHOICE, YOUR RELATIONSHIP
> WITH YOUR EMOTIONS COULD BE YOUR GREATEST
> LIABILITY - OR YOUR GREATEST ASSET.

CHOOSE YOUR OWN EMOTIONAL ADVENTURE

Let's circle back to the dilemma at hand. If the game you're playing is maximizing what matters most (aka living your best life), then your mission is to make the most powerful and effective choices possible. To become a boss-level choice-maker. That starts with being very clear about what's possible in your moments of choice.

You now know you have a choice between kinds of pain whether you choose option 1 or option 2. Yet, a lot of people mistakenly frame the dilemma of pain as a simple choice between 'courage and comfort.'

But there's actually much more at stake here. In the short term, making choices that temporarily keep you comfortable may not seem like a big deal. But when avoiding discomfort or distress becomes your preferred strategy, you're limiting what's possible and missing opportunities you may never get back. You could miss out on designing your best life.

For example, your boss asks you to speak in front of a large group of potential investors about a new product design you're prototyping. This is a moment of choice. But you immediately decline since you hate speaking in front of large crowds and it feels like avoiding that discomfort or distress is what matters most. And while saying no helps you avoid the aversive experience and brings you immediate, momentary relief, you have also just avoided the pain that goes with moving toward what you value more: pursuing all possible paths towards disseminating a life-saving technology.

When you unplug from the emotional matrix, you can choose your own emotional adventure. Do you want the unnecessary additional pain that comes from trying to avoid the pain you actually can't escape, and missing out on what might be possible? Or, do you want the kind that comes from challenging yourself and moving toward your innermost interests, desires, and yearnings?

IF YOU UNPLUG FROM THE EMOTIONAL MATRIX, YOU CAN CHOOSE YOUR OWN EMOTIONAL ADVENTURE. DO YOU WANT THE UNNECESSARY ADDITIONAL PAIN THAT COMES FROM TRYING TO AVOID THE PAIN YOU ACTUALLY CAN'T ESCAPE, OR THE KIND THAT COMES FROM CHALLENGING YOURSELF AND MOVING TOWARD YOUR INNERMOST INTERESTS, DESIRES, AND YEARNINGS?

Again, choosing option 2, aka the emotional 'red pill,' will seem like the obvious choice. But in real-time choice-making it's not that easy. It takes real skill to play at an expert level. It's easy to get entranced by default emotional reactions that move you toward comfort and pleasure. Especially when unhelpful defaults kick in and obscure what matters most in any moment. And with a 98% default rate, this glitch in the code can be very, very costly.

This means you can unwittingly end up acting on bad intel instead of harnessing the opportunities that exist in each moment.[4] You'll be more likely to stay in that relationship that just isn't working because it's painful to end it. Or choose Netflix over the gym. To override the pull of the default world and freely choose your actions, you need the skillfulness that comes from a powerful relationship with your emotions.

DECODING THE SIGNAL FROM THE NOISE

It may be news to you that you're in a relationship with your emotions. In any moment, you're interacting with your emotions, and they are interacting with you. As your primary motivational system, emotional messages shape what you pay attention to, how you interpret what's happening, what you think is possible in your life, and what you do.

This explains why they wield so much influence over your choices – from the food you eat, the hobbies you love, the religion you follow, the careers you pursue, the candidates you endorse, the friends you unfriend, to the romantic partners you pick, the games you play, and the battles you fight.[5,6] They tell you about what you know and what you *believe* you know. How you relate to your compelling, complex, ever-changing emotions determines how you navigate your moments of choice, especially in times of intense stress or distress.

Here's how it works. Your emotional programming comes prewired from birth and sends you messages (aka triggers) that motivate you to act in certain ways. Those messages are also influenced by everything you learn as well as the actions you rehearse that can hold you in predictable emotional patterns. This programming and their patterns make up your very own complex emotional network, aka, the emotional matrix.

When your network deploys emotional triggers they motivate you to act in several ways: in line with reactive *defaults* or in line with freely chosen *values* (and sometimes even both). If you don't realize these messages can be inaccurate and you can't decode which ones you want to listen to, you're more likely to default in unhelpful ways. When default messages are loud, it can be a lot harder to hear your values.

And, until you become a master decoder, differentiating your unhelpful defaults from helpful defaults and your values can be really tricky.

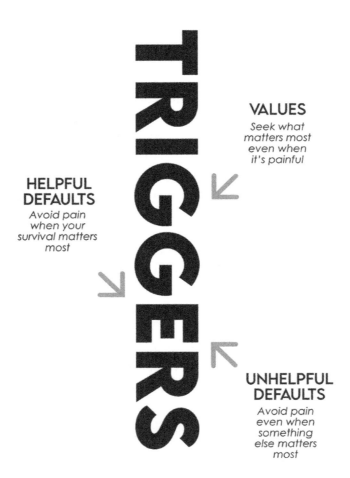

TYPES OF
EMOTION TRIGGERS

VALUES
Seek what matters most even when it's painful

HELPFUL DEFAULTS
Avoid pain when your survival matters most

UNHELPFUL DEFAULTS
Avoid pain even when something else matters most

Consider that, in any moment, your emotions not only deploy life-affirming messages and mission-critical directives; they also deploy 'fake news.' As their name suggests, emotional defaults can sometimes be faulty – even when they feel right, natural, obvious, and urgent. Like a fire alarm screeching when there is smoke but no fire. Noisy, but not so helpful. In this way, emotions are always giving you valid (even if at times unsophisticated and unhelpful) messages about what you're experiencing.

... IN ANY MOMENT, YOUR EMOTIONS NOT ONLY DEPLOY LIFE-AFFIRMING MESSAGES AND MISSION-CRITICAL DIRECTIVES; THEY ALSO DEPLOY 'FAKE NEWS.'

To break this down we'll explore the three types of messages your emotional network will send you. First up are the helpful defaults. These defaults help you act quickly on your feet when there's a threat. In smaller moments they can feel so familiar, they are often unnoticeable and require little to no effort on your part. Their job is to help you survive.

But defaults can also sometimes be unhelpful. They are not always smart about what matters most in a given situation. Unhelpful defaults may work to keep you comfortable or in more predictable and practiced patterns, even when that disconnects you from what matters most. Unhelpful defaults will urge you to do the wrong thing at the wrong time in the wrong situation. For example, say anytime you hear someone around you raise their voice, you automatically start yelling back. This fast automatic reaction, though understandable, may not be helpful in context.

Even if you're not aware of it yet, you get messages from helpful and unhelpful defaults all the time, ranging from urges to stretch out your arms to brace a sudden fall, or to raise your voice if someone is yelling at you, or to unwittingly procrastinate on a potentially life-changing project because you're afraid of failing. You don't even have to think about these choices. They can be helpful or unhelpful, depending on the context.

Meanwhile, values send you messages about what you care about in context – your innermost authentic interests, desires, and yearnings in the moment. Because values are freely chosen and ever-changing, they require continuous conscious inquiry and deeper listening – like hearing a signal through the noise. It's their job to help you thrive.

For example, your values might send you messages to work on your relationship instead of calling a divorce lawyer, to stay in a stable job versus trying something new (or vice versa), to skip the after-dinner chocolate on Tuesday, Wednesday, and Thursday but have it on Friday, or to respond with patience to the person raising their voice because they've mistaken you for someone who isn't listening. Sometimes your values can be obvious, but other times hearing their signals is like trying to hear your friend telling you about a fascinating encounter with your favorite celebrity over a bad internet connection on Zoom.

DEFAULTS DON'T ALWAYS 'READ THE ROOM'

You can understand your emotional coding this way. Imagine yourself at a party with all of your emotions as friends. The 'helpful' defaults are like that friend who, even in the middle of all the good vibes action, will be quick to see flames lapping at the door, yank you out of whatever you're doing and lead you to the nearest exit while you're still wondering if you have time to finish your drink. When it comes to survival and protection, helpful defaults always have your back.

In the other corner, you have 'unhelpful' defaults. They are like that friend who sometimes just cannot read the room. They have a knack for saying exactly the wrong thing at exactly the wrong time.

When everyone at the party is having a laugh, they mention how terrible the news has been lately. Or when a friend is sharing about their recent traumatic divorce, they ask *who wants a drink?*

Meanwhile, values are like your more sophisticated, nuance-savvy, and context-sensitive friend. They can really 'read a room'. Not only do they know what matters most to you, they will urge you to stick with whatever is priority #1 in a given situation – even when that comes with an increase in discomfort or distress.

Values are the friend who spots you being chatted up by your boss when what matters most to you is networking with your coworkers. But also knowing your value of Respect, your values will support your painstaking listening to your boss's 20-year plan for the agency with absolutely no interest in your reaction for a 'respectable' amount of time.

Even though you're counting the seconds until it's over. They may even motivate you to snag some tasty appetizers passing by to ease the tedium and create a momentary diversion to help you stay the course.

And, in the interest of prioritizing what matters most in context, values will then motivate you to interrupt your boss's filibuster and move you back into circulation, so you can mix with colleagues you rarely get to socialize with.

... VALUES ARE LIKE YOUR MORE SOPHISTICATED, NUANCE-SAVVY, CONTEXT-SENSITIVE FRIEND. THEY CAN REALLY 'READ A ROOM'.

Again, it's worth noting that your defaults are not *always* at odds with your values. Sometimes helpful default messages line up with what you care about most in real time. In these moments, running on autopilot works just fine: *I feel uneasy walking through a dark alley, so I'll walk faster to get back onto a main street to stay safe.* Your reflexive reaction to get to a safe street matches up with what matters most.

And while it's great when this happens, when defaults don't align with your innermost interests, desires, or yearnings, you can end up creating the very opposite of what you really care about. *I feel irritated by my friend who can't stop checking her phone, so I leave our dinner date early even though what I most value is connecting with her.* Decoding emotional messages on an expert-player level takes skill and practice.

Here's an example of how subtle this can be. As I write this, I have an urge to get up and make a second cup of coffee – totally valid given I've been sitting for three hours straight and my love affair with brown happiness water. But let me give you more context.

After a big push to get into my writing flow, getting up right now would break that focus without any assurance I could find my way back. It would feel most natural to get up and grab coffee. But when I get curious about my choice, I can drop down and decode the more context-sensitive signals of my values. Finishing this book absolutely matters most to me – more than having a second cup in this moment.

So, while the default urge to break is valid and tempting, and my well-rehearsed pattern of obliging this urge makes it even stronger, breaking doesn't represent what matters most to me in this very moment. And if I weren't a highly practiced values-based choice-maker, my coffee urge would hijack my opportunity to keep writing.

And in higher-stakes moments of choice, when your unhelpful defaults are way noisier than a coffee craving, being able to hear the signals your values send can be even more challenging.

Bottom line: your default emotional reactions don't always serve up the messages you need to be a boss-level, values-based choice-maker.

> BOTTOM LINE: YOUR DEFAULT EMOTIONAL
> REACTIONS DON'T ALWAYS SERVE UP
> THE MESSAGES YOU NEED TO BE A
> BOSS-LEVEL, VALUES-BASED CHOICE-MAKER.

This is complicated by the fact that your emotions and all their messages, by design, *feel* true. When you're plugged into the emotional matrix, default reactions and their patterns reign supreme – regardless of whatever else may actually matter:

> You may struggle with self-destructive habits or addictions, feel helpless to overcome them, and give up. *It may seem like what you feel is all there is.*

> You may experience tragedy or hardship and feel disconnected from meaning to the point where you shut down and withdraw. *It may seem like what you feel is all there is.*

> You may have so much chronic pain that any recovery feels hopeless so you stop moving your body at all. *It may seem like what you feel is all there is.*

> You may have a life that looks good on paper but feel empty and lost and become riddled with guilt that you're not happier and more grateful. *It may seem like what you feel is all there is.*

You might be highly motivated to learn and grow but feel uninspired about improving your performance so you settle for where you've gotten. *It may seem like what you feel is all there is.*

You may win a contest, a job promotion, a dream partner, or even the lottery and feel so lucky or invincible that you take some impulsive, high-stakes risks. *It may seem like what you feel is all there is.*

When you believe *everything* your emotions tell you, it can really muck up your choice-making and limit what you create with your life.

> WHEN YOU BELIEVE *EVERYTHING* YOUR EMOTIONS TELL YOU, IT CAN REALLY MUCK UP YOUR CHOICE-MAKING AND LIMIT WHAT YOU CREATE WITH YOUR LIFE.

YOUR EMOTIONS ARE NOT PROBLEMS

In case it sounds like I'm saying you should never trust your emotions, or that defaults are all bad, that's not it at all. Emotions are always telling you about actual experiences you are having. You really do feel whatever you feel. What I *am* saying is, a good part of the time, your emotions may not be accurately 'reading the room.' And all these moments add up.

When you don't know how to decode your emotional messages – differentiating unhelpful defaults from helpful defaults and values – you can end up far away from the life you want. Since your emotions are always working on your choices, you can unwittingly end up acting on bad intel, instead of harnessing the opportunities that exist in each moment. In each of your 35,000 daily moments of choice, you'll be more likely to do whatever comes most naturally. You're likely to act on whatever you feel, without deeper inquiry.[7]

Even so, your emotions are never the problem. It's how you *respond* to them that can be problematic. You can end up creating exactly what you *don't* want and miss opportunities to create what you do want.

... YOUR EMOTIONS ARE NEVER THE PROBLEM. IT'S HOW YOU *RESPOND* TO THEM THAT CAN BE PROBLEMATIC.

You're probably already aware of this on some level.
For example:

Maybe you become irritated and snap at your mother when she's trying to give advice about your job interview despite the fact she hasn't done one in 30 years. But, what matters most to you is asking for the empathy you want or showing appreciation for her consistent support.

This is unhelpful defaulting.

Or, maybe you get an annoying last-minute request from your boss as you're leaving work and you stay an extra hour out of an irrational fear of getting fired, even though what really matters to you is getting home to prepare dinner and help your kids with their homework.

Again, unhelpful defaulting.

Say you've been sober for a year, but you go out with new friends which triggers your social anxiety, and you impulsively decide to drink when what really matters more to you is learning to cope with your social discomfort.

Unhelpful defaulting.

Or your child is blocking the door when you're leaving them alone for the first time with a babysitter and you chastise them, even though reassuring them matters more than being five minutes late.

Unhelpful.

Or you and a colleague are up for a promotion at work, and in a company-wide meeting you undermine them when what really matters to you is being a team player and not having everyone hate you if you get promoted.

Unhelpful.

Or, let's say you've been at the same job for 10 years, but have always wanted to try something else, and you don't want to go the rest of your life wondering 'what if ... ? But you let the fear of failure boss you into choosing the certainty and comfort you know.

You get the picture, and what's at stake with each choice.

The trance of reactivity will have you relating to *all* your emotions as if they are messages from the universe itself. Even when sometimes unhelpful urges lead you away from your truest interests, desires, or yearnings ... and in some cases, life itself. When you believe that what you feel is all there is, there is no authentic choosing. You can't see what else is possible.

This is life inside the emotional matrix.

The good news is, as soon as you understand this, the trance is broken.

You can begin to see *what else there is.*

The emotional matrix loses its power.

This is why your relationship with your emotions is so important.

WHEN YOU BELIEVE THAT WHAT YOU FEEL IS ALL THERE IS, THERE IS NO AUTHENTIC CHOOSING. YOU CAN'T SEE WHAT ELSE IS POSSIBLE.

When you relate powerfully to your emotions, you'll stop relying on unhelpful default emotional reactions that urge you always and ever toward comfort and pleasure and away from pain. You'll be able to choose to either heed your automatic default emotional reactions, or pause and inquire about what matters most to you *in context* so you can design your actions accordingly. When you have a powerful relationship with your emotions, you can:

· harness your choices as opportunities for flexible, intentional, and creative action

· decode the signals of your innermost interests, desires, and yearnings through the noise of unhelpful defaults

· align your actions with your authentic values, even when it's painful.

Being powerful with your emotions can make even your worst moments some of your best opportunities. You can become millions of moments of choice more powerful.

WHAT ELSE IS POSSIBLE: LIVING BY DESIGN

A new client once came to a session with me and promptly asked why he should care about his emotions (a wildly intoxicating question for a bona fide emotion science nerd like me).

Here's what I told him: 'Your emotions are at the heart of every choice you make and every action you take. This means how you relate to your emotions – especially painful ones – shapes the entire course of your life. This is where your ultimate power lies: doing what matters most in any moment of choice, even in the face of intense stress, challenges, or pain.'

As a psychologist, coach, and consultant, I've had countless opportunities to observe this firsthand. I've witnessed both in research and in real time how people's relationship with their emotions impact their lives. It can tell you really interesting things like:

· whether you can differentiate your deepest values from automatic default reactions

· whether you view emotion triggers as threats to be avoided or as opportunities to be harnessed

· how well you stay focused on what matters and where you want to go

· how often and how much you get knocked sideways by emotion triggers

· how much you suffer from trying to change things you have no control over

· how much you dwell on the past or worry about the future

· how willing you are to endure discomfort and distress for the sake of what you care about

· how you perform in high-stakes situations or moments of intense stress.

This is why learning to relate to your emotions powerfully can be such a significant quality-of-life upgrade.

It's a radical paradigm shift to go from operating on autopilot to flexible, intentional, and creative living … from default to design. From believing everything your emotions tell you in any moment to realizing *what you feel is not all there is.*

This is why I created emotional efficacy training.

WHY EMOTIONAL EFFICACY?

If there's anything I know from my experience as a professional and as a human being, it's that life can be a challenging experience and can come with so much suffering when you don't have a powerful relationship with your emotions.

I've spent more than 25 years working with diverse clients and teams with varying levels of skillfulness with their emotions in a variety of high-stress, high-risk environments, including US Members of Congress, C-level executives, global entertainers, artists, as well as civic and non-profit leaders, teachers, and students.

Throughout my life, and especially during my doctoral training, I've been obsessed with the question of why some people seem to thrive while others stagnate or struggle. I focused on emotion science, contextual behavioral research, neuroscience, the science of wellbeing, and learning theory. My studies all led me to this: efficacy with emotions is central to how people behave and is related to their level of wellbeing and performance.

I developed the construct of *emotional efficacy* (aka emotion efficacy) to help measure how well people navigate their emotions to maximize what matters in context.

The construct of emotion efficacy overlaps with several popular constructs you might recognize:

- *emotional intelligence* (effectively regulating yourself and your interactions with others)
- *psychological flexibility* (effectively adapting behavior to values in context)
- *resilience* (effectively persevering in the face of difficulty).

With the support and encouragement of my dissertation chair, Matthew McKay, PhD, I developed and piloted the original skills training protocol *Emotion Efficacy Therapy* (EET), which draws from key processes and interventions found in the most cutting-edge evidence-based behavioral treatments, including *Acceptance and Commitment Therapy* (ACT), *Dialectical Behavioral Therapy* (DBT), and *Exposure Therapy*.[8]

The results have been very promising. In a pilot study and several randomized controlled clinical trials, people who learned emotional efficacy skills reported significant improvements within a brief period (eight weeks) – with a range of chronic health and mental health challenges, including significant levels of anxiety and depression, mood dysregulation, unprocessed trauma, addiction, obsessions and compulsion behaviors, and patterns of interpersonal instability. Specifically, people reported that they could better tolerate distress, regulate their emotions, and do what matters most, with the bonus of often feeling less anxious, depressed, and stressed.[9]

Another trial showed significant decreases in internet addiction, and another showed a 50% reduction in relapse rates in people struggling with drug and alcohol dependency and mental health challenges after just eight weeks of emotional efficacy training.

This original research along with countless other studies suggests that higher levels of emotional efficacy correlate with *flexibly, intentionally, and creatively* being able to maximize what matters most in context. In other words, by leveling up your emotional efficacy, unhelpful defaulting decreases and values-based choice-making increases.

... BY LEVELING UP YOUR EMOTIONAL EFFICACY, UNHELPFUL DEFAULTING DECREASES AND VALUES-BASED CHOICE-MAKING INCREASES.

It makes sense. I've seen low emotional efficacy do everything from constraining what's possible for people to causing ruinous consequences. I've seen low emotional efficacy cause people to miss big opportunities they didn't see right in front of them. I've seen low emotional efficacy destroy relationships and shatter lifelong dreams, topple promising start-ups, create silos of crippling loneliness, and block creativity and flow for writers, performers, and artists. I've seen low emotional efficacy keep leaders overly focused on achieving results and end up burning through the employees they need to reach them. I've seen low emotional efficacy keep people stuck in destructive patterns and addiction. I've seen low emotional efficacy stop policymakers from taking action to improve the welfare of hundreds of thousands of lives. The list goes on ...

And beyond what I've observed, years of research highlight the negative impact and suffering that comes from low emotional efficacy. For example, more than 75% of people who seek psychotherapy suffer from problems with their emotions, and between 25% and 50% of executives who seek coaching struggle with significant levels of anxiety, stress, and depression.[10,11] Chronic emotional reactivity and dysregulation significantly decrease the quality of life for people – from depression, anxiety, and impulsivity, to suicide,[12,13,14] lower social functioning,[15] substance abuse,[16] low lifetime achievement, low sense of emotional self-efficacy,[17] more frequent deliberate self-harming behaviors,[18,19] increased distress and restricted life functioning,[20] increased suffering and pain,[21] and diminished contact with meaningful and valued life activities.[22]

I also know this suffering firsthand. I've been on a lifelong quest to develop a more powerful relationship with my big, beautiful, mysterious, entrancing, and sometimes terrifying emotions. I've worked hard to heal early childhood trauma, from several early medical catastrophes to relentless bullying in formative years that left me scared, scarred, armored up, and vulnerable to the hopelessness and helplessness of depression. At times I have related to my emotions in ways that not only didn't serve me, but that even created the very experiences I didn't want to have. I've watched people I love struggle with low emotional efficacy that left them vulnerable to chronic depression, addiction, crippling anxiety, and interpersonal problems. A few did not survive.

And, I can also look back and see times when my relationship with my emotions was an asset that allowed me to do things that mattered even when they were hard – from taking terrifying career risks as a 20-something female on Capitol Hill, to leaving a powerful religious community and losing the respect of many dear personal friends and formidable professional allies it had afforded me. Being able to skillfully navigate discomfort and distress also gave me the willingness to change careers several times to pursue work I loved, and to tolerate all the uncertainty that came with it. Skillfully navigating periods of grief and depression allowed me to see my emotional pain as messages to be read, and to discover what I desired and yearned for most. And increasingly, even if imperfectly, I've been able to harness many moments of choice to expand what matters most.

I've seen others with high emotional efficacy persevere in the face of many difficulties, including scant social or economic resources, physical and mental health challenges, unpredictable setbacks, and unspeakable trauma. I've seen high emotional efficacy transform moments of pain and suffering into opportunities. I've seen people with high emotional efficacy repair relationships that seemed ruptured beyond hope. I've seen executives with high emotional efficacy disrupt organizational patterns at the deepest and widest levels, paving the way for increased employee engagement, value-added performance, wellbeing, and profitability. I've seen high emotional efficacy help performers and artists unlock and express new levels of creative potential. And I've seen high emotional efficacy propel political leaders to positions of influence where they've had lasting, positive, and prosocial impact.

The research backs this up. Skillfully relating to your emotions has also been shown to lead to better performance, mental health, and personal and social functioning (think emotional intelligence).[23,24,25,26,27,28,29,30] And in the workplace, flexibly, intentionally, and creatively relating to your emotions can lead to higher levels of performance, job satisfaction, and engagement, and lower absence rates;[31] decreases in stress and increases in physical health and wellbeing;[32] reduced burnout;[33] reduced emotional exhaustion and depersonalization;[34] reduced depression;[35] reduced anxiety and stress;[36,37,38] and improved cognitive flexibility, social support, life meaning, and active coping.[39] Individuals with higher emotional competency also demonstrate the highest performance, including self-regulation, agency, and greater emotional resilience.[40]

5 STEPS TO INCREASE EMOTIONAL EFFICACY

People are often relieved to discover there is so much more possible than they realized. If you're looking to level up your performance or you have long believed that you are emotionally 'broken,' learning you've been trapped in the emotional matrix can be a happy revelation.

That said, sometimes, the realization that your actions have been unwittingly driven by a less-than-powerful relationship with your emotions can feel demoralizing. If this is you, be gentle with yourself. Keep in mind that alongside any sense of regret about the past is also a world of possibility available to you as you build your emotional efficacy. You have the technology – you just need to learn how to use it.

YOU HAVE THE TECHNOLOGY –
YOU JUST NEED TO LEARN HOW TO USE IT.

It would also be understandable if you already feel like you're drinking from a firehose. Stay with me. In not so many pages, you've just downloaded the problem, opportunity, and technology to help you optimize your moments of choice.

In the next nine chapters, we'll be unpacking all the skills you need until it feels more manageable. Whether you're someone whose emotions often interfere with your wellbeing, or you want to tap your full potential and optimize performance, this book is for you.

What follows is a 5-step evidence-based program to increase your emotional efficacy for anyone interested in building a more powerful relationship with their emotions, by moving from defaulting to valuing, to design your best possible life.

Through a combination of psychoeducation and experiential practice, emotional efficacy training will give you the skills to:

STEP 1:   *Unplug* from the emotional matrix and decode
           your defaults (chapters 2–4).

STEP 2:   *Surf* emotion waves instead of defaulting (chapter 5).

STEP 3:   *Clarify and act* on your values in moments of intense
           stress or distress (chapter 6).

STEP 4: *Regulate* your emotions when needed so you can act on what matters (chapters 7–9).

STEP 5: *Play* infinite games to pivot to what matters most and what's possible in any moment of choice (chapter 10).

When you master emotional efficacy skills, it will look something like this:

EMOTIONAL EFFICACY **MODEL**

EMOTION **AWARENESS**
I can tune into all parts of my emotional 'STUF': sensations, thoughts, urges and feelings

VALUES-BASED **ACTION**
I can decode what matters most in context and design my actions to align with it

HIGH EMOTIONAL EFFICACY

EMOTION **SURFING**
I can hang out with my emotional 'STUF' without acting on unhelpful urges

MINDFUL **COPING**
After surfing I can regulate my emotions until I can take values-based action

Before you read further there are a few things about this book you should know:

1. *This book is a journey.* Building your emotion efficacy muscle is a lot like going to the gym and activating your body to build strength and muscle. You start by learning how to use the machines or weights. Then you begin at a very easy pace. Gradually you'll turn up the intensity. Similarly, this book starts with foundational knowledge and skills and then builds on them. Each of the skills chapters contains brief psychoeducation, examples, client dialogues, and some

guided experiential skills practice (with links to more), and follows the same sequence:

- You'll learn a new skill.
- You'll be asked to reflect on how to apply the skill.
- You'll practice the skill in an activated state.
- You'll be given challenges to put your learning into action so it stays with you.
- If you're willing, you'll practice IRL (in real life).

2. *All of the information and skills in this book are based on a foundation of scientific evidence.* In keeping with my ethical commitment to disseminate evidence-based research and practice, everything you'll learn in this book has been tested, both in the emotional efficacy protocol, as well as in other therapy and coaching interventions which focus on emotional experience, wellbeing, and performance.

3. *Where relevant, the names and identifying details for any client examples or dialogues in this book have been changed, adapted, and combined to protect their privacy.* Any similarities to any individuals are coincidental.

4. *Increasing emotional efficacy requires experiential practice.* It's one thing to know *about* emotional efficacy skills, and quite another to use them, especially when you're triggered. This is why you'll learn to practice the skills in a moderately emotionally activated state so they will 'stick.' As an adjunct to the skills training in this book, you'll also be able to access guided experiential practice for each emotional efficacy skill at www.drapriliawest.com/practice.

5. *You'll want to dedicate a journal or note in your phone to write in.* Throughout the book you'll be given prompts and reflections to deepen your understanding of the skills and apply them in your own life. You'll also be asked to reflect after each guided experiential practice and be given challenges at the end of each chapter. This will help you carry the learning forward and get the most out of the book and your practice.

6. *At the end of the book, there's a Glossary of Nerdy Terms defining a lot of the words you'll see.* I use these 'nerdy' terms not only because I want you to become fluent so we can speak the language of emotional efficacy together, but also because there aren't good enough ways to describe some of the skills without them. Some of the language may seem awkward at first, but these terms are repeated throughout and will eventually feel familiar.

7. *This book is a self-help guide for informational purposes only and not a substitute for psychological services.* This book is intended for people who can do their own work without professional support. It is not intended to diagnose or treat any formal condition. You can read and do the exercises, or stop at any time based on what works for you. If at any point while reading this book you begin to experience too much discomfort or distress, you may benefit from seeking professional help. (You can find a therapist or coach trained in contextual behavioral approaches who could work through this book with you through here: www.contextualscience.org). Finally, if you are currently under the care of a licensed mental health professional you should consult them before reading this book or doing the experiential practice to discuss whether it's right for you.

8. *Increasing your emotional efficacy is a lifelong endeavor.* Developing a more powerful relationship with your emotions can happen immediately, but it's not something you ever perfect. It's an ongoing journey. Once you've completed this book and practiced all the skills, you'll have what you need to continue leveling up your emotional efficacy.

CHAPTER 01 LEARNINGS

- Life is created by moments of choice in which you can choose to move closer to or further away from what matters to you.

- Emotional pain is inevitable for humans; how you respond to pain determines what happens in the course of your life.

- How you respond in any moment of choice depends on your relationship with your emotions.

- Humans have an interesting dilemma: to choose the pain that comes with trying to avoid pain and add a layer of unnecessary suffering, or to choose the pain that comes with doing what matters, even when it's hard.

- In any moment of choice, you're operating by *default* or by *design*.

- When you experience intense emotion triggers, your choices can be hijacked by defaults, which may or may not help you align with what matters most to you.

- Emotions are messengers that come from hardwired and learned reactions (defaults) which can be helpful for surviving, but not always thriving, and your deepest interests, desires, and yearnings (values) which help you design your best life.

- *Emotional efficacy* is maximizing what matters most in your moments of choice.

- When you have high emotional efficacy, you can be flexible, intentional, and creative in your moments of choice.

- When you don't believe everything your emotions tell you, you can see what else is possible.

02

INSIDE
THE
EMOTIONAL
MATRIX

You have to understand. Most people are
not ready to be unplugged. And many of them are
so inured and so hopelessly dependent on the system
that they will fight to protect it.

Morpheus to Neo in *The Matrix*

BY NOW YOU MIGHT BE WONDERING, how is it that our most excellent, evolutionarily-evolved motivational guidance system (aka, your emotional network), upon which all of humanity has depended seems to be serving up faulty data?

Short answer: we evolved this way.

And to give credit where it's due, emotional default processes are responsible for our survival. Default reactions come in really handy in high-threat situations where you need to act fast in the face of threat. But while defaults help us *survive*, they don't always help us *thrive*.

Here's how this works: your emotional network 'is built more for avoiding than for approaching.'[1] This means your default reactions will motivate you to avoid emotional discomfort or distress to help you survive.[2] And they are so 'good' at their job, they will send alarms at even the slightest hint of a threat to get you ready and able to react.

This mostly worked well in the past, where default messages could save you from the frequent threats that could end a life. But, as psychologist and author Rick Hanson explains, this 'reactive mode evolved to be a brief solution to immediate threats to survival – not a way of life.'

Also, present-day threats are not so dangerous. Default messages today are just as likely to come from threats to how we want to show up, how we want to think about ourselves, how we want others to perceive us, and the impact our actions have. And while these might be understandable upsets, they aren't lions, tigers, or bears. Again, this leads to errors in choice-making. And less than your best possible life.

DEFAULTS CAN BE HELPFUL OR UNHELPFUL

To briefly recap, because of this coding, humans inherited defaults that are unreliable and inaccurate because they are not sensitive enough to the actual context. Our emotional networks haven't yet evolved to better 'read the room.' As a result, these unhelpful defaults can trump the ability to see what else is going on, what really matters, or what else is even possible.[3] In the emotional default world, it can feel like the house is on fire when actually the frying pan is just smoking and needs to be doused.

Sometimes unhelpful defaults create so much *noise* that they drown out the less urgent *signal* coming from what you value. When you're likely to act on whatever message is loudest and feels most threatening you can easily botch any of your 35,000 daily choices. You'll over-index on safety, certainty, coherence, comfort, and pleasure, even when something else matters more.

> SOMETIMES UNHELPFUL DEFAULTS CREATE SO MUCH *NOISE* THAT THEY DROWN OUT THE *SIGNAL* FROM WHAT YOU VALUE ... YOU'LL OVER-INDEX ON SAFETY, CERTAINTY, COHERENCE, COMFORT, AND PLEASURE, EVEN WHEN SOMETHING ELSE MATTERS MORE.

This is why over-relying on what you *feel* is not effective.

It won't give you the flexibility, intentionality, and creativity you need to stretch for what matters most in context. And, unless you get good at overriding these unhelpful defaults, it's more likely than not your default emotional reactions will have their way with your choices.

This is the grip of the emotional matrix.

Understanding how this happens is the first step to unplugging. In this chapter you'll learn how to decode the messages that come from hardwired or learned defaults especially when they are unhelpful in context.

Once you recognize them, they won't have as much power over your choices. (And that means you will have more.)

Eventually you'll be better able to differentiate unhelpful defaults from your values, which means you'll be more capable of designing your actions in line with what you really care about.

You'll be better able to decide whether you want the pain of moving away from your values or the pain of moving toward them.

Fair warning: what you're about to read is the most dense and jargon-heavy of all the chapters in this book. It's jam-packed with lots of new terms and ideas. But they are foundational for the skills training that follows. Just as Morpheus told Neo when he was feeling overwhelmed by so much new information: 'I didn't say it would be easy … I just said it would be the truth.' And, my guess is, since you're still reading, you want the truth.

THE CONTEXT OF THE EMOTIONAL DEFAULT WORLD

The hidden context of your emotional default world is always shaping your choices, and therefore your actions. This context is made up of hardwired and learned factors that determine how you feel, and often, how you choose to act. In 'Matrix' terms, this emotional coding creates a simulation where it seems like what you feel *is* all there is, making it tricky to discern what matters most in context. It can be hard to tell the helpful defaults from the unhelpful defaults from the values.

> IN 'MATRIX' TERMS, THIS EMOTIONAL CODING
> CREATES A SIMULATION WHERE IT SEEMS
> LIKE WHAT YOU FEEL *IS* ALL THERE IS, MAKING
> IT TRICKY TO DISCERN WHAT MATTERS
> MOST IN CONTEXT.

Here's how this works. Our emotional networks have been evolving for some 600 million years. To survive, our ancestors' emotional networks adapted to motivate them to avoid threats; for example, running away from lurking predators, or slowing down to rest and recover from illness. Their emotions also motivated them to forage for food and engage in social connection to cooperate and procreate. Over time, these emotional reactions became defaults, and were hardwired from birth.

Your defaults have one job: to help you survive. To do this, your defaults send you emotional messages to move you toward pleasure and away from pain. Your defaults want safety, certainty, coherence, comfort, and pleasure – and when do they want them? *Now.* If you listen carefully in any given situation, you can almost hear them grunting like bossy cavepeople sizing things up: 'Good!' 'Bad!' 'Right!' 'Wrong!' 'Safe!' 'Danger!' Again, in context, this can be helpful or it can be unhelpful – even destructive.

YOUR DEFAULTS WANT SAFETY, CERTAINTY, COHERENCE, COMFORT, AND PLEASURE - AND WHEN DO THEY WANT THEM? NOW.

We'll explore decoding the signals of your values a little later in the book. But first, let's explore three major types of defaults that can exert helpful or unhelpful influence over your choices. To make it easy to remember, we'll call this formidable trio the '3Bs':

- *biases*
- *beliefs (about emotion)*
- *biology.*

EMOTIONAL **DEFAULTS**

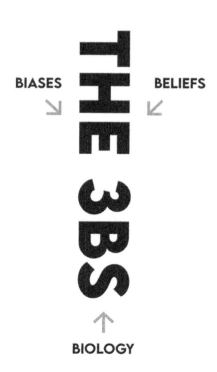

DECODING BIASES

The first type of defaults are predetermined, prejudiced reactions known as *biases*. And while they aim to help you move away from pain and toward pleasure, they also interfere with boss-level choice-making. Biases love to be 'right.' And they will do almost anything to convince you as much, even when they aren't reading the room.

We won't explore all the hardwired biases (since by some counts there are over 175 of them),[4] but there are three that commonly influence your choices, especially in the presence of real or perceived threat:

· negativity bias

· confirmation bias

· emotional reasoning.

Negativity bias

First up is the almighty negativity bias.[5] Over time humans became hard-wired to pay attention to what could go wrong in any given situation. This negativity bias urges you to rush to worst-case conclusions so you will err on the safe side and avoid any potential harm. You could think of the negativity bias as a magnet that attracts any threatening data, and then sticks with you until you do something with the information (heed it or dismiss it).

There are many subtle or more obvious ways you might notice your negativity bias in action. It's more obvious when something triggers you, and your emotions motivate you toward a fight, flight, or freeze reaction to neutralize the perceived threat. But this bias is so powerful that it can rev up even at the subtle suggestion of a real threat. If you just *feel* like there is the possibility of a threat, your negativity bias will be at the ready with guns a-blazing.

The negativity bias's motivation to look for what could go wrong is also why you remember negative experiences more clearly.[6] And again, it may help you survive, but looking for evidence of what's wrong and building a case for threats can also lead to significant errors in judgment, such as:

- Overestimating threats as being bigger or worse than they are. (For example: *If I am called on to present at this meeting, I'll mess up and get fired.*)

- Underestimating the resources you have to face the threat effectively. (For example: *I won't remember anything if I present off the cuff, even though I know the material well.*)

- Missing what's possible and the opportunities in front of you. (For example: *I'll keep a low profile in this meeting because I don't want to give my boss anything to be critical of* (even though it's a huge opportunity to show them what you can do.))

Not coincidentally, overestimating threats, underestimating resources, and missing what's possible is a recipe for unworkable stress, depression, and anxiety. One of my clients, 'Eve', struggled with depression most of her life. When we investigated, what we found was, following some difficult childhood events, her negativity bias had been running hot. By the time she came to work with me, she had felt so threatened over such a long period that overestimating potential threats and underestimating her resources had become her main operating mode. And this meant she had missed many opportunities to expand what really mattered to her. Avoiding any threat had left her stuck in a smaller and more painful version of her life than was possible.

Confirmation bias

Confirmation bias, aka *my-side bias*, is another way humans tend to misread or prejudge what's happening. The crafty confirmation bias, like all 'dedicated' biases, is trying to have your back by motivating you to maximize your safety, certainty, coherence, comfort, and pleasure. By relying on past experiences, it will motivate you to look for evidence to confirm what you have already decided you believe – even in the absence of any evidence to support it, or in the face of new information that contradicts it.

This means you'll pay attention to information that supports what you already think based on prior experiences. (And no, it doesn't mean you're any less smart if you do this … like all the biases, this is innate to humans and has no correlation with intelligence.)[7]

For example, you might observe the preconceived notions of the confirmation bias at work when you make judgments about something or someone you have very little information about. Your focus will shift away from curiosity to searching for data to support what you already think is happening or predict will happen.

It can be as outlandish as, you dated a redhead who was unfaithful, and you're now looking for signs that the current redhead you're dating is cheating on you.

Or you failed a math class, so now anytime you do something math-related you look for any errors to support the idea that you are bad at math.

Or, you can probably think of people who assume that all people from one political party are evil, and all people from another are good, and then they look for evidence to support that.

While one or the other would be enough to get you defaulting in a moment of choice, the negativity bias and confirmation bias will happily double-team your judgment and choice-making. For example, maybe you had a bad experience getting lost on a hike with your community youth group. Ever since, anytime you go hiking in a new place, you not only look for evidence of what could go wrong, how incapable you might be of navigating your way back, and miss opportunities to enjoy nature or your company, but you could also be looking around for evidence to confirm you've already lost your way, even when you're on a clearly marked path.

Emotional reasoning

My personal favorite, and the original inspiration for this book, is the bias of *emotional reasoning*. As a dutiful bias, it runs in the background, constantly working on all your emotional experiences. It tells you that whatever you feel is true, no matter how illogical it may seem and without any supporting evidence.

In my work as an executive coach, therapist, consultant, and mediator, I've seen the handiwork of this bias with errors of judgment and choice-making over and over. Whether it's couples in conflict who unwittingly use their feelings as a compass to determine their partner's intentions, managers who assume their feelings of paranoia about their coworkers mean that collaborating is risky, diplomats whose feelings of discomfort about their colleague's belief systems lead them to abandon peacemaking efforts, or companies who fail to merge because one side takes offense at the other's proposal, and concludes they are being 'played for fools.' It's as if people are convinced, *if I feel it, it must be true.* This makes us meaning-making machines that – despite efforts to be 'rational' – never cease to reason based on our feelings.

> IT'S AS IF PEOPLE ARE CONVINCED,
> *IF I FEEL IT, IT MUST BE TRUE.* THIS MAKES US
> MEANING-MAKING MACHINES THAT - DESPITE
> EFFORTS TO BE 'RATIONAL' - NEVER CEASE
> TO REASON BASED ON OUR FEELINGS.

Emotional reasoning is powerful because whatever you feel significantly impacts what you focus on, what you believe, and what you choose. As explored prolifically by Nobel Prize–winning psychologist and author Daniel Kahneman, emotional reasoning can lead you to jump to conclusions with limited evidence and draw erroneous conclusions or make irrational choices.[8]

My client 'Kai' had struggled with depression, to the point where he would go through periods where he would struggle to get out of bed for weeks at a time. When we first met, he was in the middle of such a period, and when I asked him what he wanted or was looking forward to, he came up empty. He told me that he didn't feel life was worth living. Interestingly, when I asked him what was wrong with his life, he also came up empty. He had everything he needed: food, shelter, money, a kind loving partner, a job he excelled at. But because he felt hopeless and helpless, he emotionally reasoned that it must be true. So he stayed in bed.

The overreliance on what you feel makes it (too) easy to perceive threats where they don't actually exist. You can get triggered by the smell of smoke when there is no fire. And when that happens, your emotional network can shift into overdrive, narrowing your focus to avoid a threat.

For example:

You hear a car honking, get startled, sense the hair on the back of your neck stand up, and you stop to look for a threat, even in the absence of evidence you're in real danger.

Or in work meetings when people's facial expressions appear to be anything less than enraptured – or even just neutral – with what you're saying, and you feel threatened, you could interpret this as a sign you're being negatively evaluated.

Or you could feel threatened when you first shift to healthier eating patterns because you feel the discomfort from sensations of hunger, even if you're just experiencing the natural discomfort of change.

Or, in more extreme cases, if you've been depressed and in pain for a long period of time, you could feel so threatened, you might decide life isn't worth living, even if it's possible your circumstances could improve.

Ironically, these three biases – with their prejudices, errors in judgment, and fast automatic choice-making – are largely where our 'need to be right' comes from. This makes sense from an evolutionary perspective, since the cost of being wrong in caveperson times could be certain death. But this also means we can approach choices with self-righteousness, rigidity, and narrow thinking when we get triggered.

An obvious example of this is how hard it is to change people's minds about subjects that evoke intense emotion – think politics or religion. The idea that we could be wrong about things that seem important can feel so very threatening. It's the high-stakes emotional equivalent of feeling like, *I could die from being wrong about this!* Even if 'this' is just the side-eye your senior partner at work seems to be giving you when you leave the office at 4:55 p.m.

This is also why the fear of being 'wrong' can make you feel vulnerable to being kicked out of your social circles (the modern-day equivalent of the tribe). This would have meant for you death thousands of years ago. An aversion to rejection or negative evaluation became evolutionarily hardwired to help you survive. So much so, that you will make up explanations for why you think what you think, even when you lack the evidence to support it.[9]

At times, the biases may even triple team you in order to convince you they're right. When you're emotionally triggered, chances are your negativity bias, confirmation bias, and emotional reasoning are all in play. In these cases, you'll easily confuse or mistake the threat of discomfort and distress for dysfunction or danger.

> WHEN YOU'RE EMOTIONALLY TRIGGERED, CHANCES ARE YOUR NEGATIVITY BIAS, CONFIRMATION BIAS, AND EMOTIONAL REASONING ARE ALL IN PLAY. AND YOU'LL EASILY CONFUSE OR MISTAKE DISCOMFORT OR DISTRESS FOR DYSFUNCTION OR DANGER.

As an example, let's say you're at an amusement park with friends and they all want to ride the Full Throttle rollercoaster with you. And while you're standing in line waiting to brave up for the ride, just looking at the epic inclines, declines, and loops leads to a cascade of reactions: your heart races, a knot forms in your stomach, and the thought, *what if this just happens to be the ride that actually breaks mid air?* appears and creates a big wave of emotion. Without even trying, your emotional reasoning bias will tell you that because you feel this way, the ride must be dangerous.

But just in case you're not that easily convinced, your negativity and confirmation biases will come from behind to reinforce the emotional reasoning bias. Your negativity bias will start looking for anything that could go wrong, and remind you that *being inverted at 160 feet is really just never a good idea.* It will have you scanning for possible signs of danger – the squeak of the cars rolling over the tracks, the teenager responsible for the ride scrolling his cellphone while people are barreling past at a bazillion miles per hour – to motivate you to dip out.

And let's also say your cousin had a scary experience on a roller-coaster when she was 12, where she got stuck at the top for 30 minutes. Ever since then you've been suspicious of amusement park rides. This gives your confirmation bias all the evidence it needs to offer up evidence that there's going to be a problem, moving the threat level from substantial to critical. Of course all of this negativity and confirmation then re-triggers your emotional reasoning bias, which tells you that based on what you're feeling now, it's even more dangerous than you thought.

By this point you're officially in bias overdrive. By the time you strap into the janky cart, it's more likely than not you've developed an award-winning case of the jitters that would persuade any judge and jury that this could be your last ride.

REFLECTION: HOW BIASES SHAPE YOUR CHOICES

Recognizing these biases when they're in play will keep you from being as captive to their messages. Take a moment here and reflect on how these biases could be shaping your choices. Recall a situation where you were triggered (had a big emotional reaction) using the three questions below:

- Were you overestimating threat, underestimating your resources, and/or missing an opportunity? *(negativity bias)*
- Were you looking for evidence to confirm what you already think or believe? *(confirmation bias)*
- Were you using your emotional experience to inform your belief about what was happening? *(emotional reasoning)*

DECODING BELIEFS ABOUT EMOTIONS

All humans develop beliefs about many aspects of life, including beliefs about emotions. Unlike your biases and biology, which are hardwired, beliefs are learned from what you make up about experiences you have. And, not surprisingly, just like all your 3Bs, they can powerfully impact what you do in moments of choice, especially when you're triggered.[10]

You glean your emotion beliefs from experiences with yourself, your social circles, your culture, and your environment. You could think of them as rules or stories about how things are, or that predict how something or someone will behave. When your beliefs about emotions become ingrained they can shape your moments of choice: how much you pay attention to various emotions, which ones you enjoy, which ones you endure, and which ones you avoid.[11]

For example, difficult, challenging, or traumatic events can shape beliefs about certain emotions; for example, you became majorly depressed after the death of your first pet, and it may have been so painful that you developed the belief that the experience of grief is intolerable and to be avoided at all costs. Or, you may have developed a belief that feeling excited is dangerous because you have experienced excitement in the past as a set up for disappointment when things did not go the way you expected.

In addition, many of us grow up in families who have specific beliefs about certain emotions. It's possible that only positive or negative emotions were encouraged or discouraged. Or, perhaps any emotional expression was unappreciated and believed to be a sign of irrationality or cowardice.

On a family and cultural level, beliefs about emotions based on gender can also be stark. For example, you may have heard the message that 'boys don't cry.' And if you grew up identifying as male, you may have worried about looking 'weak' and avoided any experiences that could lead you to feel vulnerable. Or, if you grew up identifying as female, you may have gotten the message that 'anger is ugly and undesirable.' As a result, you may have suppressed moments when you were upset or when your boundaries were crossed.

Following are examples of common beliefs people have about emotions:

- If I let myself feel my emotions, I'll lose control.
- Containing my emotions is intolerable.

- People don't actually care what I'm feeling.
- It's doesn't matter what I'm feeling.
- I feel too much.
- Feeling good is a set up for disappointment.
- I need to be certain about what I feel.
- Things that bother me don't bother other people.
- I must be rational and logical.
- If I let myself have strong feelings, they might not go away.
- I have to guard against certain feelings.
- It's dangerous to express my feelings.
- If I relax, I won't be safe.
- As a male, I should never show vulnerability.
- As a female, I should never show anger.

These beliefs powerfully impact how you relate to your emotions (ergo, what you do in moments of choice) in subtle and obvious ways. On a broad level, if you believe emotions are dangerous and overwhelming, you'll relate to them as dangerous and overwhelming, and then experience them as dangerous and overwhelming. And, if you've ever felt really out of control with emotions you may become 'emotion phobic,' believing *all* emotions are to be avoided at all cost.

But if you believe emotions are momentary experiences that come and go, then that's exactly how you'll relate to them, and you'll experience them as temporary and ever-changing. Or, if you believe emotions contain valuable information, you'll experience them as opportunities to get curious and listen in. That's how powerful beliefs about emotions are.

For example, if you believe the feeling of excitement is a set up for eventually being disappointed, you'll try to avoid letting yourself feel too excited. Or, if you believe the feeling of anger will cause you to lose control, you may work hard to suppress any hint of irritation.

Like the biases, beliefs about our emotions *feel* true, even when they're not accurate or helpful in context.

... IF YOU BELIEVE EMOTIONS ARE DANGEROUS AND OVERWHELMING, YOU'LL RELATE TO THEM AS DANGEROUS AND OVERWHELMING, AND THEN EXPERIENCE THEM AS DANGEROUS AND OVERWHELMING.

As an example, a client of mine, 'Alexi,' had a belief that feeling relaxed was dangerous based on past experiences where she had been blind-sided by traumatic events. As a result, she had an aversion to relaxation which was interfering with her new job, where she was struggling to fit in because she was preoccupied with staying on top of everything and avoiding letting her guard down, even in lighter moments. As a result, she was coming off as being high-strung and hypersensitive with coworkers. In our sessions, we also discovered that even taking deep breaths would immediately bring a wave of fear and anxiety. She described that it felt like she was making herself vulnerable to harm by relaxing, even without any evidence to support her belief.

In addition to developing your own rules and stories, certain beliefs are reflected and reinforced through wider cultural messages about emotions. One glaring example in the US is the idealization of positive experiences and the devaluing of so-called negative experiences. This stems from a growing but erroneous belief that feeling good (as much as possible) is good, and feeling bad is bad and has no value.

In their book *The Upside of Your Dark Side*, Todd Kashdan and Robert Biswas-Diener highlight the 'not so hidden prejudice against emotional states.'[12] We are told that being happy is paramount, outrage is always jus-tified, and being sad or down is socially undesirable. And not surprisingly, this leads to downplaying and minimizing the experience and expression of negative emotions and a belief that they should be concealed.

Anyone scrolling social media can see this reflected in inspirational quotes emphasizing positivity, without regard for context and sometimes at the expense of honoring difficult experiences or even tragedies. Forced positivity is also all over the self-help industry. A lot of spiritual teachers and influencers advocate that the good life exists in maintaining positive emotional states. They advocate 'good vibes only,' and some even say 'negative' emotions, regardless of circumstances, are bad juju and can cause you to manifest misfortune and adversity. This belief reinforces the idea that you should avoid any 'negative' experiences. Yet, once you truly understand the purpose of uncomfortable emotions, you won't want to get rid of them.

For starters, aversive or so-called 'negative' emotions have important functions. They can motivate you to be socially sensitive, to reflect on the impact of your behavior, to mourn losses, to withdraw to recover, to problem solve, and to remind you what you care about. They motivate you to cooperate with others and peacefully coexist.

They also help you survive. Sometimes discomfort and distress are exactly what you need to snap into effective action: if a bus is careening toward you, you want a huge honking dose of fear and adrenalin surging through your body to urge you to get out of the way – not warm fuzzies.

In this way, painful emotions guide you and are essential for tending to your safety, certainty, coherence, comfort, and pleasure as well as your innermost interests, desires, and yearnings – your values. You may not want them, but you need them to survive, and to thrive. You need 'all the feelings' to decode what matters most in moments of choice.

> ... ONCE YOU TRULY UNDERSTAND THE
> PURPOSE OF UNCOMFORTABLE EMOTIONS,
> YOU WON'T WANT TO GET RID OF THEM ... YOU
> NEED 'ALL THE FEELINGS' TO DECODE WHAT
> MATTERS MOST IN MOMENTS OF CHOICE.

For all these reasons, the notion of 'positive' and 'negative' emotions being good or bad is not helpful. It underplays the value and usefulness of emotions such as sadness, self-doubt, anxiety, grief, guilt, and shame, all of which are important messages that help you grow and develop.[13] It can be unhelpful and even destructive to avoid negative emotional experiences.

Focusing on an unrealistic endeavor like getting rid of so-called 'negative' or unwanted emotional experiences can distract you from what matters. It interferes with tending to your most important values, leading to less meaning and more unhappiness. And, when forced or feigned or superstitious positivity becomes a pattern, it can leave you disconnected from what you need to thrive (much more on this next chapter). It's more helpful to think of emotional 'pain' as the natural feelings that come with facing any stress, challenges, or distress.

REFLECTION: HOW BELIEFS SHAPE YOUR CHOICES

Becoming aware of your beliefs about your emotions will help you further unplug from your emotional matrix and decode them more skillfully. Spend a moment here to take an inventory about your beliefs about emotions:

- What is your favorite or least favorite emotion(s)?
- What are the messages you received about these emotions when you were growing up? Were pleasurable and aversive emotions valued equally? Were emotions considered to be important and valid, or were they minimized as bothersome, inconsequential, or a waste of energy?
- Did people (such as family, friends, or teachers) respond differently when you expressed pleasurable emotions compared to when you expressed distressing emotions? Were some emotions considered to be bad or off limits?
- How did people in your family or social circles manage their emotions? Did you notice people trying to hide their emotions from each other? Or did you notice people struggling to contain their emotions? Was showing emotions considered to be challenging? Shameful? Comfortable? Selfish? Normal?
- What were the messages you saw on TV, the internet, or other media about emotions in general? Were messages about emotions different based on your gender, ethnicity, or culture?

DECODING BIOLOGY

In addition to hardwired biases and learned beliefs about emotion, a lot of your experience is preset from the moment of conception via genetic coding. You come biologically wired with fast, automatic reactions, ranging from blinking when something gets in your eye to having a sympathetic nervous system response where your heart rate speeds up with a burst of adrenergic energy when you wake up to find you've overslept the morning of a major work presentation.

In addition to this universal coding everyone has, biology also shows up in individual and unique ways. Everyone's DNA is different, making each of us biologically 'special.' This custom blend of genetic loading makes up what is called a continuum of *neurodiversity*. Despite the diagnostic labels and TV shows about people who are 'atypical,' we are all neurodiverse, and some of us are more neurodiverse than others.

Neurodiversity in humans is just like the natural diversity you see in flowers of the same species: some are smaller or larger, and more or less colorful, some have many leaves, some have few leaves, and some have none at all. Like humans, flowers are impacted by evolution, and will express themselves differently depending on their physical environments, and other contextual factors.

For example, for purely biological reasons, your emotional experience will be shaped by specific characteristics or tendencies. You can be more or less sensitive to touch, to sight, to sounds, or to taste. You may prefer salty things, sweet things, or savory things, or love them all. You may naturally like to be around lots of people or prefer solitude and quiet. Some people prefer more novelty, while others prefer routines. Some of us tend to be more balanced and even keeled, while others are more reactive. Some of us are even born with inexplicable phobias or aversions to certain stimuli. (Mine happens to be *koumpounophobia* – a fear or disgust of buttons. Seriously – it's a thing. Look it up.)

As you might imagine, your level of neurodiversity impacts your emotional experience. Your biology can account for predispositions or vulnerabilities related to certain types of anxiety or mood instability, or with features of clinical diagnoses such as depression, bipolar 'disorder,' substance abuse, psychosis, and the autism spectrum. Some people adapt effectively to their environments in spite of their neurodiversity – through trial and error and/or with the support of other people. And some people will seek therapy or coaching.

As an example, my client 'Josh' had been described as having a particularly sensitive temperament since he was a baby. In his teens, he had been given a diagnosis of generalized anxiety disorder which was thought to be organic in nature (versus learned), and a less well-known neurological condition called Macropsia, sometimes referred to as 'Alice in Wonderland' syndrome, where distortions in visual perception can cause certain sections of an object to appear larger than normal. This perceptual distortion can result in the person feeling smaller than they are.

As a result of both conditions, Josh was more reactive to sensory stimuli, especially anything that led him to feel less safe or certain of his surroundings. Despite his desire to connect with people and try new things, he struggled to put himself in new and unpredictable situations, and experienced groups of people as overwhelming.

Another example of neurodiversity can be found in people who meet criteria for the autism spectrum disorder (ASD). My executive coaching client 'Jewels' had a diagnosis of high-functioning ASD (formerly known as Asperger's type). As a result, she experienced people's feelings and motivations as mysterious and often illogical. Her neurodiversity had impacted her social interactions most of her life. She would frequently miss common facial expressions and behavioral cues, making it more difficult for her to accurately read social situations. She also struggled to mentalize (imagine) what other people were experiencing. And she had a very low tolerance for the emotional experience of uncertainty and incoherence.

This made it challenging for her to effectively manage her executive team. She told me that when she couldn't understand the internal rationale for her colleagues' behavior, she had a hard time responding with patience and empathy. She was also highly critical of herself and her difficulties, all of which led to a consistently higher baseline of anxiety.

Biological defaults can influence your emotional experience in different ways throughout your lifespan. My client 'Paige' was a management consultant in her late 30s who was traveling nonstop for work when she hit early menopause. She was blindsided by sudden hormonal changes, including hot flashes, brain fog, and episodes of melancholy, irritability, and insomnia, which her doctor diagnosed as early perimenopause. Her stellar reputation for being extremely flexible, patient, and grounded was threatened. Her experience was turned upside down, and she could no longer depend on her emotions to support her in staying on top of her game.

REFLECTION: HOW BIOLOGY SHAPES YOUR CHOICES

Before you move forward, take a moment here to reflect on the influence of biological coding in your own life:

- Do you notice any innate preferences, or inexplicable fears, phobias, or interests that seem to be hardwired (versus learned through experiences)?
- How, if at all, do you notice your biology impacts how you experience emotions (for example, mental health, phase of life, or medical conditions)?
- How does your neurodiversity seem similar or different from other people you know?

YOUR PERSONAL DEFAULT SPECIAL OPS TEAM

By this point, you may be noticing how 'thick' the context of your emotional default world is. When it comes to your survival, the default reactions from your biases, beliefs, and biology are akin to having an emotional Navy SEALs special ops team at the ready.

Your biases can trigger or reinforce your beliefs about emotions, your beliefs can affect your biology, your biology can trigger or reinforce your biases, and so on, in any possible combination. These multilayered default processes are always working (often together) on your emotions, and therefore, your moments of choice.

At any moment, your 3Bs will recruit each other to neutralize a threat – even when it's a false alarm, or when the actual threat doesn't require a response.

No wonder humans have survived.

However, the problem arises when our defaults are so compelling, you become entranced by them, making it hard to focus on what matters most in your moments of choice. It's easier and feels more natural to default, even when it's not helpful. Again, this makes it harder to thrive.

And, when you add messages from your values to the picture, this makes each one of us our very own context for an incredibly complex and interactive confluence of factors, all of which work on our choices in any moment. And since all emotional messages feel true and right in any moment, it makes sense why people may not take kindly to the invitation to get unplugged.

> ...THIS MAKES EACH ONE OF US OUR VERY OWN CONTEXT FOR AN INCREDIBLY COMPLEX AND INTERACTIVE CONFLUENCE OF FACTORS.

Understanding all these forces exerting their influence on your choices is critical for learning to shift from defaulting to valuing in your moments of choice. In the next chapter you'll learn how to identify unhelpful default patterns and how you can use your built-in technology and emotional efficacy skills to disrupt them.

CHAPTER 02 CHALLENGES

- Identify a recent distressing situation and see if you can decode any biases, beliefs, or biology that could have been in play.

- Based on all your understanding of your beliefs about emotions, write a one-sentence summary of your beliefs about emotions; for example, *Emotions are welcome when they are positive, but dangerous when negative.*

- Find at least three opportunities when you next encounter a triggering situation to pause and practice naming any of the 3Bs in play. Also notice if your awareness of these defaults shifts what you do next.

- Identify a recurring example where you tend to avoid discomfort or distress. Was avoiding in this case an example of unhelpful defaulting (versus moving toward what actually mattered most to you)?

- To lock in the learning, share what you've learned about helpful and unhelpful emotional defaults with someone you know, and what it means to you so far.

CHAPTER 02 LEARNINGS

- Your default emotional programming is shaped by three encoded processes, aka the '3Bs': biases, beliefs about emotion, and biology.

- Recognizing your defaults is the first step toward being able to disrupt them when they are unhelpful.

- The negativity bias can lead to three specific unhelpful behaviors: overestimating threats, underestimating resources, and missing opportunities for what else is possible.

- The confirmation bias leads you to search for evidence to support what you already believe and think.

- Emotional reasoning leads you to believe that whatever you feel is true.

- Beliefs about your emotions can shape the way you experience them.

- Unhelpful beliefs about emotions can cause you to confuse danger and dysfunction with discomfort and distress.

- You have your own unique confluence of biological predispositions and vulnerabilities that make up your neurodiversity.

- Your biological coding impacts your experience in different ways throughout your life.

- Your defaults (3Bs) often function as a team to ensure your survival in the face of any real or perceived threat.

03

DISRUPTING UNHELPFUL DEFAULT PATTERNS

No problem can be solved from the
same level of consciousness that created it.

Albert Einstein

IT'S A WHOLE DIFFERENT LEVEL of consciousness to be able to observe the entire context of your emotional matrix. Without this expanded awareness, your 3Bs can wield a lot of power over your moments of choice, even when they aren't helpful.

Even when your deeper interests, desires, and yearnings matter more.

When you over-rely on what you feel, without the skillfulness to decode your emotions, unhelpful defaults will remain large and in charge of your 35,000 choices each day.

IT'S A WHOLE DIFFERENT LEVEL OF
CONSCIOUSNESS TO BE ABLE TO OBSERVE THE
ENTIRE CONTEXT OF YOUR EMOTIONAL MATRIX.

Over time, unhelpful defaulting can lead to behavior patterns that are rigid, scripted, and constrained.

They won't read the larger context of what matters most in the here and now. And they won't help you design your best life.

It's no wonder there are errors in the code.

Fortunately, you're not stuck in a default simulation where all you can do is send #thoughtsandprayers to your moments of choice. While you can't get rid of default settings, you can learn to override the unhelpful urges that come with them. Being powerful with your emotions – especially the unwanted triggering kind – will transform them from pain you're trying to escape into opportunities to pivot toward what else is possible.

If you're not quite sure you've got the hang of the 3Bs yet or are feeling a bit like you've been slipped the 'red pill' without proper warning, don't give up. Putting all this learning together takes time and experiential practice to really sink in.

After all, if unplugging from your emotional matrix felt natural, you would have already done it.

In this chapter, you'll learn how to spot your unique unhelpful default patterns, and how you can disrupt them using experiential practice.

HIJACKED CHOICES CAN BECOME UNHELPFUL PATTERNS

Not all your default patterns are problematic. Some of them overlap with your values; for example, sticking with a health routine, brushing your teeth every day, or showing up for your friends even when its inconvenient or uncomfortable. But for now, you'll focus on recognizing unhelpful default patterns that hijack your moments of choice.

So, what exactly *are* unhelpful default patterns? Quite simply, they are well-rehearsed actions driven by hardwired and/or learned responses to emotion triggers that don't sync up with your values. They motivate you to *avoid unwanted emotional experiences* – even when something else matters more. And, they always come with an urge to do what it takes to avoid a perceived or actual threat to your safety, certainty, coherence, comfort, or pleasure.

You could think of unhelpful patterns (or any patterns you rehearse) as software that gets embedded within the emotional matrix. Because you've run it so many times, this coding is what is most accessible and familiar. It might not even occur to you to check in or consult with your deeper interests, desires, or yearnings about other courses of action.

This pattern of programming makes it more likely to act on the emotional urge that comes with unhelpful defaults, creating patterns of errors in judgment and choice-making. Unless you upgrade or rewrite the software, you'll miss what you more authentically care about.

UNHELPFUL DEFAULT PATTERNS

EMOTION TRIGGER → AVOID UNWANTED EXPERIENCES

SHORT-TERM RELIEF

PAIN COMES BACK OR INTENSIFIES

Over time, these patterns can become so deeply ingrained it's hard to even imagine acting any other way; for example, not picking up your baby when they cry, even when sleep training is more important. Or not scratching an incessant itch, even though the mosquito bite is now bleeding.

One of my clients, 'Tom', is a performing artist and has a biological vulnerability to depression. Based on his past experience of feeling hopeless and helpless during a depressive episode, he formed a belief that the emotion of 'sadness' is dangerous. Now when he starts to feel the slightest sadness, his belief about the emotion of sadness activates his hardwired biases, which are only too happy to support the belief that danger (triggered by sadness) has arrived.

In response to these unhelpful default messages, Tom developed an ineffective pattern of trying to get rid of the sadness he is already having through binge drinking, staying as busy as possible, and attempting to control his schedule and his environment to avoid potential 'sadness triggers.' This in turn takes his focus away from what really matters when he is on tour; for example, being rested enough to perform, enjoying his fans, and being resilient enough to navigate intense travel and interpersonal demands, as well as so many other things that inevitably don't go to plan.

Ironically, all his attempts to avoid feeling sad leave him even more exhausted, more anxious, and feeling less in control. To boot, he now also feels sad that he is tired and isn't enjoying himself, and so he ends up even sadder. This intensifies his distress, making him more anxious about being sad. Tom's avoidance creates and maintains a cycle of pain that adds a layer of unnecessary suffering. His unhelpful default pattern has led him even deeper into the very experiences he was trying to avoid.

Like you and me, Tom is a reasonably smart dude. So how does this happen? It's important to note that this unhelpful avoidance loop gives Tom the sense that he is escaping a threat. He gets the short-term relief that *feels like* he is escaping a threat. And, like you and me, he just has a blind spot when it comes to the consequences of his unhelpful default patterns. He doesn't always connect his actions to their consequences.

This can look a lot of different ways. Your unhelpful default patterns might have you avoid something as innocuous as the annoyance of returning another email, or suppressing uncomfortable sensations in your body. Or, you might avoid by numbing distress about loneliness through drugs or delaying painful, scary medical treatment with a long list of fake reasons something else is more urgent.

In each case, you're avoiding experiences that naturally come with acting on what matters: the tedium of returning the email that matters, the discomfort of bodily sensations that signal you need to tend your wellbeing, facing the distress of loneliness head on to find company, and enduring the discomfort of necessary medical treatment.

This is how these patterns are created … naturally and innocently, as your emotional matrix keeps you heeding the legion of unhelpful default messages it deploys. Over time, the patterns become the path of least resistance.

THE FUTILITY OF CHRONIC AVOIDANCE

So what? What if sometimes you avoid connecting with certain feelings because something else matters more?

It can be the case that, at times, avoiding an unwanted emotional experience *is* what matters most. Avoiding my feeling of concern about a personal contract negotiation can be really helpful when I'm in the middle of a complex team coaching session where helping to mediate a conflict is what is most important. In this case, to focus on repairing the rupture, pushing away from concern about the contract becomes what matters most in that context.

But if avoiding unwanted experiences becomes a default pattern, in certain contexts I might not do what matters most, and I might miss out on opportunities altogether. All because I am always and ever moving away from painful experiences and toward pleasure.

The fancy clinical term for trying to control, get rid of, or move away from unwanted emotional experiences is *emotional (or experiential) avoidance*.

Here's why it's problematic – especially when it becomes a pattern:

· it doesn't always work
· it often only provides short-term relief
· it can be exhausting
· it can disconnect you from the things that matter more
· it often intensifies discomfort and distress.

And now that you know how clandestine – and ineffective – your emotional default messages can be (even when they *feel* rational), it won't surprise you how frequently you fall into these unhelpful default patterns that don't work well in context.

Let's dig deeper into the pitfalls of avoidance:

· *Avoiding unwanted emotions doesn't reliably work.* Often doing things
  to avoid discomfort and distress will give you the illusion you are
  escaping it. Let's say you and I are walking through the woods, and
  I know you're afraid of snakes, so I say to you, 'just don't think about
  them.' Chances are you'll spend a lot more time on our walk thinking
  about not thinking about snakes, you'll still feel scared – maybe even
  more scared than if you just accepted the fear – and you won't really
  be able to relax and enjoy our walk. With emotional avoidance, to
  try to get rid of something or move away from what you don't want
  to experience, you actually have to focus on not having what you
  already have or are afraid of having. (And that often leads to *more* of
  what you don't want.)

· *Avoiding unwanted emotions only leads to temporary relief.*
  One reason avoidance is so seductive is that it can be effective at
  keeping unwanted experiences at bay in the short term, even if not
  for the long term. And I don't have to tell you that as creatures of
  comfort, short-term relief can still be very compelling for us humans.
  Let's say you decide to knock back five shots of tequila over a few
  hours after an argument with your partner, to get away from your
  distress. By the second shot, the argument you had may feel galaxies
  away, and you might bask in the relief of feeling less heavy about

the words exchanged between you. You may even begin to revel in seeing yourself as being 'in the right.' But assuming there's something you care about that's still unresolved the next morning (if not sooner), alongside your desire for Advil are the very same distress feelings. Or let's say in general you avoid anxiety by double and triple checking that the stove is turned off before you leave your home. You might feel better for a few moments, but most likely the distressing thoughts show up again after you leave, especially if you've trained yourself to avoid the uncertainty of not checking. You may have delayed the anxiety, but the distressing emotional experiences you want to avoid usually come back around.

- *Avoiding unwanted emotions is exhausting.* Attempts to avoid unwanted emotional experiences take a lot of focus and energy. Think about a time when you had to be in a social situation when you were anxious, sad, mad, or bored and you tried to hide your feelings. Most likely it took real effort. And, just like not thinking about snakes in the woods, you have to continuously think about the very thing you don't want people to notice to be sure it's not noticeable. You spend energy masking the discomfort, hoping your face doesn't give you away, or you spend energy laughing just the right amount at the dad jokes your colleague keeps serving up. You're probably having to concentrate on making sure your body language doesn't communicate just how much you'd rather be home giving your cat a bath. You might be scanning for signs that people are seeing through your act. If you're masking your true feelings on a routine basis, a lot of your energy probably gets used up this way. Trying to avoid what you're already experiencing is not only ineffective, it's usually not sustainable. And when it's a recurrent, ongoing default pattern, it depletes you and even leads to burnout.

- *Avoiding unwanted emotions can disconnect you from what matters most.* This is the problem with avoiding your experience. It not only disconnects you (temporarily) from what you're feeling, but also from what matters most. It can lead you to focus on trying to escape a threat, even when it's not actually there. And when you're busy avoiding your emotions, you miss out on what's in front of you, whether that's an actual threat to be evaded, or something that matters more than avoiding. When the pattern is longstanding, you become disconnected from your innermost interests, desires, and yearnings, which are essential for decoding and acting on your values.

· *Avoiding unwanted emotions can paradoxically increase them.* Maybe you've heard the saying, 'what you resist persists'? That applies in spades to emotional avoidance. When you try to stop or control something that is already happening, the resistance can actually *increase* your emotional discomfort and distress. In other words, trying to avert an emotional experience sometimes just gives you more of it.[1] For example, say you're so afraid of feeling 'abandoned' that any time you sense that someone might be pulling away, you pull away harder. And let's say in response, they disconnect from you. By trying to avoid this experience, you end up exactly where you didn't want to be. You get so focused on avoiding what you don't want that you end up convinced it's already happening, and then you unwittingly create it.

AVOIDING UNWANTED EMOTIONS CAN PARADOXICALLY INCREASE THEM.

When emotional avoidance is unhelpful and repetitive, it can have significant and life-interfering consequences:

· You may have difficulty adapting to change or uncertainty.

· You may become preoccupied with past regrets or future fears.

· You could have trouble labeling what you feel.

· You could struggle to connect with what matters to you.

· You could relate to all your emotional messages as directives you *must* heed, even when they don't serve you.

- You could develop toxic, destructive, compulsive habits, relationships, or addictions.

- You could end up with increased depression, anxiety, panic attacks, and chronic pain.

- You could find it difficult to regulate your emotions, or struggle with being impulsive or in constant fear of losing control of your actions.

- You could regularly struggle with motivation in the form of procrastination, overwhelm, or risk aversion.

- You could miss out on experiences with certain people, places, things, or other opportunities that are important to you.

- You may be consumed by hopelessness, helplessness, fear, or overwhelm and not see any other options.

- You could stagnate in your work and wonder why your performance doesn't improve.

And that's the short list. Ultimately, defaulting to avoidance in the absence of a real threat doesn't work well, exhausts you, makes you more miserable, and distracts you from what's possible. Left unchecked, these unhelpful default patterns can unwittingly make you an expert-level avoider – moving you constantly and consistently away from any and all unwanted emotional experiences, and what you really care about.

Research suggests emotional avoidance is a core driver in psychological distress and actually creates a lot of significant life-interfering problems.[2] Unhelpful patterns of emotional avoidance have been correlated with higher levels of depression, anxiety, and psychological distress;[3,4] increased chronic pain;[5] reduced quality of life; impaired memory and problem solving;[6] decreased ability to tolerate distress;[7] diminished contact with meaningful and valued life activities;[8] and decreased psychological wellbeing.[9] In contrast, when people learn to accept unwanted emotions, they experience significant decreases in anxiety, stress, depression, and loneliness, and increases in their ability to tolerate distress, regulate emotions, and engage with values-based living, as well as greater overall wellbeing.[10,11,12]

ULTIMATELY, DEFAULTING TO AVOIDANCE IN THE
ABSENCE OF A REAL THREAT DOESN'T WORK WELL,
EXHAUSTS YOU, MAKES YOU MORE MISERABLE,
AND DISTRACTS YOU FROM WHAT'S POSSIBLE.

COMMON AVOIDANCE STRATEGIES

To uncover your unique unhelpful behavior patterns, let's explore some common avoidance strategies and emotional coping styles.

Most simply, emotional avoidance strategies are specific ways you move away from unwanted emotional experiences. And these strategies can be carried out in private or public. You can avoid in ways that only you know about, or in ways that other people can also see.

For example, whatever you do internally with your thoughts or feelings or sensations in your body to get rid of discomfort or distress are examples of *private* avoidance strategies. And whatever you do that can be observed by others (such as leaving a party, checking a lock several times, yelling) are examples of *public* avoidance strategies.

Here's what this looks like. Emotional avoidance is always prompted by an aversive emotional trigger. As you know, triggers can come from defaults through perceived or actual threats to your safety, certainty, coherence, comfort, or pleasure; or obstruction of your values – your innermost interests, desires, or yearnings.

Say you get emotionally triggered by a falling out with a friend who disclosed something that you shared in confidence. Understandably, upon learning this you become triggered and have an immediate urge to confront her.

Using what you now know about where emotional triggers come from, you could first decode that you're not in danger (it's not a helpful default trigger). Next, you could decode whether the impulse to confront her comes from an unhelpful default urging you to avoid your emotional experience by trying to change, control, or alter your reaction or the situation itself. Or, you could decode whether the impulse to confront your friend comes from what matters most: your value of Trust, and your desire to restore it. You might even notice you're triggered by both.

Either way, let's say even though Trust is what matters most to you, what's louder and stronger is the urge to avoid the pain that comes with the situation.

Enter avoidance strategies.

Instead of pulling her aside and having a curious and respectful but firm conversation intended to clarify what happened, or ask for an apology, you may do whatever it takes to disconnect from the emotional pain.

If you default to avoiding, you may try to discharge your emotional distress by calling your friend out in front of everyone, to try to get rid of the emotional pain.

Or, you might resort to binge drinking all evening to numb the pain.

Or, you might shut down and withdraw or go to sleep to distance from the pain.

Or, you might try some combination of these avoidance pitfalls that keep you from acting on what you really want.

Unfortunately, if you don't learn to catch yourself first, you'll tend to deploy avoidance strategies when you're triggered, no matter the context. And since whatever you practice grows stronger, the next time something like this happens, it will feel easier to avoid in similar ways you've now rehearsed.

Now you've created an unhelpful default pattern. Unless you can decode what's happening in the moment.

Take a few moments now to familiarize yourself with some of the most common 'frequent flier' emotional avoidance strategies and see if you recognize any of them as your own reactive patterns:

- Distancing from stressful situations, places, or people (physically or in your mind).
- Ruminating about uncertainty to give yourself the illusion of controlling it.
- Suppressing distressing thoughts, images, or memories.
- Disconnecting or resisting physical sensations or anything that triggers them.
- Acting on urges to try to discharge a distressing emotion; for example, yelling or hitting something.

- Performing certain rituals and routines; for example, repeatedly checking that the stove is off or excessively seeking reassurance in an effort to decrease discomfort or distress.
- Numbing out through alcohol, food, drugs, sex, gambling, or exercise.

We humans can be very creative – even crafty or cunning – with finding ways to avoid emotional pain. To disrupt unhelpful default patterns it's helpful to know what types of avoidance strategies you're looking for.

REFLECTION: IDENTIFYING YOUR UNHELPFUL EMOTIONAL AVOIDANCE PATTERNS

To drill down on how emotional avoidance shows up in unhelpful patterns, take a moment to respond to the following prompts:

- What are some common strategies you use to avoid unwanted emotions when it's unhelpful (moves you away from what matters most)? You can use the list above or come up with your own examples.
- Recall the last time you avoided unwanted emotions; what were some of the unwanted consequences or costs?
- Take five minutes right now to pause reading and notice any urges to avoid something you don't want to experience.

EMOTIONAL COPING STYLES

Often people have an observable style in the way they attempt to avoid unwanted emotions, especially when they are triggered. Your hardwired and learned defaults can also lead you to develop your very own signature patterns of avoiding unwanted emotional experiences. These patterns are called *coping styles*.

Like all unhelpful default patterns, when coping styles are extreme, they tend to be automatic, rigid, limited, and are usually not sensitive to context. This also means they rarely expand what matters in moments of choice.

EMOTIONAL **COPING STYLES**

OVERCONTROLLED   UNDERCONTROLLED

◄ ·· ►

FLEXIBLE

More specifically, these signature coping styles range from overcontrolled (think: inhibited, reserved, measured) to undercontrolled (think: uninhibited, dramatic, impulsive). Most people tend toward a signature coping style. You might recognize these styles in yourself or others, from being 'buttoned up' to 'letting it all hang out.' When your style is more extreme or when you are triggered they are most observable.

For example, if you tend to be overcontrolled, you may often be hard to read, and when you feel threatened you'll tend to avoid unwanted emotions by going quiet, concealing what you're experiencing, and even shutting down your own emotion awareness. Or, on the other end of the spectrum, if you tend to be undercontrolled, you'll tend to avoid unwanted emotions by becoming more expressive, and you may even go into attack mode, verbally or physically.

To illustrate, if you are someone who tends toward 'overcontrolled' patterns of avoidance, you'll tend to respond to emotion triggers by working to control and suppress them. Even when it's not effective or helpful. Or, if you're someone who tends toward 'undercontrolled' patterns of avoidance, you'll tend to respond to emotion triggers by trying to discharge them, sometimes in visible ways. Even when it's not effective or helpful.

But here's what's not always so obvious: in either case, you're usually acting in subtle or obvious ways to avoid experiencing the discomfort and distress the emotion trigger has created. And as with any emotional avoidance, this will not help you expand your interests, desires, or yearnings. Responding the same way in every situation won't help you make your most powerful choices. Based on the emotional efficacy model, in your moments of choice you want to be able to move up or down the coping style continuum *flexibly*, so your actions align with what matters most.

> RESPONDING THE SAME WAY IN EVERY SITUATION WON'T HELP YOU MAKE YOUR MOST POWERFUL CHOICES ... YOU WANT TO BE ABLE TO MOVE UP OR DOWN THE COPING STYLE CONTINUUM FLEXIBLY, SO YOUR ACTIONS ALIGN WITH WHAT MATTERS MOST.

This flexibility sometimes makes it necessary to express yourself in more or less 'controlled' ways. For example, you might choose to contain yourself when someone else is having an outburst because what matters most is not escalating the situation.

Or, you might choose to express yourself when your partner is pleading with you to share your feelings, even though you have the urge to withdraw. The goal is to be flexible enough with your responses that you can act on what matters most in each situation.

But even if you're not someone who consistently responds in a predictable way, it's likely you have visited one end of the continuum or the other.

UNDERCONTROLLED COPING STYLE: DIFFICULTY CONTAINING EMOTIONS

My client 'Dana' was referred to me by the HR department at her company for help with 'emotional intelligence' and interpersonal conflict. She told me she struggled to get along with coworkers and to maintain friendships. She spoke very fast with high energy, and at one point I had to ask her to slow down so I could keep up with everything she was telling me. When I explored the feedback she was getting from coworkers, I discovered she was aware she wasn't making much effort to contain what she thought or felt, and even moreso when she was triggered. She said she found it difficult to contain her feelings. She told me her face was a dead giveaway and often got her into trouble.

Dana also described growing up in a 'chaotic' household, with parents who often fought openly. Dana coped with her emotional discomfort through trying to discharge it by yelling back. A lot of arguments at home would end up in shouting matches until someone got tired and gave up or left. Over the years this began to feel like a 'normal' way to interact when someone got upset.

At work, Dana had continued this unhelpful pattern. She was regularly in conflict with coworkers, whether just collaborating on projects, or whenever they suggested changes or pushed back on any of her ideas. In addition to not being receptive to feedback, she would sometimes openly criticize anyone who disagreed with her.

At times, to avoid yelling, she would have to excuse herself to go to her office to calm down. A few times she left work because she was unable to regulate herself after a disagreement. As much as she cared about her job and wanted to be an effective team member, she couldn't seem to interact with people without things blowing up. Dana had developed an undercontrolled emotional style.

OVERCONTROLLED COPING STYLE: DIFFICULTY OPENING TO EMOTIONS

'Ryan' reached out to me because he was feeling depressed and was struggling to make friends or go on dates. In our first meeting, I discovered he had a difficult time putting words to his feelings, and that he rarely opened up to other people. He told me his friends and coworkers sometimes dropped comments here and there about how he was hard to read. During our session, I couldn't see much in his facial expressions, his speech was measured, and his body was still and a bit rigid in the chair. Had he not told me he was feeling melancholy and distressed, I would never have known.

I observed Ryan's coping style throughout the session; for example, I noticed that when he became uncomfortable, he would stop making eye contact or skillfully change the subject. He also told me when he felt hurt, he tended to withdraw or distract himself. He shared (in a matter of fact way) that he would sometimes get in his car, turn his music up very loud, drive very fast on the highways, and scream to blow off steam. But in general, Ryan kept his emotions tucked away. He told me he felt lonely most of the time, and the only time he felt comfortable opening up was when he was drinking with friends.

Ryan grew up in a family with a mother who struggled with compulsive drinking and was volatile and unpredictable. Whenever his mother sensed anyone was being critical of her or was judging her, she would get very upset and verbally attack them. To avoid provoking her emotional outbursts, Ryan and his father walked on eggshells. He told me it never felt safe to talk about feelings with anyone in his family. As a result, Ryan had developed an overcontrolled coping style.

By this point you may know where your coping style tends to fall on the continuum. Or, if you're still not sure, think about any feedback you've received from others.

Have people ever told you that you need to open up more, or that you seem unemotional?

Have people ever told you that you are too much, or 'extra'?

If you hang out on the overcontrolled end of the continuum, you may have a pattern of avoiding unwanted emotional experiences by pulling in, containing, and even withdrawing.

If you hang out more toward the undercontrolled end of the continuum, you may avoid emotional experiences by acting out, 'dumping' your emotions on others, and being impulsive to act on any urges.

And it's usually the case that if you tend toward being undercontrolled, your coping style will be easier to spot. When you're overcontrolled your actions aren't as observable to others.

While Ryan and Dana are more clear-cut examples at the extreme ends of the emotional coping continuum, even if you have a preferred style, you might not always respond the same way.

For example, depending on the context, even if you tend toward overcontrol, you might still explode by raising your voice with your coworker if you get angry enough. And even if you tend toward undercontrol, you might be able to contain intense emotion if you're worried about the consequences of exploding with your coworker. The point here is simply that you may have a preferred pattern of inflexibility that shows up in your relationship with your emotions.

Of course, if you're already the Goldilocks posterchild for emotional efficacy you respond flexibly, intentionally, and creatively in ways that are neither too overcontrolled nor undercontrolled, but *just right* for the situation.

> IF YOU'RE ALREADY THE GOLDILOCKS POSTERCHILD FOR EMOTIONAL EFFICACY YOU RESPOND FLEXIBLY, INTENTIONALLY, AND CREATIVELY IN WAYS THAT ARE NEITHER TOO OVERCONTROLLED NOR UNDERCONTROLLED, BUT *JUST RIGHT* FOR THE SITUATION.

That said, most of us tend toward certain styles when we are triggered – especially when we feel intensely threatened. And the potential cost of any unhelpful behavior pattern is that it may shape your actions in ways that don't align with what matters most to you in context.

If someone is threatening you, containing what you're feeling may help de-escalate the situation.

Or if someone is struggling to understand you, sharing your feelings can be helpful for creating connection.

In context, there will be times when containing works best, and other times when expressing works best.

If you're not sure you have a distinct emotional coping style, don't sweat it. The goal is always the same: to get to the place where you optimize your responses for what matters most, in any moment, in any situation.

With practice, you can adapt to any context you're in, and adjust your responses to match what matters.

REFLECTION: IDENTIFYING YOUR EMOTIONAL COPING STYLE

Take a few moments to reflect on how your preferred coping style might show up when you're triggered. Imagine the following scenarios:

- Maybe you got so anxious about a brief conversation at a wedding that you withdrew and missed out on enjoying the party? (overcontrol)
- Perhaps someone interrupted you during a big presentation causing you to lose your flow, so you lashed out at them after the meeting? (undercontrol)
- Maybe someone failed to respond to your post on social media, and you sent them a chastising DM and unfriended them? (undercontrol)
- Perhaps you failed to back a coworker pleading his case in an important meeting because you were afraid of showing how strongly you feel in front of your boss? (overcontrol)
- Maybe you turned to binge eating, binge drinking, drugs, or compulsive shopping after a disappointing date or an upsetting interaction with a friend? (undercontrol)

YOU HAVE THE TECHNOLOGY: EXPERIENTIAL PRACTICE

Just knowing you need to disrupt your unhelpful default patterns to shift from unhelpful defaulting to valuing is a start.

And, it's not enough.

When it comes to behavior, past is often prologue.

As Morpheus says to Neo, 'There's a difference between knowing the path and walking the path.'

Walking the path is a whole other level of skillfulness. If you don't practice making different choices, it can be very challenging to act differently– especially in moments of intense stress and distress.

WHEN IT COMES TO BEHAVIOR, PAST IS OFTEN PROLOGUE ... IT CAN BE VERY CHALLENGING TO ACT DIFFERENTLY - ESPECIALLY IN MOMENTS OF INTENSE STRESS AND DISTRESS.

Consider what's happening when you become emotionally triggered by unhelpful defaults, and notice the urges that follow. By their very nature, the urges to avoid uncomfortable or distressing experiences will be compelling – seductive, even – because it's their job to keep you alive and well. Their sole mission is to get you to do whatever your emotions say.

This explains why overriding default urges can seem so unnatural, even preposterous. Some people characterize this intense emotion activation as a hypnotic state. Whatever you feel intensely is designed to entrance you, making it seem like what you feel is all there is.

But what if I told you ... your emotional network is *neuroplastic*?

In fact, even your well-rehearsed, deeply ingrained, unhelpful avoidance patterns can change, grow, and reorganize – with experiential practice.

This is very, very good news.

This will help you override the pull of the emotional matrix.

REWIRING AND RECODING

Here's the nerdy nitty-gritty. The experiential skills training in this book is drawn from cutting-edge research about how people effectively learn new skills in an activated state.[13] It turns out that practicing skills (new actions) in response to emotion triggers improves learning, retention, and recall. It helps the skills 'stick'.

This is because while you can't erase anything you've learned, you can overwrite it with new learning which weakens the original learning.[14] In other words, by practicing new actions when you have at least a moderate level of emotional activation, you can rewire your emotional network.[15] The neural architecture can change with your new experience.

Ultimately, activating and rewiring your emotional network is what allows you to develop new (more flexible) patterns of behavior. You can think of it as rewiring and recoding what you have access to when you're triggered. The skills you practice and the emotional state you're in become linked.[16,17] And once your skills and specific emotional states are rehearsed together enough, they become *networked*.

When you activate enough of the linked parts – for example, how the light looks at a certain time of day, the sound of the intro of a memorable love song, what you smell in the moment, or even certain words or phrases – all these parts come 'online' to form an emotional network. This gives you easier access to the skills the next time you're in that state.

You might think of it as heating up honey. It's not very malleable when it's cold. But add even a little heat, and it easily spreads over the whole piece of toast.

It's the same with your emotional networks. When they get going, they get flowing. In this 'heated up', activated state you can more easily change the structure of neural pathways and all their related parts. As you practice new behaviors, the relationship between the structures and parts involved are strengthened. This means they are more likely to come online together whenever enough of them show up.

As the saying goes, neurons that fire together wire together. It's as if Rachel and Monica are at the coffee shop in the TV show *Friends*; you're likely to see Ross, Phoebe and Chandler show up.

Or think of it this way: you're forging a new path through the woods. At first it might feel somewhat challenging to navigate. The route has never been taken before. It may be narrow and confounded by bushes, weeds, leaves, and fallen trees in your way. You see the other older, easier, more familiar paths and it may feel crazy to be making a new one. But you try it anyway. And the more often you take this path the wider, more familiar, and easier to follow it will become. Over time, even when you see the other paths, the new one may become the obvious way to go.

It's the same with any behavior patterns. When doing whatever your urges tell you feels like the most obvious way to go, it will feel difficult to choose anything else.

But with experiential practice you can pivot. You can learn to relate to your unhelpful defaults as faulty smoke alarms when they're not what matters most. And over time and with practice, you can rewire your emotional networks to stay the course, even in rough waters.[18]

This makes sense when you consider learning a new skill takes practice. If I wanted to learn how to throw kettle bells, I'd need to do more than just read about it. Reading about it would just give me an idea about proper technique. And while mentally rehearsing how to throw them could begin to build new neural pathways, to master this skill, I still need to go into a gym and have all the emotional experiences that go with that.

As with learning any new behavior, if knowledge and insight were enough, you wouldn't be defaulting in unhelpful ways. More than the knowledge or insight, you need experiential skills training to expertly navigate your moments of choice. Practicing in an emotionally activated state will shift your relationship with difficult emotional experiences so you can better design your actions.

When you practice responding in line with your values (instead of unhelpful defaults) in an emotionally activated state, you're networking emotional experiences you have with actions you can take. This creates new relationships in your emotional network. And over time, new (more helpful, effective, and flexible) ways of responding. It will become easier and easier to make different choices, even when you're triggered.

The more you practice, the more natural it will feel to respond differently.[19]

... IF KNOWLEDGE AND INSIGHT WERE ENOUGH, YOU WOULDN'T BE DEFAULTING IN UNHELPFUL WAYS.

THE POWER OF YOUR IMAGINATION

Experiential practice using your imagination is a powerful practice used in both therapy and performance coaching. Just visualizing events can bring your emotional networks online so you can rewire them with new actions. Because your imagination is so powerful, you can activate your emotional networks just by visualizing how you act in a difficult moment of choice.

I stumbled into the power of experiential practice years before I trained in psychology. Between high school and college, I decided to learn how to play lacrosse through a local summer league. While I had never played, my high school boyfriend played lacrosse. I had thrown the ball with him and watched him play, but women's lacrosse was a different beast. If you've never seen it, it's more of a game of grace and endurance compared to the brute strength of men's lacrosse. You have to cradle the ball in a very small, flat net using centrifugal force, while also running up and down the field, pursued by opponents, to either retrieve the ball or take it to goal.

I was really nervous. When I went to sleep the night before the first game, I vividly dreamed for what seemed like a full eight hours that I was playing lacrosse. I imagined the feel of the weight of the stick with the ball in it while running and cradling. I could feel the heat of the sun hitting my face and the summer heat as my lungs heaved from running up and down the field to follow the action. I felt the anxiety and excitement with the loud crack of wood on wood as an opponent tried to check my stick to knock the ball out of it, and as I changed levels to pivot around them. I saw myself pirouetting around any defensive players who tried to 'pick me off.' And I could feel the friction of scooping the ball off the bumpy field, bringing it up into a fierce cradle and then sprinting for a fast break to score.

The next day I was still very nervous. I had the urge to chicken out as soon as I arrived. I'm so glad I didn't. As crazy as it may sound, as soon as I stepped onto the field, it was if I had access to all the 'practice' from my dream. It was as if I had already played, and play I did. I cradled, I scooped, I sprinted, I passed, I pirouetted, and I even scored two of our four goals.

I credit most of my performance that day to the experiential practice from my dream. I lucked into a vivid dream state that primed my emotional network – and gave me access to the actions needed – to meet the demands of the game.

Experiential practice will help you override your unhelpful patterns of unhelpful defaulting by rehearsing new actions in your moments of choice. You'll be using emotion activation to rehearse the emotional efficacy skills throughout the rest of the book. By activating 'trigger scenes', with moderate levels of emotional intensity, you will do guided experiential skills practice to rehearse new choices in moments when you're triggered.

At the end of each chapter, you'll find a script to practice the experiential learning on your own, or you can use the recorded practices available at: www.drapriliawest.com/practice. Staying in the mid-range of activation is what research suggests is most effective. It makes sense: with too little emotion you're less likely to bring your emotional network fully online. And with too much emotion, you're more likely to get flooded and struggle to rehearse the new skill.

Skills practice in an activated state is like downloading new software that will give you access to more flexible, intentional, and creative choices, even in intense emotional states.

You'll learn to surf the urges that come with intense emotion triggers instead of acting on them.

And eventually, you'll respond with values-based action – and mindful coping when that's helpful.

This is where your emotional adventure begins. It may not be easy, especially if you're disrupting longstanding patterns of avoidance that formed from intensely painful experiences. But disrupting them will release you from the grip of the emotional matrix.

The choice is yours.

Will you choose the pain that comes with avoidance, or keep reading to learn how to skillfully navigate the pain that inevitably comes with doing what you care most about?

If you choose option 2, the next seven chapters will show you how.

CHAPTER 03 CHALLENGES

· Identify a recent trigger you responded to by avoiding unwanted experiences. See if you can identify one or two avoidance strategies you used from the list of 'frequent fliers'. Then see if you can clarify what mattered most in the situation: avoidance of discomfort and distress, or an interest, desire, or yearning.

· Identify a recurring situation in your life where your emotional coping style is in play and is leading you to act in inflexible ways. Make a plan to do one opposite action (for example, if you are clamming up in a conflict, express one thought or feeling, or if you are impulsively responding to constructive criticism, count to three and ask for further clarification).

· Make a list of recurring trigger scenes you use in experiential practice as you learn each new skill. For best results, pick situations that activate a 'moderate' level of intensity (around 4–6 on a scale of 1–10). You'll reference this list when you do the experiential skills practice later in the book.

· To lock in the learning, share with someone you know and feel comfortable with what you've learned about unhelpful patterns of avoidance, your frequent strategies and coping style, if any. Ask them about theirs.

CHAPTER 03 LEARNINGS

· Not all default patterns are problematic. Sometimes your helpful default patterns and patterns of valuing overlap.

· Your default processes (the 3Bs) lead to emotional (or experiential) avoidance – anything you do to alter, control, or move away from unwanted experiences.

· When you're defaulting in unhelpful ways, you'll run into avoidance pitfalls and the pain that comes with being disconnected from what matters.

· When you're valuing, you'll run into unwanted emotional experiences that go with doing hard things that matter.

· Unhelpful default patterns form from avoidance strategies and avoidant coping styles.

· Unhelpful avoidance strategies usually aren't effective; they typically provide short-term relief (if any), are exhausting, and can disconnect us from meaning.

· Emotional avoidance, paradoxically, can sometimes lead to more of what you're trying to avoid.

· Emotional coping styles are automatic, rigid, and limited patterns of responding to emotions, ranging from overcontrolled to undercontrolled.

· Your emotion network can be rewired through experiential practice.

· Activating a moderate level of emotional activation while visualizing or practicing new actions can improve learning, retention, and recall of new skills.

· You will default to easier and more familiar patterns unless you practice different behaviors in your moments of choice.

04

GETTING EMOTIONALLY 'WOKE'

Coach, I got a feeling we're not in Kansas anymore.

Ted Lasso

THAT YOU'VE MADE IT THIS FAR means you've fully committed to unplugging from the emotional matrix. Welcome to what else is possible when what you feel is not all there is.

Throughout the rest of this book, you'll learn specific emotional efficacy skills to help you optimize your moments of choice. You're now ready to free yourself from unhelpful default patterns and to choose the pain that comes with acting on your values. You'll learn to surf through the pain that naturally comes with stretching for what matters most, even when it means doing hard things. You'll learn to hear the signals of your values through the noise of your defaults, to align your actions with your interests, desires, and yearnings. And, you'll learn to regulate your emotions to help you stay focused on what you really care about in context. You'll become a boss-level choice-maker who can design your best life and unlock your full potential.

Becoming aware of and understanding your important, complex, and ever-changing emotional life is essential for developing all the skills that follow.

The first skill, emotion awareness, is fundamental because when you're not tuned in to your experience, you're more vulnerable to choice-making glitches.

You'll run on autopilot.

You'll be more likely to confuse discomfort or distress with dysfunction or danger.

You'll be entranced by unhelpful urges to default.

You'll struggle to know what you care about or even want in any moment.

… WHEN YOU'RE NOT TUNED IN TO YOUR EXPERIENCE, YOU'RE MORE VULNERABLE TO CHOICE-MAKING GLITCHES … YOU'LL RUN ON AUTOPILOT … YOU'LL BE MORE LIKELY TO CONFUSE DISCOMFORT OR DISTRESS WITH DYSFUNCTION OR DANGER … YOU'LL BE ENTRANCED BY UNHELPFUL URGES TO DEFAULT … YOU'LL STRUGGLE TO KNOW WHAT YOU CARE ABOUT OR EVEN WANT IN ANY MOMENT.

EMOTIONAL EFFICACY **DECISION CHART**

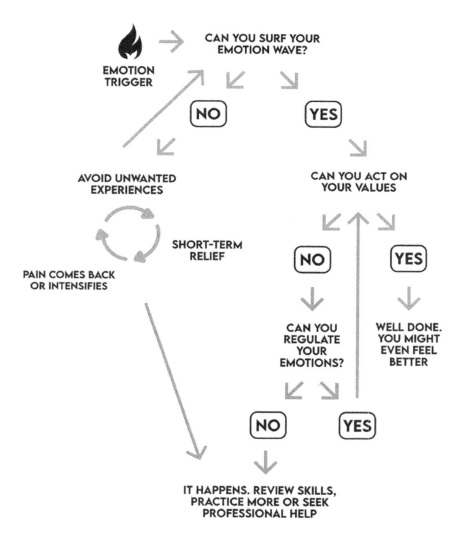

EMOTION TRIGGER

CAN YOU SURF YOUR EMOTION WAVE?

NO

YES

AVOID UNWANTED EXPERIENCES

CAN YOU ACT ON YOUR VALUES

SHORT-TERM RELIEF

PAIN COMES BACK OR INTENSIFIES

NO

YES

CAN YOU REGULATE YOUR EMOTIONS?

WELL DONE. YOU MIGHT EVEN FEEL BETTER

NO

YES

IT HAPPENS. REVIEW SKILLS, PRACTICE MORE OR SEEK PROFESSIONAL HELP

In this chapter, you'll learn the importance of tuning in to your emotions by recognizing an emotion 'trigger' as soon as it happens, and observing all parts of your emotional experience.

As a guide you can use the decision tree on the previous page to see how you'll practice responding to emotion triggers using the emotional efficacy skills so you can endgame the moments of choice that follow.

TUNING IN

Being able to connect to what's happening in the present moment is essential for decoding emotional messages. The reason is simple: there's not enough context to make effective choices when you're not aware of what's happening emotionally in the 'here and now.'

Tuning in to your experience in the present moment will help you wake up and smell the emotional coffee – to differentiate false alarms from what authentically matters. Eventually, awareness with your emotions will help you listen deeply enough to pivot to values-based action.

You probably already notice when emotion triggers happen, even if you don't know what they are. By design, they are meant to get your attention either via a (helpful or unhelpful) threat alert from your 3Bs, or an important signal from your values. And yet, if you're not someone who is already tuned in, true emotion awareness can feel like a big stretch.

> THERE'S NOT ENOUGH CONTEXT TO
> MAKE EFFECTIVE CHOICES WHEN YOU'RE
> NOT AWARE OF WHAT'S HAPPENING
> EMOTIONALLY IN THE 'HERE AND NOW.'

'I NEVER REALLY LIKED MY HUSBAND'

'How did I never realize I didn't really like my husband?' my client 'Kristen' asked. She and her husband had married in their early 20s, and now after 25 years she was empty-nesting and had 'hit a wall' where she felt she could no longer stay in her marriage.

She said, 'I knew I didn't have "butterflies" in my stomach when I married him, but I told myself he was smart, reliable, from a good family, and that feeling in love was the stuff of fairytales.'

Over the years she had chalked up her irritability and annoyance with him to 'immature male behavior' and rationalized her experience as typical challenges in coparenting and marriage.

Having been raised in a family that leaned toward emotional overcontrol and where rationality was highly valued, Kristen (over)relied on her intellect for making choices. As a result, she hadn't learned to decode her emotions. Instead, she did everything by the book. She did what she thought she should. She went to the 'right' college, took the 'right' job, and married the 'right' guy – in the eyes of her family and her larger social circle.

Now, all these years later, Kristen was full of grief about what might have been. She was spending hours each day ruminating about how her life might have unfolded if she had known how to listen more deeply to what her emotions could tell her about her values. Instead, she let her belief that 'emotions are liabilities and being rational is strong' guide her choice to marry someone who 'looked good on paper.' Only after becoming close to a male colleague at work did she start to feel what she was missing with her husband, and she was terrified she was going to have an affair if she didn't leave.

Like Kristen, people can go long periods – or even their whole lives – without realizing that something or someone is just not working for them.

Or that they're missing out on meaningful opportunities and what else might be possible.

They push aside feelings or ignore them to follow what 'seems' right to them, or what other people say they 'should' do.

All because they don't take their emotions seriously or understand what's possible from paying closer attention.

Being tuned into your emotions is powerful on many levels, not just for decoding your triggers. Research shows that being able to describe and talk about your feelings is therapeutic.[1] This makes sense if you imagine the joy of being a small child who suddenly discovers language to express themselves. You might even remember when you were first able to communicate, or maybe you've witnessed children putting words to their experience for the first time.

This is what it's like for anyone who discovers emotional fluency later in life. Putting words to your feelings not only helps you figure out what you feel, and what matters to you, it can also increase your sense of safety, certainty, coherence, comfort, and pleasure. It shifts your experience.

> PUTTING WORDS TO YOUR FEELINGS
> NOT ONLY HELPS YOU FIGURE OUT WHAT
> YOU FEEL, AND WHAT MATTERS TO YOU,
> IT CAN ALSO INCREASE YOUR SENSE OF SAFETY,
> CERTAINTY, COHERENCE, COMFORT, AND
> PLEASURE. IT SHIFTS YOUR EXPERIENCE.

I'll never forget happening into this realization as a staff songwriter for a big music publishing company in the early 2000s. My job (amazingly) was to write songs every day. This meant digging deep into my own life experience to come up with ways to describe lots (and lots and lots) of feelings. At the time I wasn't aware of the clinical research showing that being specific and describing 'all the feelings' can be very cathartic. It turned out I was unwittingly doing some version of my own therapy by deep diving into my experience – past heartbreak, loneliness, excitement, inspiration – and putting words to the whole gamut between hope and despair.

I distinctly remember one song I wrote just after an argument with my then-boyfriend. I walked away from it confused about my feelings and what mattered to me. I went into my modest home studio, put all my 'triggered energy' into exploring and expressing, and 90 minutes later I emerged emotionally 'exorcised'. What had felt threatening and confusing ended up becoming liberating and meaningful.

It doesn't always come that easily. Depending on your current level of emotional fluency, putting words to feelings can take some practice.

Sometimes you might struggle to connect to what you're experiencing, and you could end up feeling confused and more disconnected.

And sometimes, getting in touch with your feelings – especially if you don't do it on the regular – can be more like getting a root canal … you know you need it, and that you'll feel better on the other side, but it doesn't feel fun, especially the anticipation. The fact is, because of the way emotions work, once you're 'in your feelings,' the only real way out of pain is through (more on this in the next chapter).

> THE FACT IS, BECAUSE OF THE WAY EMOTIONS
> WORK, ONCE YOU'RE 'IN' YOUR FEELINGS,'
> THE ONLY REAL WAY OUT OF PAIN IS THROUGH.

And if you're clear that there will always be discomfort and distress (whether you're avoiding unwanted emotional experiences or expanding what matters most), you can tap the willingness to tune in. Even when your emotions are painful.

TAKING YOUR EMOTIONS SERIOUSLY

Most of us listen to our emotions just enough to avoid disaster and distress and make the most of pleasurable experiences. But this doesn't help with errors in judgment that come with unhelpful defaulting. Especially when they're telling us really important things we need to know, not just to survive, but also to thrive.

Practicing emotion awareness requires breaking with the 'normal' pace of life long enough to slow down and notice what's happening. This is easier said than done. Turning in can feel like that disappointing downshift to 15 mph on a long road trip when you've been happily buzzing along at 65 for several hours. But when we are cruising along in autopilot, we don't always see what's happening until it's too late to choose something else.

So, for example, had my client, Kristen, paid more attention to her emotion triggers, she may have registered that she was deeply unhappy and done something about it years ago. Tuning into your emotions and decoding their messages is essential for clarifying what matters most. Without getting present and tuning in, you won't be able to harness your moment of choice to design your actions in line with your values. The first step is to slow down and to master tuning in to whatever is happening for you emotionally. This doesn't happen without effort and practice.

In my own life, I've seen the cost of not having better emotion awareness. I remember a situation in my 20s with a colleague from Capitol Hill who was flirty with me. It started with compliments that felt a bit too intimate. And over time, he started making sexual advances. Several times, even when I would say no and tell him he had the wrong idea, he would persist until I physically removed myself from his presence. When it happened I was in shock and didn't register (and I probably didn't want to register) how deeply uncomfortable I was. My natural reaction was to shut down and disconnect from my feelings. I didn't want to face the fact that this person, whose work I respected immensely, was committing a huge #boundaryfail. Instead I avoided being alone with him, which didn't always work. Eventually, my work took me out of DC and it ceased to be an issue.

Years later I ran into him at a restaurant. He picked right up where he had left off, flirting and even trying to pull me close. When I resisted, he leaned in to try to kiss me. But by this time my emotion awareness was dialed in. I immediately sensed the tension in my stomach; I noticed my thought, *who does he think he is?!* And I noticed my urge to slap him as I felt the swell of indignation and anger front and center. While I chose not to act on the (well-deserved) urge to leave, I did what mattered most: I found my 'no.' And I let it out, loudly. Loudly enough for everyone around us to hear, in no uncertain terms, the consequences of him ever trying that again.

MORE THAN A FEELING: THE 'STUF' OF EMOTIONS

Now that you understand the concept of tuning into your emotions, let's explore *how* you can begin to do this. The Latin root for the word emotion is 'emotere', which means 'energy in motion.' You'll recognize emotional energy moving in the form of what you know as emotion triggers, which come in the form of messages sent by defaults or values. Emotional messages provide data about what your mind and body are experiencing in context. Triggers can be on the pleasurable or distressing ends of the emotional spectrum. When they happen, you know there's energy in motion. Your emotional network is activated, and you're feeling something.

> ## EMOTIONAL MESSAGES PROVIDE DATA ABOUT WHAT YOUR MIND AND BODY ARE EXPERIENCING IN CONTEXT.

But, here's an interesting question: when you get triggered, *how* do you know what you're feeling in any moment?

This question is often is met by a range of responses, from curiosity to blank stares to laughter by my clients. A lot of times people know what they are feeling. But, if you ask them *how* they know they are experiencing those feelings they, can't tell you.

For instance, maybe you're pretty good at noticing when you get triggered – when something happens and you get emotionally activated. You know you're feeling some kind of way. But do you actually know *what you feel?*

While most people tend to use the word *feeling* to describe all emotional experience, at any given moment you can experience emotions in at least four distinct ways that make up your emotional 'STUF':

- what's happening in your body *(sensations)*
- what you are thinking or images in your mind *(thoughts)*
- how your impulses motivate you to act in certain ways *(urges)*
- how you label or interpret the all these experiences in context *(feelings)*.

Here's what this looks like. As I write this, we've been waiting for days to hear about the final results for the 2020 presidential election in the US. I'm definitely triggered. But how do I actually *know* what I'm feeling? Through all my emotional STUF: I'm sensing tension in my neck and shoulders and energy pulsing through my body (sensations); I'm thinking, 'will there be more civil unrest in my neighborhood?' and 'where will I go if it gets dangerous?' (thoughts); I have the impulse to stay glued to the news instead of working or even eating, and to call my girlfriends (urges); and as a result, I feel nervous, annoyed, and tired (feelings). All of this emotional STUF is happening at the same time. And all the parts contribute to my experience in the moment, as well as how my emotional energy moves next.

Earlier versions of psychological science conceptualized emotional experience as just being made up of thoughts and feelings, separating your 'mind' or thoughts from your broader emotions. However, more recent research has given way to broader and more complex models of emotion,[2] and most now include not only a cognitive and affective, but also, a somatic component. However, most people still tend to think of their emotions as one big *feeling*. They don't realize their feelings are just the tip of the iceberg.

> ... MOST PEOPLE STILL TEND TO THINK OF
> THEIR EMOTIONS AS ONE BIG *FEELING*.
> THEY DON'T REALIZE THEIR FEELINGS
> ARE JUST THE TIP OF THE ICEBERG.

Emotions are actually a lot like music – sometimes simple and straightforward, and other times, rich, complex, and even mysterious. They are made up of many parts, but together they can seem like a single song.

Here are a few more examples of how you might experience different parts of emotional STUF at the same time:

- The feeling of *sadness* often comes with a constricted sensation in your throat, chest, and stomach, sometimes with thoughts about loss and regret, and often includes an urge to withdraw or cry.
- The feeling of *joy* often comes with an open and relaxed sense throughout your body, sometimes with thoughts about gratitude or revery, and often includes an urge to engage with others or celebrate.

- The feeling of *anger* often comes with a tense sensation in your chest, in your shoulders, back, and jaw, sometimes with thoughts about injustice or betrayal, and often includes an urge to withdraw or attack.

EMOTIONAL **'STUF'**

SENSATIONS

THOUGHTS

URGES

FEELINGS

Whenever you become emotionally activated, all your emotional STUF is activated. And the 'louder' it gets, the easier it is to notice each part of your emotional network.

There is a whole host of research documenting the interplay between all your STUF.[3] Not only do your sensations, thoughts, urges, and feelings get activated by internal events or events in your environment, they also play off each other.

It works like this: every part can trigger other parts, making up an incredibly interactive network of actions and reactions. Feelings can impact urges, urges can impact sensations, sensations can impact thoughts, and so on, in any possible combination. What you think about can trigger sensations in your body and an urge to act in a certain way – and this in turn can create more feelings, and also more sensations, thoughts, urges, and feelings in any possible combination.

You could think of your emotional STUF as a band – when the drummer goes faster, everyone else follows. The singer speeds up, the guitarist fumbles his difficult solo because of the pace, and the bass player plucks his strings in time with the quicker tempo. And in reverse, if the singer slows down, the bass player will loosen up, the drummer will hang back, and the guitarist will adjust to the new tempo.

> YOU COULD THINK OF YOUR EMOTIONAL STUF AS A BAND - WHEN THE DRUMMER GOES FASTER, EVERYONE ELSE FOLLOWS. THE SINGER SPEEDS UP, THE GUITARIST FUMBLES HIS DIFFICULT SOLO BECAUSE OF THE PACE, AND THE BASS PLAYER PLUCKS HIS STRINGS IN TIME WITH THE QUICKER TEMPO.

Similarly, when you experience any sensations – such as tension in your chest or a rapid heartbeat – it's likely to trigger corresponding thoughts (for example, *what's about to happen?*), urges (for example, scanning your environment for threat), and feelings (for example, anxiety, dread, or anticipation). And in turn, these thoughts, urges, and feelings can amplify or even trigger more sensations, and vice versa, in any combination. And your STUF also interacts with what's happening in your environment. It's a big feedback loop.

PRACTICING EMOTION AWARENESS

To start, you'll notice each part of your emotional STUF, one at a time. You can actually do this in any moment, but it's most helpful if you find something to act as a trigger – something to activate at least a detectable level of emotion. As you practice, you'll eventually be able to observe everything at once, just like you'd watch different parts of weather happening at the same time.

Following are a few examples of what this might look like.

Example 1: When I haven't eaten for more than eight hours (medium trigger), I might experience the following STUF:

S = I notice a *sensation* of emptiness and tension in my stomach.

T = I notice the *thought*, 'time to eat!'

U = I notice the *urge* to go to the kitchen and prepare food.

F = I notice I *feel* anxious and slightly irritable.

Example 2: If I am having a significant disagreement with a board member about the purpose of our work (medium trigger) I might experience this kind of STUF:

S = I notice the *sensation* of tension in my neck and shoulders.

T = I notice the *thought*, 'why did you volunteer if you aren't committed to our mission?!'

U = I notice the *urge* to convince them my perspective is 'right.'

F = I notice I *feel* disappointed and concerned.

Of course, you wouldn't be this fluent in this kind of 'emotion-eze' unless you've done this kind of work before. To help you out, following are brief primers with lists of examples for each part of your emotional STUF. These lists will also serve as a reference for your experiential practice toward the end of this chapter.

THE S OF EMOTIONAL 'STUF': SENSATIONS

So much emotional experience happens in your body. You may not always sense what's happening there, but you can increase your awareness by learning to watch for different types of sensations. Like all parts of emotional STUF, sensations will both trigger and react to all the other parts of emotional STUF.

Sensations can be described in many ways: *size, shape, tension, temperature, movement, uncomfortable,* and *pleasurable.* Following is a list you can use to practice describing all the various sensations you might experience in your body.

THE 'S' OF STUF: **SENSATIONS**

SIZE	TEMPERATURE	SENSATIONS that tend to be uncomfortable	SENSATIONS that tend to be pleasurable
Small	Hot		
Medium	Cold		
Big	Cool	Prickly	Calm
	Warm	Electric	Energized
SHAPE	Neutral	Tingling	Smooth
Flat	Chilled	Twitchy	Streaming
Round	Boiling	Burning	Warm
Square	Sweaty	Radiating	Cool
Ropey	Clammy	Buzzing	Relaxed
Thin		Itchy	Open
Wide	**MOVEMENT**	Dense	Light
	Shaking	Thick	Spacious
TENSION	Throbbing	Blocked	Airy
Tight	Pounding	Contracted	Releasing
Loose	Fluttering	Heavy	Expanded
Knotted	Shivering	Empty	Expansive
Heavy	Queasy	Stabbing	Flowing
Light	Wobbling	Nauseous	Floating
Constricted	Bubbling	Tender	Fluid
Clenched	Breathlessness	Achy	Releasing
Dull		Sore	Flexible
Intense		Bloated	Satiated

As you practice you might also notice how often sensations trigger an urge to adjust or change something so that you are more comfortable in your body. To dive a little deeper with sensations, you can try noticing when they are aversive or pleasurable. You might also notice a pattern of experiencing certain kinds of sensations when you're triggered.

THE T OF EMOTIONAL 'STUF': THOUGHTS

Your mind is almost always producing thoughts or images, which can range from what's happened in the past, to what will happen in the future, to what's going on right now. Your thoughts make up the 'content' of your mind. You might experience them as an inner narrator or voice in your head that's frequently talking, or as pictures like a movie in your mind.

Often your thoughts make up bigger groups of related thoughts that become longer narratives or even stories. And as you know, because of a tendency to seek safety, certainty, coherence, comfort, and pleasure, when you're feeling threatened, the content of your thoughts will often center around avoiding something, or approaching something.

Like all parts of emotional STUF, thoughts can activate sensations, feelings, and urges that motivate you to take action (for example, the thought, *I shouldn't touch that flame or I'll get burned* could trigger sensations of tension in your shoulders and chest, a feeling of fear, and the urge to move away). Your thoughts will also naturally follow other parts of your emotions. For example, if you're feeling calm, and your body is relaxed, you might notice more neutral thoughts, or that the frequency and number of thoughts decrease. Or, if you feel anxious or threatened, and your heart is beating rapidly, your thoughts will naturally speed up and increase in cadence and sense of urgency.

THE 'T' OF STUF: **THOUGHTS**

WORDS	IMAGES
I wonder when my sister will call?	(My sister's face)
Should I make another cup of coffee, or keep working?	(Favorite coffee mug)
It sure is pretty outside...	(Mountains in the background outside my window)
I shouldn't have eaten the whole pint of ice cream last night.	(Melty ice cream in a bowl)
I should stop at the grocery store on the way home to get more ice cream.	(Driving to grocery store)

Just like any unhelpful default messages, thoughts can seem like the truth even when they are false alarms. This also means when you become hooked by your thoughts, you might relate to them as 'facts' about what's happening. Some thoughts even seem like commands telling you what you should do, and it can feel really unnatural not to obey them, especially if there's any perceived threat looming. In fact, if you are someone who tends to 'buy in' to your thoughts, they will seem urgent, like alarms going off, and make it difficult just to watch them.

When you first start watching the content in your mind, it's possible you'll hear a cascade of thoughts – something like this:

> Why am I doing this exercise? This isn't relaxing at all. And I have so much to get done. I can't forget to get that memo done for my boss on Monday because last time I didn't have it on her desk by 8:20 a.m. she emailed asking for it and she probably thinks I didn't care and am not that conscientious and am I really conscientious or is she just overbearing, and oh how I wish I didn't think about these things on the weekends – it would be so nice just to relax and have fun like so many other people seem to do on social media ... I wonder if I'm doing this right? I have so many thoughts. Ugh, is this normal? Why is my mind running so fast? Is there something wrong with me? I am always worrying about stuff and am so anxious but maybe it's because my boss doesn't like me, or maybe I'll get fired and then what will I do? Maybe it's hopeless ...

To practice watching your thoughts, try slowing down to observe just one thought at a time instead of moving straight to the next thought. Be prepared that it may be tempting to get involved with your thoughts, instead of staying with the exercise. This is natural and you'll notice it gets easier to slow down and just watch your thoughts, one at a time, as you practice. (Pro tip: if you're struggling, it can help to take a few deep breaths to slow them down since whatever happens in your body affects your thoughts.)

A stream-of-consciousness thought-watching practice will have one thought at a time at a slower pace:

> *I wonder when my sister will call me?*
> *Should I make another cup of coffee?*
> *It sure is pretty outside ...*

I shouldn't have eaten the whole pint of ice cream last night.

I should stop at the grocery store on the way home to get more ice cream.

THE U OF EMOTIONAL 'STUF': URGES

Simply put, urges are impulses to act in certain ways. Every emotion comes with at least one or more urges. Your emotions always urge you toward some kind of action – to either do something or not do something. That's the job of an urge – to motivate you to do what your emotional network is reading as most important for you. As you may remember, urges can prompt private actions, known only to you in your mind or in your body, or observable actions, like talking or moving in front of another person.

Urges, by their very nature, are so compelling that not acting on them can feel really uncomfortable. Urges can seem especially obvious in moments we are intensely triggered – it's hard to imagine acting in any other way. (Again, this is why experiential learning is so powerful.) It could feel like not scratching an itch ... sometimes a very, very intense itch.

Because intense urges come from urgent emotion messages from your mind (thoughts) and body (sensations), and your interpretation in context (feelings), acting on them can feel really 'right.'

After all, who wouldn't want to act on the urge to celebrate a long, hard sought-after win?

And who wouldn't want to indulge the urge to ruminate on a story about hopelessness, helplessness, danger, and threat when they're scared?

And who wouldn't oblige the urge to climb into a cozy bed and rest when recovering from food poisoning?

Following is a list of examples you can reference to familiarize yourself with different kinds of private or observable action urges you might notice when you experience any (unwanted or wanted) emotional STUF.

THE 'U' OF STUF: **URGES**

worry	ruminate	defend
tense up	fantasize	push
run	explain	strike
jump	analyze	freeze
problem-solve	cling	plead
celebrate	leave	protect
judge	laugh	shield
procrastinate	attack	leave
justify	fight	argue
intellectualize	yell	hide
apologize	pretend	shut down
blame	fawn	check
surrender	fight	obsess
adjust	quit	solve
withdraw	anticipate	define
pretend	arrange	convince
rationalize	embrace	listen
cry	help	celebrate
detach	connect	wait
collaborate	communicate	accelerate
stay put	delegate	scratch

THE F OF EMOTIONAL 'STUF': FEELINGS

In the emotional efficacy model, the term 'feelings' refers to words or labels used to interpret emotional experience in context. Your feelings describe real and valid experiences. What you feel in any moment will depend on how you interpret what's happening with your sensations, thoughts, and urges in a given situation.

Because your feelings are always interpretations, they always depend on the context. For example, if you have the sensation of a rapid heart rate, sweaty palms, and the urge to move and discharge energy, and you're having thoughts about whether or not you're doing 'it' right, you might be feeling *anxious, scared, insecure, and vulnerable.*

Yet, in another situation with those same sensations and thoughts, your feelings might be *stimulated, fascinated, energetic, and aroused.* The first scenario might be a major work presentation, while the second might be an intimate encounter. The difference is how you interpret what's happening in context.

Or, take an even more complex example: let's say you have the sensations of a rapid heart rate, sweaty palms, and the urge to move and discharge energy, but your feelings are *hopeful, excited, amped up, and sentimental.* This could also be related to a work presentation, but maybe the context is that it's your last major work presentation in your current job.

Feelings help you read and understand exactly what you're experiencing. Sometimes you can even experience very different kinds of feelings at the same time. On the following page are examples of labels you can use to describe your feelings.

If you're not tuning in to your emotions carefully, they can obscure what really matters. You'll begin to realize that you can play the role of an observer watching all parts of your emotions. By learning to be curious and just notice your emotional STUF, you will begin to shift how much power they have over you. And this will expand what's possible in your moments of choice, especially when you're triggered (much more on this in chapter 6).

REFLECTION: NOTICING YOUR EMOTIONAL NETWORK OF STUF

Tuning into your emotional STUF is how you begin to disrupt unhelpful default patterns. Take a moment now to evaluate how much ease you have noticing all parts of your emotions:

- What do you notice when you try to tune into sensations? Do any of the 3Bs send you messages to avoid whatever you're experiencing in your body? If so, what is the exact message?

- What do you notice when you tune into your thoughts? Do any of the 3Bs send you messages to avoid any thoughts or images that show up? If so, what is the exact message?

- What do you notice when you tune into your feelings? Do any of the 3Bs send you messages to avoid labeling them? If so, what is the exact message?

- What do you notice when you tune into your urges? Do any of the 3Bs send you messages to avoid connecting to them? If so, what is the exact message?

THE 'F' OF STUF: **FEELINGS**

FEELING labels that describe unpleasant or aversive experience:	FEELING labels that describe pleasant or neutral experience:
hostile	joyful
angry	excited
rage	safe
critical	accepted
skeptical	understood
irritated	energetic
furious	playful
frustrated	alert
hurt	present
disappointed	curious
lonely	fasinated
overwhelmed	stimulated
annoyed	amused
selfish	daring
jealous	powerful
sad	proud
ashamed	respected
guilty	satisfied
suspicious	appreciated
exhausted	nurtured
regretful	hopeful
lonely	fulfilled
bored	invigorated
unappreciated	competent
apathetic	confident
inadequate	grateful
hopeless	sentimental
miserable	trusting
scared	loving
confused	responsive
helpless	relaxed
insecure	pensive
anxious	authentic
weak	protected
embarrassed	adventurous
discouraged	purposeful
disconnected	connected

Emotion awareness alone is a powerful skill. Just pausing to observe your emotional STUF can disrupt unhelpful default patterns. In fact, after emotion awareness training, the same client who originally asked why their emotions mattered described their experience this way:

> It has taken me a few weeks to be able to really track my emotional experience. Now I notice that when I can be curious about how I'm feeling, I am less irritable and reactive with my partner. And the more curiosity I have, the more in the moment I am, and the more I can slow down and feel into what I actually want and need. I can see how much my increasing emotion awareness affects my choices for the better.

With real-time emotional activation, doing experiential practice with emotion awareness will help you master tuning in to all parts of your emotional experience in an activated state, so you're ready to move to the next level. Ultimately experiential practice will accelerate your learning and make new skills easier to remember when you get triggered IRL.

THE EMOTION AWARENESS OBSTACLE COURSE

Before you start practicing, it may be helpful to know the kinds of challenges people encounter when they first start practicing emotion awareness. Don't be surprised if you experience some of the following common obstacles:

- *You may struggle with observing different parts of an emotion.* Sometimes a thought might seem like a feeling, or an urge like a sensation, or any other combination you can imagine. Or your STUF could seem like one big thing. It's natural to have an easier or harder time observing certain parts. Some people struggle to identify sensations in their body; others may not easily identify their thoughts; and some people aren't sure what they are feeling. If you find yourself struggling to identify which is what, don't give up.

Some people can identify all parts of emotion with little effort, while others struggle to observe any part. One of my clients could only identify images instead of thoughts when we first started working together. Another client couldn't identify her sensations until after several months of practice. There's no right or wrong here – there's just getting better at knowing what's happening for you. The important thing is to keep trying and being curious. Like any skill, the more you practice, the better you'll get.

· *You may worry that if you become aware of your emotions, you might have to take difficult action.* When people repeatedly disconnect from their emotions, tuning in can seem like an intimidating plunge into the unknown. You might try to reframe emotion awareness as 'harnessing opportunities to expand what really matters,' to help you find the willingness to get in touch with whatever is there. And if it feels like too much, it may mean you'd benefit from working with a trained professional.

· *You can psych yourself out before you really try.* Often people predict that the discomfort they'll experience by getting in touch with any unwanted STUF will be greater than it is. This happens when the anticipatory anxiety of deeply connecting with your emotions is way more intense than the experience itself. Knowing this in advance can be a good way of inoculating yourself and motivating yourself to do it anyway. If this is what you're experiencing, try recording the level of distress you predict you'll feel and then compare it with the actual distress you experience during practice to see if there's a pattern you can learn from.

· *You may struggle to connect to your emotions at all.* If you are someone who has avoided tuning in to your emotions, you may just be out of practice. Or, you may be avoiding emotions because of negative beliefs about them, so you tend to suppress or push away any sensations, thoughts, urges, and feelings. You can disrupt this pattern by just being kind to yourself about the fact that tuning in isn't happening naturally. Then, you might practice with one part of an emotion at a time; for example, by first just noticing the urges the music brings up. Then when you feel ready, go back and notice the rest: thoughts, sensations, and feelings. There's no medal for moving quickly ... go at your own pace. That's the beauty of being able to do this work on your own with minimal structure.

- *You may find it uncomfortable or even distressing to connect with your emotions.* It's natural to experience discomfort or even some distress when you pay attention to certain emotions. Often people find it to be odd, difficult, or uncomfortable at first. If you find this experiential practice too distressing, or, if after trying you still can't connect to any part of your emotion, this may mean you would benefit from having a professional guide you.

EMOTION AWARENESS EXPERIENTIAL PRACTICE

Let's get experiential. To improve your emotion awareness you'll want to get into a state of emotional activation. In this first experiential practice you'll use music as an emotional trigger. Pick a few songs that activate different emotions for you, from pleasurable to aversive. The important thing is you know listening to them will evoke at least a medium-level emotional response.

It may help to keep the lists of emotional STUF handy for reference. While you're listening, you'll record what shows up, as in the following example.

TRIGGER/SONG: *HURT*, SUNG BY JOHNNY CASH

EMOTIONAL 'STUF'

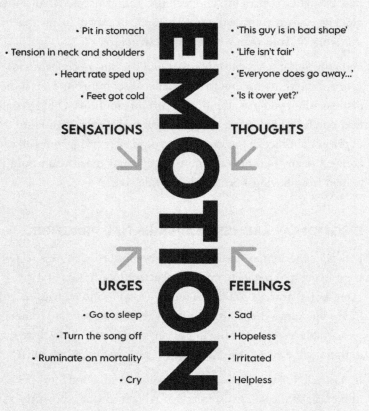

SENSATIONS
- Pit in stomach
- Tension in neck and shoulders
- Heart rate sped up
- Feet got cold

THOUGHTS
- 'This guy is in bad shape'
- 'Life isn't fair'
- 'Everyone does go away...'
- 'Is it over yet?'

URGES
- Go to sleep
- Turn the song off
- Ruminate on mortality
- Cry

FEELINGS
- Sad
- Hopeless
- Irritated
- Helpless

To rehearse the skill of emotion awareness, you can use the following script, and you can also access a guided experiential practice at www.drapr{}iliawest.com/practice.

SET UP

Find a private, quiet place and get into a comfortable position where you're likely to stay alert. For this practice, you will also need a notebook and pen so you can record your emotional STUF after you've finished listening.

SELECT A TRIGGER

Choose two songs to play that you think will trigger a medium level of emotion activation. On a scale of 1 to 10, with 10 being the highest level of activation, you want to shoot for moderate intensity, between 4 and 6.

ACTIVATE EMOTION

To activate your emotions, you'll play each song for at least 90 seconds. Then move to the next step.

OBSERVE EMOTIONAL STUF

Notice each part of your emotional STUF, one part at a time, as follows:

(Sensations)

- Notice their size and shape.
- Notice whether they're moving or staying the same.
- Notice any tension in the sensation.
- Notice if there's any temperature.

(Thoughts)

- Notice each thought or image that comes to mind, one at a time.

(Urges)

- Notice an impulse to do something or not to do something (internally or an outward observable behavior).

(Feelings)

- Label at least two feeling(s).

When you finish listening to the first song, take a few minutes to list all four parts of your emotional STUF you noticed:

TRIGGER/SONG #1

Sensation(s):

Thought(s):

Urge(s):

Feeling(s):

Now play the second song you've chosen and repeat the sequence.

Notice each part of your emotional STUF, one part at a time, as follows:

(Sensations)

· Notice their size and shape.

· Notice whether they're moving or staying the same.

· Notice any tension in the sensation.

· Notice if there's any temperature.

(Thoughts)

· Notice each thought or image that comes to mind, one at a time.

(Urges)

· Notice an impulse to do something or not to do something (internally or an outward observable behavior).

(Feelings)

· Label at least two feeling(s).

· Take a few minutes to list all four parts of your emotional STUF you noticed:

TRIGGER/SONG #2

Sensation(s):

Thought(s):

Urge(s):

Feeling(s):

REFLECT

To wrap up the experiential practice, take a few moments to reflect using the following prompts:

- Did anything surprise you?
- What, if anything, was challenging?
- What did you learn?
- Write down anything else you want to remember.

CHAPTER 04 CHALLENGES

- Over the next few days, set an alarm at three times during the day to stop whatever you're doing and tune in to the four parts of your emotional STUF: sensations, thoughts, urges, and feelings. Describe anything you notice using your STUF lists to get as detailed and specific as you can to increase your emotional fluency.

- If you notice you are having discomfort connecting to any parts of emotion, do a quick inventory of the 3Bs (biases, beliefs about emotion, and biology) to see where the threat is coming from.

- Take time to do the emotion awareness experiential practice using music at least three more times over the next week and track what parts of your emotional STUF are easier or harder to connect with. You can also use the guided practice at www.drapriliawest.com/practice.

- To lock in the learning, share what you've learned about your emotions with someone you know, and what it means to you so far. Ask them if they understand how they know what they are experiencing in a given moment. If they don't, walk them through observing the four parts of emotional STUF.

CHAPTER 04 LEARNINGS

- Emotion awareness entails tuning in and observing all parts of your emotional STUF in the present moment.

- Slowing down to tune in to emotions can be challenging if you're not in the habit.

- Listening to and naming your emotions can be a cathartic experience in and of itself.

- Emotions are made up of four parts called 'STUF': sensations, thoughts, urges, and feelings.

- Emotional STUF is interactive: each part can trigger and react to all the other parts.

- It's natural to have more or less ease watching different parts of your emotional STUF.

- With increased emotion awareness you can decode which messages tell you what matters most in a given situation.

05

THE ART OF
EMOTION
SURFING

Between stimulus and response there is a space.
And in that space is our power to choose our response.

Attributed to Viktor Frankl

BY NOW YOU MAY HAVE caught a glimpse of how much more authentic your choices can be when you're unplugged from the emotional default simulation, which sometimes obscures your deeper interests, desires, and yearnings. And how much more powerfully your actions could move you toward what you really care about.

Unless you were already an emotional efficacy virtuoso, it's likely you've already changed the level of consciousness from which you're experiencing your emotions.

But even if you're not quite sure if you're getting it or doing it right yet, if you've read this far and you're practicing the exercises, you're well on your way.

Expanding your emotion awareness by noticing how emotion triggers show up in your emotional network is a strong start. Now you're ready to face and embrace – instead of avoid – the kind of pain that leads you toward what matters.

What you'll learn here is that while you can't ever get rid of unwanted emotional experiences that come with stress, challenge, and pain, one of the things you can do is shift how you relate to them in moments of choice. In this chapter you'll learn how to hang out with painful triggers without acting on unhelpful urges that come with them.

This may sound difficult.

It can be very difficult.

But even if you don't realize it yet, you are more than your emotions. You're a human *having* emotions … your emotions don't have you.

EMOTION SURFING (TUNING IN + HANGING OUT)

Emotion surfing (aka mindful acceptance) builds on the skill of emotion awareness. If emotion awareness is *tuning in*, emotion surfing is *tuning in and hanging out*. Or, you could think of it this way: being aware of your emotions is like observing the ocean from the beach. Emotion surfing is actually being in the water and riding the waves.

Let's review the challenge – and the opportunity – here. How you respond in moments of choice between a painful emotion trigger and how you act is where the fullness of your power lies. Whenever you get triggered, you'll reliably have an urge to do something or not to do something. Even if it's subtle. What you do next is up to you.

Surfing your emotion waves means you can just ride them out, instead of acting on the default urges (the U of STUF) that always come with them. In each moment of choice, you can choose how you'll show up. Without the skills to do something other than act on an urge, not much else will be possible. You'll default to automatically seeking safety, certainty, coherence, comfort, and pleasure. An unhelpful default urge can obscure your moment of choice where you could instead just ride the wave. If you don't recognize you have a choice, there won't be one.

> IF YOU DON'T RECOGNIZE YOU HAVE A CHOICE,
> THERE WON'T BE ONE.

LEANING INTO DISCOMFORT AND DISTRESS

This is where building the tolerance needed to surf comes in. Being able to lean in and just be with an emotional experience will really help you when you're uncomfortable, overwhelmed, or scared. When the easier-seeming and familiar urges to avoid your unwanted emotional STUF kick in, pausing to observe, be curious and make space for all of the experience will help you respond with more flexibility, intentionality, and creativity.

With practice, you can learn to approach your waves of emotional pain as opportunities to be harnessed instead of threats to be avoided.

The realization that *you don't actually have to do anything* when you're distressed and upset actually blows a lot of people's minds. Being able to surf through unwanted STUF means you don't actually have to oblige the urges. You can experience intense emotion triggers without acting on the urges.

When you don't believe that what you feel is all there is, so much more becomes possible.

THE REALIZATION THAT *YOU DON'T ACTUALLY HAVE TO DO ANYTHING* WHEN YOU'RE DISTRESSED AND UPSET ACTUALLY BLOWS A LOT OF PEOPLE'S MINDS ... WHEN YOU DON'T BELIEVE THAT WHAT YOU FEEL IS ALL THERE IS, SO MUCH MORE BECOMES POSSIBLE.

To be fair, even in a more neutral state, just hanging out with your emotions can be challenging. Anyone who has ever practiced mindfulness or meditation already knows this.

Thoughts can spiral and jump from one thought to the next, like popping popcorn. You notice uncomfortable sensations – aches and itches – and that your body wants to be constantly adjusted. Your feelings may run the gamut from amusement to discomfort to even repulsion, when you're slowing down and just *being* with whatever is happening. And your urges to constantly do something, solve something, or change something can keep popping up like late night drunk texts from an ex – they don't stop even when you ask them nicely. And that's just in a neutral state.

I re-encountered this myself a few years ago, even after years of teaching mindfulness practice and emotional efficacy skills. I signed up for a daylong silent retreat and intended to use it to break from several intense work projects and to enjoy some lovely peace and quiet.

However, as the morning began, I noticed just how restless I was, how uncomfortable sitting still and being with my feelings seemed. I noticed my mind trying to drift out of the present moment and back into problem solving, rethinking several recent financial decisions, then analyzing the color and texture of different kinds of scarves people were wearing, and even counting how many days it had been since I had eaten papaya.

Except for sleeping, I had been operating in fourth or fifth gear for so long that the quiet spaciousness just made my mind seem louder, and it took me several hours to fully 'arrive' to the retreat and drop down enough to watch my experience without becoming hooked and carried away by every sensation, thought, urge, or feeling that came up.

You may have noticed similar challenges during the emotion awareness practice in the previous chapter. Just tuning in to painful emotions can feel counterintuitive or even 'wrong.' And most of us stay so emotionally 'busy' that tuning in doesn't come easy. And when you add to that the intention of hanging out with painful STUF, it can be a real challenge to ride it out.

In fact, the easiest way to explain how challenging it can be to surf a painful emotion wave is this: imagine I asked you to do the opposite of what you automatically want to do when you get triggered by something painful and your urge is to avoid (resist, ignore, control, numb) the unwanted experiences.

What would the opposite of your unhelpful default reaction look like?

You might slow your roll, open up, relax in the moment.

You might watch with great interest your default urges trying to seduce you – without acting on them.

Maybe you'd even sit back and welcome the whole painful experience – like a stunning sunset or your favorite version of Tchaikovsky's *Nutcracker Suite*.

This is the intention behind hanging out with unwanted STUF.

But in case it's not already obvious, observing and accepting painful emotions is no soft skill. It's likely the 3Bs will be telling you that something is very much *not* okay – maybe even in a life-or-death way. And, even if the painful trigger is not an unhelpful default but an emotion trigger signaling a deeper value (for example, someone you love dying, or not getting a promotion you really wanted), the first reaction to emotional discomfort and distress will usually be an urge to avoid it.

In either situation, tuning in and hanging out with emotional pain can feel at first like you're doing something wrong or even dangerous – like touching a red-hot stove you know will burn you. For a lot of people, it's a significant pivot to accept (instead of avoid) painful experiences.

Surfing your emotion waves is the key to overriding unhelpful default urges. Over time, you'll build your tolerance for unwanted STUF, recover more quickly, and become less vulnerable to having your choices hijacked and ending up somewhere you'd rather not be.[1]

This makes you way more resilient.

And eventually, you'll be primed to use your moments of choice to design values-based actions that enhance your life.

'I JUST CAN'T BE WITH THE PAIN ... '

My friend 'Lily' has a diagnosis of bipolar disorder and struggled with compulsive drinking on and off throughout her adult life. When I first met Lily, she was just out of a difficult divorce after a two-year marriage, was a struggling artist, and had little social support. She was anxious, depressed, and haunted by unprocessed traumatic events from her teen years.

She had developed a really unhelpful default pattern. To avoid unwanted emotional STUF, she would drink every day, starting at noon until she passed out at night. She also had some very unhelpful beliefs about her emotions that fueled and maintained her avoidance strategy, including a belief that she needed to be in pain to create her art, and her belief that her pain was intolerable.

Interventions and carefrontations from several friends and family never seemed to help. As a result of drinking to manage (read: avoid) painful emotions, her medication was not working well. She was regularly experiencing rapid mood cycles of very high highs and low lows, with some paranoia and visual hallucinations.

At the heart of Lily's unhelpful defaulting was her lack of skill for facing and embracing emotional pain. When I would ask her why she thought she couldn't quit or get help, she told me, *I just can't be with the pain, you know?* And she was trying to escape using the best coping strategy she knew: numbing out with alcohol. She couldn't see all the choices she was missing because her avoidance strategies were so well-rehearsed. She was unable to see that anything else was possible.

When you don't have the skills to navigate painful moments, not much else is possible. This is why it's so hard to change unhelpful patterns designed to avoid discomfort and distress. When you face and embrace unwanted emotional STUF, you're fully in contact with it. Even when it feels like an unwelcome dinner party guest you'd prefer would leave. In the same way, when you can surf a formidable emotion wave, you are bringing an intention to lean in and fully allow any sensations, thoughts, urges, and feelings – even if you didn't originally invite them.

> WHEN YOU FACE AND EMBRACE UNWANTED
> EMOTIONAL STUF, YOU'RE FULLY IN CONTACT WITH
> IT. EVEN WHEN IT FEELS LIKE AN UNWELCOME
> DINNER PARTY GUEST YOU'D PREFER WOULD
> LEAVE. IN THE SAME WAY, WHEN YOU CAN SURF A
> FORMIDABLE EMOTION WAVE, YOU ARE BRINGING
> AN INTENTION TO LEAN IN AND FULLY ALLOW ANY
> SENSATIONS, THOUGHTS, URGES, AND FEELINGS –
> EVEN IF YOU DIDN'T ORIGINALLY INVITE THEM.

In the same way, when you surf an unwanted emotion wave, you are bringing an intention to lean in and fully allow any sensations, thoughts, urges, and feelings – even if they weren't invited.

Remember, the only real way out is through. And while all waves do eventually level off and resolve, there's no guarantee it will happen while you're surfing. The good news is, you don't have to get out of discomfort or distress to keep surfing, or to choose your next best move (more on that next chapter).

PIVOTING WITH THE POWER OF CURIOSITY

So, what's the secret to building the tolerance to surf through painful emotional STUF? *Curiosity*. It's that simple. And that hard. When you're not curious about what's happening in the present, you'll notice how easy it is to get hooked by unhelpful default urges. Without curiosity, you're much more likely to fall back on familiar reactive patterns. Curiosity is the antidote to emotional reactivity. When you are hooked by emotion triggers, and you *really, really, really* want to act on the default urge, curiosity can break the trance.

There's now research about this which suggests that being curious decreases reactivity and can lead to all kinds of positive outcomes.[2] People who are regularly curious are more willing to embrace the novelty, uncertainty, and challenges that are inevitable, compared to their less curious peers.[3] When it comes to observing and accepting your emotional experience, curiosity is king. In his book *Curious?*, psychologist, author, and researcher Todd Kashdan explains, 'Curiosity creates possibilities; the need for certainty narrows them.'[4]

CURIOSITY IS THE ANTIDOTE TO EMOTIONAL REACTIVITY.

This is why facing and embracing the experience of pain is nothing short of heroic. Remember, your defaults want you to believe that acting on their default urges is a life-or-death matter. They will send messages en masse to make you feel that way. But when you slow down and pause to get interested in what's happening, you immediately disrupt your default reaction. You can see triggers as opportunities instead of pain to avoid. When you realize every trigger is a moment of choice, you'll naturally become more curious.

With curiosity I've been able to powerfully navigate many moments of choice when I was triggered. As one such example, several years ago I participated in a 360-feedback assessment as part of a leadership training certification. (I always do the assessments I give my clients first.) Several of my colleagues participated. But unbeknownst to me and one former colleague – due to a misunderstanding – their responses were not anonymous. I could see how they responded compared to the other participants. And if you can sense where this is going, this colleague's perceptions of my competencies and growth were markedly different from other colleagues' feedback, and my impressions.

While I tend to think of myself as being practiced at receiving direct and constructive feedback, I won't pretend that when I first saw this colleague's responses, I was anything but distraught. As context, I had worked with this person for several years, and we had also spent time together socially. They had even given me stellar endorsements, referrals, and recommendations over the years. It was a total shocker.

As you might imagine, my defaults kicked in, and all my unwanted emotional STUF came online, further prompting me to see the feedback as a potential threat I needed to neutralize. Even comparing the critical feedback with the glowing feedback from many more recent colleagues didn't put it in perspective. I could hear default urges pleading with me to find my way back to safety, certainty, and coherence, comfort, and even pleasure.

Thankfully I was able to get curious and lean in instead.

I tuned in and hung out with all the unwanted STUF. Making space for the sensations of numbness in my face and heat across my chest, I watched thoughts like, *how could they say this? ... maybe they didn't fill out the survey correctly?* and, *seriously?* – and let them go. I sat with the urge to confront the colleague and demand to know what the hell did they mean in an effort to somehow determine this had all been a big mistake. I made space for feelings of shock, disappointment, confusion, and even some fear.

While I kept surfing, I didn't exactly 'hang ten.' I had the urge to cry (and I did a little). And, I became hooked by a few thoughts (read: avoided), which actually made my distress more intense. But when I would catch myself ruminating, I could shift back into surfing again. And with continued curiosity about my STUF, I was able to see my pivotal moment of choice.

Instead of acting on the urge to confront my colleague in a heated state, I decoded what mattered most: preserving our relationship. And it was clear talking with them while I was that upset would not help. So I surfed until the wave leveled off (it didn't completely resolve for a few hours) and I was able to get back to what I was doing.

Over the next few days as I sat with the feedback, the whole experience became incredibly interesting to me, and eventually led to a conversation that put the feedback in better perspective for both of us.

REFLECTION: CULTIVATING CURIOSITY

- Take a moment right now to reflect on a trigger situation where you gave into an unhelpful default urge. Imagine what it would have looked like if you had brought curiosity (openness and interest) to the experience of being triggered before you reacted. What would you have noticed?

- If the trigger situation involved another person, what might you have noticed or done differently by bringing a curious mindset?

- What do you think might have happened differently? Would the outcome have changed? How?

THE ALCHEMY OF EMOTION SURFING

So, why does emotion surfing work? Because your network of emotional STUF is so interactive, how you respond to triggers shapes what happens next emotionally, and how you experience it. This means being curious and tuning in and hanging out with all your emotional STUF doesn't just change how your emotion wave behaves once it's in motion.

It can also change the context in which it is occurring, in this case … you.

Here's what I mean. When you just surf your emotion wave, two things can happen:

- The emotion wave will eventually change in intensity, duration, and type. And if you keep surfing, the wave will eventually level off or peter out.

- How you experience the wave will change. Even if at first it seems threatening, as you sit with it you'll stop seeing it as an experience to be avoided. It might even become interesting.

THIS MEANS BEING CURIOUS AND TUNING IN AND HANGING OUT WITH ALL YOUR EMOTIONAL STUF DOESN'T JUST CHANGE HOW YOUR EMOTION WAVE BEHAVES ONCE IT'S IN MOTION. IT CAN ALSO CHANGE THE CONTEXT IN WHICH IT IS OCCURRING, IN THIS CASE ... YOU.

This fascinating phenomenon is described in physics and psychology as the 'observer effect.'[5] It has been seen in both quantum experiments with waves and particles, as well as psychological experiments, where the thing or person being studied changes its behavior as a result of being watched. It's the same with your emotions: the mere observation of your emotions changes them, as well as your experience of them. And many times, I've seen this happen at lightning speed.

This is how the alchemy happens. By changing your behavior – how you respond to your emotion triggers – your emotion wave will also change its behavior, which in turn changes your experience of it, and vice versa.

Knowing this can motivate you to become a better emotion surfer ...

... to lean in ...

... feel the burn ...

... and ride it out.

'IT JUST FADED OUT. LIKE IT'S BARELY THERE ...'

CLIENT: When I think about the conversation I have to have again with my mom about her going to rehab, I feel really scared. I notice the thought, *she'll be hurt that I'm still so angry about the way she is handling it.*

ME: Yes, so there's a thought she may be hurt because you're angry. Can you let that thought go and come back to hanging out with what else is here?

CLIENT: I still notice fear.

ME: Okay, so the feeling is fear. Can you validate that feeling?

CLIENT: Yes, it makes sense that I'd be feeling afraid since in the past when she gets hurt, she gets very critical.

ME: That does make sense.

CLIENT: My urge is to avoid the conversation altogether.

ME: Good noticing. And what happens when you just sit with that urge?

CLIENT: I still feel the fear.

ME: Where does that fear show up in your body?

CLIENT: My stomach is knotted up and it feels like someone is pressing on my chest.

ME: Okay. See what happens if you just lean in … Let those sensations be there, without resisting them, trying to control them, or judging them as being bad or wrong. Maybe you could even try inviting them to be there and stay as long as they like?

CLIENT: That sounds scary, but okay … I'll try.

ME (about 30 seconds later): What's happening for you now?

CLIENT: I notice when I relax my stomach, I have the urge to tense up again.

ME: Good noticing. So, see if you just let that urge to tense up be there. And refocus on the sensation in your stomach by sensing if there's any temperature … warmth or coldness?

CLIENT: It's just neutral.

ME: Okay, neutral. Now, see if you can tell if that tension is moving or staying the same?

CLIENT: Yeah, it's just staying the same.

ME: Okay, just keep being curious. See if you can tell if the tension is the same in the middle as it is around the edges?

CLIENT: It's a little more tense in the middle.

ME: Good noticing. Imagine just leaning into that tension. Just watch whatever it does …

CLIENT (nods, and pauses about 20 seconds): Whoa …

ME: What's happening?

CLIENT: It just faded out. Like it's barely there …

While I can't make any guarantees, in my experience most clients who practice emotion surfing eventually experience this emotional alchemy. Either the unwanted emotions, their relationship to the distress of them, or both, morph or ease up.

The concept of surfing emotion waves has been adapted from the science of mindfulness, and the benefits have been intensively researched. This non-reactive practice of facing and embracing whatever emotional STUF shows up can lead to increased wellbeing. When you develop this capacity to fully allow your experience, you are generally less stressed, more content, and more resilient.[6] In fact, emotion surfing can lead to increased resilience by:

- supporting the curiosity needed to unhook from unwanted emotional STUF
- helping you tolerate discomfort and distress without defaulting
- helping you recover more quickly when big emotion waves hit.

To briefly summarize: you can let an emotion wave take its course by curiously hanging out and leaning into the experience until it shifts, changes, or passes. In this way, as you turn toward your emotional pain, your relationship with it also changes. You'll naturally have less distress about your distress. Eventually this creates the space to pivot from surfing to valuing (more on this in the next chapter).

THE LIFESPAN OF AN EMOTION WAVE

There are some very cool things to know about emotion surfing that can help you level up your practice:

- *Emotions always come in waves.* Emotion waves are just like waves in the ocean. They are triggered by energy, build momentum, peak, and eventually resolve. If you just ride out a wave of unwanted STUF,

WHAT YOU FEEL IS NOT ALL THERE IS

instead of resisting or trying to control or alter your experience, it will taper off on its own. In the same way, if you resist it or try to stop it, you'll be splashing around in an even bigger wave and potentially get pulled under.

- *Emotion waves can be relatively short-lived.* They can resolve much more quickly than you might think. Some research suggests that the chemical process of an emotion wave can work its way out of your system in as little as 90 seconds.[7] This means that unless it's a tsunami, your experience after the initial trigger is a result of how you're reacting to it ... and by now you know what that means – you're trying to avoid the experience you're already having, which will increase its intensity and duration.

- *Emotion waves arise from one or more triggers.* Every emotion wave is triggered by something that happens either privately (for example, activated sensations, thoughts, urges, or feelings) or observably (other people's actions, environmental events). While emotion triggers happen all the time (without you even noticing them), you'll usually notice the medium-to-large triggers.

- *When you try to alter, control, modify, or repress what you're already feeling, this serves to fuel your emotion wave.* Attempts to avoid experiencing unwanted STUF will act as additional triggers that can intensify and prolong your emotion wave. You end up adding unnecessary suffering to the already painful emotion trigger. And if you keep avoiding, you can create multiple waves that sometimes last for days on end. #whenwavesbecomemoods

This is why learning to lean into your discomfort and distress is so powerful. When you *don't* surf, and you try to avoid what you're already experiencing, you create that extra layer of pain – 'unnecessary suffering'.

In gamer terms, you can think of surfing big emotional waves as a 'boss fight.' You 'defeat' these more powerful bosses by figuring out their pattern of attack. It's the same with powerful emotion waves. The waves might *feel* more powerful than you. But once you understand their lifespan you can use the predictable pattern of their movement and momentum to your advantage – like emotional aikido. In this way, the waves become something to ride, instead of them riding you and pulling you under with unhelpful default urges.

> THE WAVES MIGHT *FEEL* MORE POWERFUL THAN YOU. BUT ONCE YOU UNDERSTAND THEIR LIFESPAN YOU CAN USE THE PREDICTABLE PATTERN OF THEIR MOVEMENT AND MOMENTUM TO YOUR ADVANTAGE - LIKE EMOTIONAL AIKIDO.

Here's an example. Imagine you've just gone through a breakup and you're still feeling pretty raw. A few nights later you're listening to music and hear a track you and your ex considered to be *your song*.

What happens?

Most likely an emotion wave is triggered and all the painful unwanted emotional STUF you've been working hard to get past shows back up:

You might sense a constriction in your chest and belly.

You might have the thought, *we used to listen to this cuddling in bed together at night.*

You might experience the urge to cry and call your ex.

You might feel lonely or sad.

This is a moment of choice.

You could either surf the wave, or you could act on the (unhelpful) urge to call your ex at 2 a.m. If you practice the aikido of emotion surfing in response to a painful emotion trigger, the lifespan of your emotion wave might look something like this:

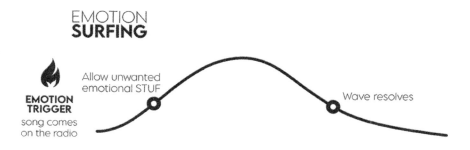

EMOTION
SURFING

EMOTION
TRIGGER
song comes
on the radio

Allow unwanted
emotional STUF

Wave resolves

To surf the wave:

You'd notice and make space for the physical constriction in your chest.

You'd notice and let go of the thought of cuddling in bed.

You'd also notice and let go of the thought, *he understood me like no one ever will again.*

You'd avert the seduction of your unhelpful default urge to call, and sit with the discomfort instead.

You'd notice and label your feelings – loneliness and sadness – validating them, saying something like, 'it makes sense I'm feeling all this.'

And if you kept surfing, you'd eventually see the emotion wave level off or soften or, over time, your distress about the wave would decrease.

But let's say you *don't* surf. Let's say in the scenario with your ex you defaulted to struggling with the pain and the unhelpful urge to call your ex. Things might go very differently.

To start, you might resist the tension you sense in your belly and chest. This would intensify the emotion wave, because as you know, 'what you resist, persists.'

You might also ruminate about how much you miss your ex, even though you were unhappy in the relationship. And more painful thoughts, like *what if I was wrong about him?* would serve as additional triggers that fuel your wave.

You might act on your urge to call your ex, and ask to get back together. But unless 1) he answers the phone, and 2) says something like, 'I'm so glad you called, I feel the same,' this could trigger even more distress.

Lastly, you might judge – rather than validate – your feelings of sadness and loneliness. Now you're in a whole new level of pain.

In this second scenario, you're defaulting to avoidance strategies that may seem natural if they are familiar and well-rehearsed. As you can see in the image following, responding to painful emotion triggers with avoidance strategies tends to make emotion waves go higher and last longer. You can clearly see the zone of unnecessary suffering it creates.

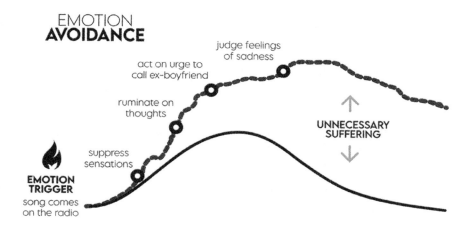

As you'll remember from the previous chapter, avoidance strategies can provide an emotional fix, even if it is short-lived. That's why they can be so compelling when you're triggered. For example, using avoidance strategies – such as seeking reassurance from a friend, performing certain rituals, or numbing out with drugs or alcohol – can temporarily decrease the emotion wave.

But even if you get some momentary relief, when it stops or you sober up, you're back to facing emotional pain. You're right back on the wave, stuck in an avoidance loop that maintains your pain and unnecessary suffering. Not to mention, you're missing opportunities to explore what matters more in your moment of choice.

SAY SOMETHING ... ANYTHING?

ME: Today we agreed we would use the experiential practice for emotion surfing using the argument you keep having with your partner as your trigger scene.

CLIENT: Yes, I really need that. We got into it again last night.

ME: Okay, so can we work with that?

CLIENT: Sure.

ME: Okay, if you would, close your eyes, and go back to the scene from last night, to the moment you noticed you got triggered. You could imagine replaying it like a movie and freeze on that frame.

CLIENT: Yeah. We were working on a presentation for our mutual clients, and it was the moment he said he didn't like what I had written. And very quickly I asked what he didn't like about it, but he just kind of froze up and couldn't tell me. Which, as you know, is a pattern. And I'm beginning to think he just doesn't like me having any control or power.

ME: Okay, well, before we get into thoughts, check in with yourself and see how activated you are just thinking about that, on a scale of 1 to 10, with 10 being as activated as you could possibly get.

CLIENT: I'm a solid 6.

ME: Got it. Let's cut off the scene here, and surf through all parts of your emotional STUF: starting by making space for any sensations you notice; naming any thoughts and letting them go; sitting with any urges to do something or not to do something; and labeling any feelings without judgment.

CLIENT: Okay. So, first I'm noticing this urge to reach out and put my hands on his shoulders and shake him while imploring him, *say something ... anything!*

ME: Okay, so you noticed that urge. What sensations go with that urge?

CLIENT: I feel hot in my neck and chest, and I feel energy coursing through my whole body, and tension in my forehead.

ME: Good noticing. Let's slow this down a bit. See what happens if you just allow the heat in your neck and chest to be there. Can you lean into it without trying to change or alter it in any way?

CLIENT: I'm trying ... but it just got a little hotter.

ME: So see if you can just be curious about that, and what it's going to do next, with an intention to allow whatever happens.

CLIENT (after about 20 seconds): Well, it's definitely cooler now, but I still have tension in my forehead.

ME: Okay, let's shift your attention to your forehead, and again, just allow the tension to be there without trying to change or alter it in any way. Just be curious about it. What's that like?

CLIENT: It's definitely an unnatural feeling to do that. Like, the opposite of what I would normally do, like at least rubbing it or something.

ME: Good noticing. Can you stay with that for a few moments?

CLIENT: Yes … and now it suddenly shifted to my jaw.

ME: Okay, so just follow the sensation, wherever it goes. You're just hanging out with it.

CLIENT: Okay.

ME: You might even bring the intention of welcoming it.

CLIENT: Whoa, that's different.

ME: What do you notice now?

CLIENT: Well, it just kind of dissolved.

ME: Good noticing. Let's stay in a place of curiosity here … what else do you notice?

CLIENT: That thought just came rushing back: *just say something, anything!*

ME: Okay, and what happens if you let that thought go? Can you do that? Or if it's helpful, you can shift your attention back to your breath, noticing the inhale or exhale to unhook from it?

CLIENT: Yeah. I can do that. But now there's another thought right behind it.

ME: Okay, good noticing. So just come back to your breath first to slow this down.

CLIENT: Okay. I'm on the exhale.

ME: Great. Now what's the thought that shows up?

CLIENT: I'm having the thought that *he doesn't respect my ideas.*

ME: Okay. And see if you can unhook from that thought, just letting it go.

CLIENT: Yeah. Hmmm.

ME: What's there now?

CLIENT: I just went from feeling so angry, to feeling sad and even a little scared.

ME: Good noticing. Angry to sad and a little scared?

CLIENT: Yeah.

ME: What else?

CLIENT: I notice I'm having the thought that *we just aren't a good match.* And the thought that *I need someone who can collaborate on my level.*

ME: And again, unhooking from those thoughts and letting them go …

CLIENT: Yes. And I'm refocusing on my breath.

ME: Great. Now, what else is here?

CLIENT: I notice an urge to comfort myself.

ME: Ahhh. That's a big shift, huh?

CLIENT: Yeah.

ME: And what's the feeling that goes with that?

CLIENT: Compassion, for how difficult this whole situation feels.

ME: Good noticing. And what sensations go with compassion?

CLIENT: I guess, I just, feel softer, less tense.

ME: Okay. And any thoughts that go with the urge to comfort yourself, the feeling of compassion and the softening of sensations?

CLIENT: I notice the thought that *I know what to do, and I need to stop avoiding it.*

ME: Okay. Let's pause here. Where are you on the emotion wave now? Scale of 1 to 10?

CLIENT: I'm probably around a 3.

ME: Okay, great. Take a deep breath, open your eyes, and then bring your attention back to the room.

REFLECTION: RECOGNIZING YOUR MOMENTS OF CHOICE

Recall a recent emotion trigger that resulted in a big wave.

Rate how intense it was on a scale of 1 to 10.

See if you can recall which of your unwanted STUF was the loudest.

Identify the exact moment of choice, when you chose to act on the emotion urge or to face and embrace the pain.

If you're motivated, you can actually practice emotion surfing any time you get triggered, no matter how small the wave is. #ranoutofketchup And, because your imagination can activate your emotions, experiential practice is really accessible, even in the absence of a real-life trigger.

Some people find it helpful and interesting to rate the intensity of their wave before and after to track what's happening. This can tell you not only what's going on with your wave, but also your tolerance of it. You can use a 10-point rating scale, with 1 being no observable emotional activation, and 10 being as triggered as you can imagine. Remember, the goal in any experiential practice is to stay in the 4 to 6 mid-range of intensity. This makes it easier to connect with what's happening, but keeps you from becoming overwhelmed.

As you practice, you'll notice how simple emotion surfing is in theory. But when you're activated, by your imagination or in IRL, it's more complex and challenging. With time and practice, it will get easier and easier, and you'll be able to ride out bigger and bigger waves – without being pulled under.

THE EMOTION SURFING OBSTACLE COURSE

It's helpful to anticipate some of the common obstacles that show up for people learning to surf their emotion waves:

- *Sometimes you bow out early or wipe out.* Allowing unwanted emotional STUF can seem so unnatural and threatening. It's only natural to fall back into avoiding. You might catch yourself tuning out or getting hooked by STUF, and that's totally understandable. But it won't help build your distress tolerance. Sometimes it can help to set a timer for just 15 seconds, and gradually work your way up. Keep increasing your time on the wave until you can do a full 10 minutes or longer. There's no shame in wading in slowly. The important thing is to keep going until you start to see how your emotional experience shifts when you just hang out with it.

- *Sometimes, when you watch your thoughts, they can hook you.* It's so easy to get drawn in or almost hypnotized by what your mind makes up. Some thoughts are especially hard to let go of, especially if you're intensely triggered. It may be helpful to acknowledge that you're having a 'sticky' thought, and then let it go. You can also bring your attention to your breath, noticing if you're on the inhale or exhale to reset. If the thought comes up again, try not to judge; remind yourself that it's natural to struggle with letting go of thoughts that come with a sense of urgency. Just keep practicing unhooking and letting the thoughts go, using your breath as an anchor as needed.

- *Sometimes your emotion waves stay intense, even if you surf them.* While most emotion waves will at least level off if you surf them, even the most practiced emotion surfers still have waves that sometimes stay high, despite expert-level leaning in. Don't fret – this doesn't mean you're doing anything wrong. By staying with your unwanted STUF you're still increasing your ability to tolerate distress without acting on any urges. And it doesn't even mean you can't still pivot to valuing (more on that next chapter).

- *It might seem like you're trying to allow a painful experience that might not be okay at all.* When you are really triggered, it might seem like you're being asked to invalidate or ignore your experience and surrender to what's happening. Assuming you're not getting true red alerts, the practice of emotion surfing takes courage and willingness. Often there isn't anything easy or comfortable about it. But there's a huge potential payoff just ahead: the shift from unhelpful defaulting to valuing.

In the previous chapter you used music as the activating trigger for experiential practice. Going forward, you'll select a trigger scene and use your imagination to get into an activated state. You'll want to choose trigger scenes with moderate levels of intensity to optimize your experiential practice. Refer to the list of trigger scenes you made if you need help picking one. When you're ready, you can also practice the skills sequence when you get triggered IRL.

EMOTION SURFING EXPERIENTIAL PRACTICE

For this emotion surfing experiential practice and the ones that follow you'll pick a recurring scene you can reasonably predict will trigger a wave of unwanted emotional STUF. You'll want to choose something ahead of time that you know will bring up unwanted emotions at a medium level of intensity (between 4 and 6 on a 10-point scale).

To rehearse the skill of emotion surfing, you can use the following script, and you can also access a guided experiential practice at www.drapriliawest.com/practice.

SET UP

Find a private, quiet place and get into a comfortable position where you're likely to stay alert. Close your eyes or find a single spot in front of you to focus on by just softening your gaze.

SELECT A TRIGGER

Choose a trigger based on a memory or recurring event to activate a medium intensity of discomfort and distress. (Keep in mind, in the low range you can struggle to access your emotional STUF, and in the high range you can be easily overwhelmed.)

ACTIVATE EMOTION

Set your trigger scene by imagining it as a movie, and describe what you notice as if it's happening in real time, including:

· where you are

· what time it is

· who you are with.

1. Go to the exact 'frame' where you anticipate you'll get emotionally activated.

2. Describe anything you are seeing, hearing, touching, tasting, and otherwise doing in as much detail as possible, frame by frame, until you reach a medium level of activation.

3. Stop the scene and shift to emotion surfing.

EMOTION SURFING

Surf your emotion wave by bringing an intention of curiosity to hanging out with each part of your emotional 'STUF' for two minutes each.

(Sensations) For at least two minutes, scan your body from head to toe for any sensations that stand out to you:

· Notice their size and shape.

· Notice whether they're moving or staying the same.

· Notice any tension in the sensation.

· Notice if there's any temperature.

Bring an intention of allowing the physical experiences that go with sensations. Imagine making space for them, or welcoming them to be there and do whatever they want to do. Be curious about how they behave when you are just watching them.

(Thoughts) Shift your attention from sensations to noticing thoughts for at least two minutes:

· When a thought shows up, say to yourself 'there's a thought' and then let the thought go.

- Refocus on your breath as a way to place a pause between thoughts.
- And then watch for the next thought to show up, and repeat.

(Urges) Shift to watching any urges for two minutes:

- When you notice one, get curious about how intense the urge is: low, medium, high?
- Notice what it's like to just sit with the impulse to do something or not do something.
- Rate the discomfort on a scale of 1 to 10, with 1 being as relaxed as you can imagine and 10 the most uncomfortable you can imagine.
- Notice if the urge changes in intensity as you sit with it.

(Feelings)

- Label each feeling.
- Validate and welcome the feelings, saying something like: *It makes sense I'm feeling* [insert label]. Or, *it's okay for the feeling of* [insert label] *to be here.*
- Get curious about whether there are any other feelings, underneath the first feelings you noticed.

REFLECT

To wrap up the experiential practice, take a few moments to reflect using the following prompts:

- Did anything surprise you?
- What, if anything, was challenging?
- What did you learn?
- Write down anything else you want to remember.

CHAPTER 05 CHALLENGES

·   Make a commitment to pause the next time you are triggered, and
    to tune in (emotion awareness) and hang out (emotion surfing) with
    all parts of your unwanted emotional STUF. Notice the moment
    of choice where you could act on the unhelpful emotion urge, or
    override it and keep surfing. If you're curious, set a timer and see
    how long the emotion wave lasts after you start surfing.

·   Referring to your list of 'frequent flier' avoidance strategies, identify
    which one(s) you're most tempted to use while you're surfing the
    emotion wave for at least five minutes.

·   Lock in the learning by sharing with someone you know and feel
    comfortable with what you've learned about emotion waves and how
    you respond to them.

·   Practice using emotion surfing using the guided experiential at least
    three times before you move forward. Notice which parts of your
    unwanted emotional STUF are easier or harder to hang out with (it
    will often be the same as the parts you have trouble tuning in to). For
    extra credit, after the practice, work through the 3Bs inventory to see
    how they might be in play in the trigger scene you used.

CHAPTER 05 LEARNINGS

- The second core skill of emotion surfing adds 'hanging out' to the tuning in of emotion awareness.

- By surfing your emotions, you'll override the unhelpful urges that come with emotion triggers.

- Emotion surfing also builds your tolerance for discomfort and distress, helps you to recover more quickly from big emotion waves, and increases your resilience.

- Curiosity is the antidote to emotional reactivity.

- The lifespan of an emotion wave can be relatively short-lived if you don't respond with avoidance strategies.

- Strategies to avoid a painful emotion wave are likely to make the wave more intense and last longer.

- There is an alchemy where emotions shift and change simply by being observed.

- When you learn to watch the pattern of a wave, you can more skillfully ride out the pain.

- Experiential practice with emotion surfing uses emotional activation with imaginal or actual skills practice to accelerate learning and help you skillfully navigate moments of choice.

06

KEEP CALM
AND
VALUE ON

We can't live into values that we can't name …
living into values requires moving from lofty aspirations
to specific, observable behaviors.

Brené Brown

AT THE RISK OF SOUNDING overly obvious, knowing what matters to you matters a whole lot. Maybe more than you realize … yet. So many people I work with don't *really* know what they care about. Especially moment to moment. Often, they are living lives that are rote, predictable, and devoid of the kind of meaning that leads to optimal vitality and well-being. They might even be dissatisfied, but it doesn't naturally occur to them this suffering is a lack of connection to meaning.

Think of it this way:

If your values are 'signal' and your helpful and unhelpful defaults are 'noise' – your emotional life is likely to be a lot (up to 85%) more cacophonous than clear. Defaults can be so noisy that you don't even realize any other interests, desires, or yearnings exist. These louder default messages can obscure what you authentically care about in context.

The distorted guitars of your defaults easily drown out the sometimes more delicate value signals of the harp. Or, like an old radio, your values 'stations' can be harder to find than the static from your defaults.

Hopefully by now it's clear that you may fail to hear your innermost signals because you'll tend to believe that what you feel is all there is. And in general – and even more when you're triggered – the signals about what matters most are naturally softer, because while they lead you to thrive, they aren't always necessary for you to survive.

> … THE SIGNALS ABOUT WHAT MATTERS MOST
> ARE NATURALLY SOFTER, BECAUSE WHILE
> THEY LEAD YOU TO THRIVE, THEY AREN'T
> ALWAYS NECESSARY FOR YOU TO SURVIVE.

That said, you now know how to choose to override the default urge and hang out with your emotions. This opens up a whole new opportunity. Now you can surf through an emotion wave of pain and figure out how you want to show up. This is why being able to override unhelpful urges and designing action in line with your values is such a potentially potent life upgrade.

Designing your actions aligned with your values is the apex of emotional efficacy. When you master the skills you'll develop boss-level choice-making by increasing:

- *Flexibility*, to help you adjust your actions when your situation and what matters most shifts or changes.
- *Intentionality*, to give you a clear direction in context.
- *Creativity*, to harness the opportunity to expand what matters in as many ways as possible.

In this chapter, you'll learn the next core skill: *values-based action* (aka VBA or valuing). You've heard me reference the skill of values-based action throughout the first five chapters; for example, 'doing what matters most in context', 'doing what is most meaningful', 'moving in the direction you really want', 'moving toward interests, desires, and yearnings', or, 'doing what you really care about'.

Here's how the skills sequence progresses now: as soon as you notice you're triggered, you'll tune in and hang out (emotion surfing), decode the signal for what matters most, and design your actions accordingly (values-based action).

WHAT YOU REALLY, REALLY WANT

You've probably never heard anyone say, 'My life is truly amazing … everything is just so meaningless.' Most people instinctively believe that meaning is important, even if they don't understand why or the extent of it. As it turns out, being connected to meaning is a key factor in wellbeing.[1]

It's so important that even when people just *search* for meaning, they report higher levels of happiness and self-actualization.[2] And people who report lower levels of meaning tend to have lower levels of life and relationship satisfaction, desirable feelings, and social connectedness, and higher levels of unwanted feelings and depression.[3]

Building a more meaningful life will energize you, sustain you, and pull you through difficult patches and unforeseen challenges.[4] It will build your resilience. This makes being in sync with your values a formidable built-in protection against any threat or loss, and a real asset to achieving your best life. (Who wouldn't want that?)

But in case the mere topic of values causes your eyes to glaze over or summons images of pithy posters with aspirational quotes or memories of learning the 'golden rule' as a child or virtue-signaling do-gooders, I invite you to become more curious.

It's not a luxury to learn how to clarify values and put them into action. When you take this seriously, it's what gives you a life you can look back on knowing you played 'full out,' rather than a life you look back on with remorse. People don't tend to retrospectively regret how they felt, but they do regret past choices that didn't align with what mattered most to them.

> PEOPLE DON'T TEND TO RETROSPECTIVELY
> REGRET HOW THEY FELT, BUT THEY DO
> REGRET PAST CHOICES THAT DIDN'T ALIGN
> WITH WHAT MATTERED MOST TO THEM.

Living flexibly, intentionally, and creatively requires knowing what you care about. When you don't know what really matters, you won't know how to align your actions.

Alice: 'Would you tell me, please, which way I ought to go from here?'

The Cheshire Cat: 'That depends a good deal on where you want to get to.'

Alice: 'I don't much care where.'

The Cheshire Cat: 'Then it doesn't much matter which way you go.'

As this excerpt from *Alice in Wonderland* illustrates, if you don't know where you want to go, you'll struggle with what action to take, making you more vulnerable to unhelpful defaulting. Your values-based actions are the 'moves' you make when you're triggered in the direction of your innermost interests, desires, or yearnings in a given situation.

... VALUES-BASED ACTIONS ARE THE 'MOVES' YOU
MAKE IN THE DIRECTION OF YOUR INNERMOST
INTERESTS, DESIRES, OR YEARNINGS IN
A GIVEN SITUATION.

FREELY CHOSEN VS 'FAKE' VALUES OR OLD VALUES

But before we get too far ahead, let's define what values are, and what they're not. For our purposes, values are *freely chosen intentions to embody and express what you care about most in context*. You could think of your values as the 'why' or purpose behind any intentional action you take. They represent the greater meaning behind your choices.

Values are powerful for two reasons:

· they give your actions meaningful intention and direction
· they give you the willingness to do hard things that matter.

For example, the 'why' for writing this book comes from my core value of Possibility – how much I care about helping people to learn to maximize what's possible for their lives. And I can tune in and hear this signal, which then motivates me even when, say, I'm tired or my shoulder is killing me, or when it seems really hard to translate my nerdy jargon into more engaging language because there's a new episode of *Ted Lasso* in my queue, or I don't feel like I can sit in front of my computer squinting at the screen for even one more hour. My value of Possibility gives me direction and motivation.

If I wasn't an experienced values-based choice-maker, I'd be out. Fortunately for me, because I know the book matters most, even in the face of discomfort, I'm able to override the urge to go hang out with the adorable, inspiring and beautifully flawed Ted, Rebecca, Roy, and Keely, and stay with my writing.

WHAT VALUES ARE NOT

The concept of values may seem fairly straightforward – until you realize what values are *not*. Because your values are freely chosen, they are not inherited from your family or social circles. Values are also not based in what you think you *should* care about ('fake' values). And they are not based in what a former version of yourself may have cared about ('old' values).

If identifying values seems complex, that's because it's some next-level expert emotional decoding.

You'll know when you are being bamboozled by old or fake values because you'll notice that you're 'shoulding yourself,' and it may feel really uncomfortable to admit that something else matters more.

For instance, say you've always been told you should be Modest. It may then understandably feel weird to learn you care more about Self-Expression, and for example, choose to wear a low-cut shirt or get a tattoo in a visible area. You might even judge yourself for considering it – even if the Self-Expression of getting a tattoo matters more. And, if your fake or old value of Modesty is deeply embedded, you might end up judging yourself harshly for even considering it, leading to an epic 'should-show' about what you think you're supposed to want. Just becoming aware of this will make you a better values-based choice-maker. Letting anything other than your true values guide your actions can wreak havoc on your choice-making accuracy.

To figure out what matters in a moment of choice, you'll drop down and listen for any signals you may not have previously identified. (You may need to give yourself permission to do this). Listening for these signals can surprise you, and it sometimes leads to life-changing choices: to leave a relationship, to get a new job, to move to a new place. It can also radically change how you show up for yourself, and your relationships. And, it will help you figure out if what you care about is worth the pain of moving toward your values – will you 'do you' or forego the tattoo because of what your mother might say?

As long as you're not doing harm or acting in antisocial ways, there's no right or wrong to values. This is why the ongoing act of dropping down and listening deeply to yourself can be so powerful.

For example, maybe you think you value Adventure more than anything else. But when your dad starts pressuring you about the upcoming family trip, you notice you get triggered. This is where you can get curious.

Maybe Adventure is just what your dad cares about most and you learned this value from him.

Or, maybe the old you did really care most about Adventure.

Or, you might feel like you *should* value Adventure. Your dad might be really disappointed if you sit out on this year's annual family hike to Mount Kilimanjaro.

But upon closer inspection, you drop down and listen to what matters more to you and discover that, in context, it's actually Stability. And working that extra week could help you pay down your second mortgage. Or, maybe present-day you is much more interested in Family, and you could focus your extra energy and time there.

With deeper inquiry you can find your way.

THE WILLINGNESS TO DO HARD THINGS

Meaningful intention and direction is not all your values give you. One of the superpowers of values is that they can significantly increase your motivation. This is because when you're inspired by what you care about, you'll be more willing to do whatever it takes to move toward it with your actions.

As a straightforward example, let's say you have a goal of doing the dishes every night before bedtime (even though you despise doing dishes) because you value having an orderly kitchen. Let's also assume it would be easy to default by reading the discomfort of doing them as a threat (presumably to comfort and pleasure) and just leave them for the morning. And if avoiding the discomfort of doing them when you're tired is well-rehearsed your default pattern will be in full support.

However, once you remind yourself why it matters to do them – how much you enjoy a clean kitchen first thing in the morning – you've now linked doing a monotonous chore to your value of Orderliness, transforming the aversive dishwashing into something rewarding. You've brought the meaning of doing the dishes into clear view.

This linking of actions to values is motivating when you're trying to disrupt difficult unhelpful default patterns. Because it makes your actions meaningful to you.

Remember, to change a behavior – especially one you've rehearsed a lot – you have to tap the willingness to tolerate the discomfort and distress that comes with making the change. Linking actions with meaning can be a game-changer. And it's easy to miss this powerful step – especially when you're triggered.

It comes down to this: it's hard to do hard things. You might need boatloads of motivation to persist through the inevitable discomfort and distress that comes with stretching for what matters. And it's even harder if your actions aren't obviously connected to what really matters to you. If you don't have a clear enough rationale for why you're willing to tolerate unwanted STUF and 'value on' anyway, it's near impossible to persevere.

You get to choose.

The pain of avoiding and a smaller life.

Or moving toward what matters and bringing the pain with you.

> IT COMES DOWN TO THIS: IT'S HARD TO DO
> HARD THINGS ... AND IT'S EVEN HARDER IF YOUR
> ACTIONS AREN'T OBVIOUSLY CONNECTED
> TO WHAT REALLY MATTERS TO YOU.

There's a reason I'm making such a big deal about this: when your goals and actions are linked to your values, it can supercharge your motivation. The actions shift from neutral or tedious to also being inspired and purposeful. You're more likely to hit your targets. This is why values are so much more powerful than goals (which are not always obviously linked to meaning). Values-based actions become *naturally rewarding*, no matter how challenging or even irritating they might feel. Even when they're hard, you can tap the willingness to do them anyway.

As an example, I have a goal of doing daily physical therapy exercises to rehab an old injury. However, every time I get ready to do them, all sorts of unwanted emotional STUF shows up:

Sensations: Tension in my stomach and a drop in energy

Thoughts: *Will these boring exercises even help? Will I ever be able to run again?*

Urges: Do *anything* else

Feelings: Frustration, boredom, and hopelessness

As you can see, doing these PT exercises brings me zero joy. My 3Bs are quite sure that my certainty, comfort, and pleasure are under threat, even when I just think about doing them. It makes sense. Doing PT isn't naturally meaningful to me. In the short term, the only reward it offers is getting it off my mental to-do list. For this reason, whenever I lose sight of the 'why' behind doing my PT, I really struggle to be consistent.

So how do I keep going, even when I am triggered by an emotion wave urging me toward the couch or into some less purposeful activity after a long day of work? With the willingness that emerges as soon as I link my PT with the greater meaning of my values of Health and Adventure. The act of connecting them to being able to enjoy a higher quality of life transforms the dreaded clamshell and bridge exercises from a tedious routine into a tedious routine I can tolerate for the sake of my bigger 'why.'

This illustrates a key point about your primary motivational system (aka your emotions): you can shoulder the weight of a lot of actions that are disconnected from values for a certain amount of time. But to tap the willingness to do what matters in a triggered state, you need to connect your actions to a 'why' that goes beyond hitting a meaningless target. Your values will give you meaningful intentions and directions, and the motivation. Especially when there is no short-term reward.

> ... TO TAP THE WILLINGNESS TO DO WHAT MATTERS IN A TRIGGERED STATE, YOU NEED TO CONNECT YOUR ACTIONS TO A 'WHY' THAT GOES BEYOND HITTING A MEANINGLESS TARGET. ESPECIALLY WHEN THERE IS NO SHORT-TERM REWARD.

BRINGING YOUR 'STUF' WITH YOU

To be clear, overriding an unhelpful default urge to take VBA can seem like the very opposite of what you feel like doing in a moment of choice.

If you're not aware of this, you could end up waiting years (or until it's too late) to do the things that really matter to you.

Make no mistake, your innermost interests, desires, and yearnings will often lead you into doing hard things. And this is further complicated by the fact that sometimes, taking values-based action can actually *intensify* your unwanted emotional STUF. You heard me right. When you move toward what matters, unhelpful defaults can escalate their messages to avoid. #dangerwillrobinson. They easily confuse your discomfort and distress for danger and dysfunction. This makes sense – otherwise it would be natural to do VBA instead of acting on an unhelpful default urge. Hitting the gym would be easier than Netflix and pizza.

This is where you can choose the pain that goes with doing what matters most to you. The reality is, *you can have all the difficult emotions while you act on your values.* You can surf a tsunami-size emotion wave of unwanted STUF, override the default urge, and do VBA anyway. Sometimes you have to tolerate the STUF you don't want to get what you *do* want. All it requires is a willingness to bring the discomfort and distress with you. And the cherry on top is that doing what matters most often leaves you feeling better afterwards.

> YOU CAN SURF A TSUNAMI-SIZE EMOTION WAVE OF UNWANTED STUF, OVERRIDE THE DEFAULT URGE, AND DO VBA ANYWAY. SOMETIMES YOU HAVE TO TOLERATE THE STUF YOU DON'T WANT TO GET WHAT YOU DO WANT.

This is especially good news for anyone who tends to rely on their feelings for motivation (yes, I'm looking at you). It's easy to fall into the trap of believing that to take difficult actions, you need to feel brave enough, relaxed enough, rested enough, smart enough, happy enough, confident enough, attractive enough, and [fill in the blank here] enough. You might recognize our familiar friend, the emotional reasoning bias, saying, *if you don't feel like doing something, then you must not be up to the task.* And it might bring along its other bias buddies as back-up. Fortunately for you, you're several chapters wiser now.

Being able to access this next level of play depends on seeing your moments of choice as opportunities to create what you care most about, and to bring any unwanted feelings along for the ride. When you approach your moments of choice this way, you can probably sense how much more is possible. Maybe even a lot more. Maybe you can even think of something important right now you'd be willing to stop avoiding because you can now link it to what matters?

Again, knowing the 'why' behind your actions will give you the resilience you need to keep going, even when it's hard, and even when your actions themselves are not rewarding in the short term.

'I CAN FEEL SCARED AND STILL DO WHAT I CARE ABOUT'

ME: So, Anna, you identified the value in your work domain as Creativity, and you want to begin looking for a job that gives you more freedom to think outside the box ... more creative opportunities?

ANNA: Yes, but I'm also terrified of leaving the security of my current job.

ME: Right. So, to even take steps toward finding something else feels scary?

ANNA: Exactly. And I'm also feeling judgy about it.

ME: Got it. You want a new job that offers more creative possibilities, and you're scared to try something new, and you're judging yourself for being scared.

ANNA: Right.

ME: It makes sense that leaving something secure for the unknown would feel scary. I'm curious, and take a moment before you answer, does it matter enough to do it anyway?

ANNA (pausing for 10 seconds): Yes, but I still haven't been able to bring myself to sit down to figure out how.

ME: Okay, so you're clear it matters, even though it's been hard to get started. Would you like to work on figuring out what your VBAs would be?

ANNA: Sure, that sounds good.

ME: Great. So, what do you think will move you in the direction of your Creativity here?

ANNA: Well, it's simple to start. I need to be able to sit in front of the computer and scroll through job listings.

ME: Okay, good, let's do some experiential practice with this VBA of researching job opportunities online. Go ahead and get comfortable and close your eyes. And take me to the scene where you imagine you'd do the research. What happens?

ANNA: I'm back from my morning walk, and I'm feeding the dog in the kitchen, and I'm choosing whether to lay down on the couch and scroll through IG, or go to my desk and the computer to do the research.

ME: Okay, good. And in this moment, what unwanted emotional STUF shows up when you think about going to the computer?

ANNA: Ugh, what *doesn't* show up?! I immediately notice tension in my shoulders and chest, and have the thoughts *there probably isn't anything worth applying for*, and *maybe it's better to stay where I am*, and then I notice the urge to grab my phone and start my social media binge.

ME: Yeah, there's a lot working on you there to get you defaulting to avoidance. Let's slow this down. What are the feelings that go with the sensations, thoughts, and urges?

ANNA: Um, mostly nervous. Also, ambivalent and scared.

ME: Okay, nervous, ambivalent, and scared. That makes sense. How intense is the emotion wave?

ANNA: Hmmm … it's a decent-sized one … about a 6 in intensity.

ME: Okay. What happens if you open up and allow yourself to fully experience the wave?

ANNA: I notice I still have the urge to go to the couch.

ME: That makes sense – acting on the urge to go to the couch would feel easier. That's your unhelpful default urge. See if you can just notice that urge, without acting on it. What else is there?

ANNA: Well, now I notice I'm having the thought that *I really, really don't like my job. I mean, I'm good at sales, but it's so boring and I hate the routine of it. And I've always dreamed of being able to do something more creative, in film or TV.*

ME: Good noticing. That's a lot of thoughts strung together there. Let's slow down and just take one at a time. You notice you really don't like your job. Can you let that thought go, and come back to your breath and see what other thought comes up?

ANNA: Yes, yes, and now I notice the thought *I really want the space to be creative.*

ME: Great. Now let that thought go, and come back to your breath again.

ANNA: I feel scared.

ME: Okay, so just notice that feeling. What's the urge that goes with feeling scared?

ANNA: To go to the couch!

ME: Good noticing. So can you have that urge, and shift from emotion surfing to doing your VBA? What happens if you visualize walking toward the computer?

ANNA: Ugh. My heart rate just sped up. But I'm imagining doing it anyway.

ME: Great. Just tell me what you notice as you imagine sitting in front of the computer and pulling up the job site.

ANNA: Well, I'm sitting down at the desk, and the urge comes to pull up my email instead. And I can feel the tension in my chest again, and the thought *why is this so hard?*

ME: Okay, so let's slow this down again and just hang out and surf a little more here ... bringing curiosity to the tension in your chest. Imagine if you draw a line around it, what shape and size it would be?

ANNA: Yes. It goes all the way from shoulder to shoulder and down to my diaphragm. And I can sense some heat there too.

ME: Good noticing. And what happens if you just hang out with the tension. Just letting it be however it wants to be? You might even imagine embracing it ...

ANNA: Hmmm. It kind of relaxes. But then the thought shows up, *why are you even trying? You know you're not going to follow through with applying.*

ME: Okay, and can you let that thought go and come back to noticing your breath, the inhale and the exhale of it?

ANNA: Okay.

ME: Now what do you notice?

ANNA: I have the urge to lie down again.

ME: Okay, and can you just sit with that urge and be curious about what it's like to have the urge, without acting on it?

ANNA: Yes ... it's hard.

ME: Can you just let it be hard?

ANNA: Yes. Yes.

ME: And what feelings are there when you just allow it to be hard?

ANNA: I'm actually feeling a weird mixture of fear and pride.

ME: Tell me about that ...

ANNA: Well, I'm having the thought that *I generally struggle to stay with things when they are hard, but I realized even practicing this is hard so I'm proud of myself for staying with it.*

ME: Okay, good noticing. And let that thought go, coming back to your breath, and notice what else is happening.

ANNA: Yeah … now I feel scared again. And that comes with another thought that *I could be making a mistake*, and I also notice now that my face feels tingly.

ME: Okay, so just notice everything that is happening. Let's keep surfing. You're feeling some fear, and noticing the thought you could be making a mistake by getting a new job, and you notice that tingling sensations in your face go with that feeling and thought?

ANNA: Yes, and now I'm back to remembering the 'why' behind this value of Creativity.

ME: Great … what's that thought?

ANNA: I'm having the thought that *even if I have to take a pay cut, doing something interesting will immediately increase my quality of life.*

ME: Well done. And just noticing the inhale and exhale of your breath. What else is there?

ANNA: The thought that *I just can't go on with my current job. It sucks me dry.*

ME: Okay. Let that thought go, and come back to your breath. What else is there?

ANNA: I can still feel some fear and some tingly sensations in my face.

ME: Okay, can you practice bringing those along with you while you visualize doing VBA?

ANNA: Yes, I'll try.

ME: Keep in mind that even imagining taking VBA can intensify your unwanted STUF. Can you feel the fear and sense the tingling sensations in your face, and pull up the jobsite anyway?

ANNA: Aaagh, okay, yeah … I see myself clicking on a link to one of the jobs. And I can see myself opening the first listing and starting to read through it to see if it meets the list of workability factors we made.

ME: Great. Now, let's run that sequence again. Can you go back to the kitchen where you feed your dog?

ANNA: Okay.

ME: Now, just imagine going from there to the computer, and notice what comes up.

ANNA: I'm warm in my chest, and I feel some tingling in my arms. I am thinking *that couch sure looks comfy*, and there's definitely an urge to lay down. But it's less intense now. Probably like a 4.

ME: Okay, and what are the feelings?

ANNA: I would say, still fear. But actually, a little hopeful now … even though it doesn't feel easy to imagine going to the computer.

ME: Okay, so see if you can let it feel challenging. Just hang out for a minute with the warmth in your chest, the tingling in your arms, the thought that the couch looks comfy, and the feelings of fear and hope.

ANNA: Okay.

ME: It's not easy … ?

ANNA: No, it's not.

ME: Can you visualize going to your computer anyway? And talk me through it?

ANNA: So I'm walking into my office, sitting down to my desk. I'm noticing the urge to open email, but I'm clicking on the jobsite tab instead.

ME: And what's happening with your unwanted emotional STUF?

ANNA: It's there, but it's down now.

ME: Okay, so where is the intensity?

ANNA: More like a 3.

ME: Okay, keep going.

ANNA: Yeah, I'm actually noticing that my urge is to just do it. To make it happen.

ME: So it's getting easier?

ANNA: Yes.

ME: Okay. So just notice the shift to wanting to get into it, to start scrolling job listings. Notice what it's like to have felt the way you did in the kitchen, and to go to your computer anyway, and to be there now with more ease.

ANNA: It's crazy!

ME: What's crazy?

ANNA: This idea that I have to *feel* like doing it has stopped me so many times. And I really like the idea that I can feel scared and do it anyway.

ME: That's powerful. Nice work. Let's wrap the experiential practice here.

ANNA: Okay.

ME: So, since doing this research may still be triggering for you tomorrow, could you commit to doing this experiential practice with VBA again tonight before you go to sleep to reinforce your willingness to do it tomorrow morning? And, even tomorrow morning if necessary if you are struggling to override the urge to avoid doing the research after your walk?

ANNA: Yes, I can commit to that.

ME: Great!

DECODING THE EMOTIONAL SIGNALS OF YOUR VALUES

With time and experiential practice, you'll master decoding your values the same way you learned to decode defaults and their unhelpful patterns. Clarifying your values requires self-inquiry and reflection. It's like connecting to your deeper intuition, or even 'listening to your heart.' Learning to drop down and hear these emotion signals is key for discerning your values in a moment of choice.

Sometimes you'll immediately know what matters to you, and you'll be skillful enough to take VBA as soon as you are triggered. Other times there can be lots of potential pitfalls to watch for, such as:

· unhelpful defaults or fake or old values will seem more important than what actually matters

· several different values will seem to be equally important, and you'll have to figure out which one to prioritize

· you'll choose a VBA that seems right in the moment, when hindsight shows you were just avoiding something painful.

As a result, taking VBA requires willingness, continuous inquiry, and a lot of experimentation.

As an example, my client 'Joanna' was debating what to do for her boss of 10 years for his upcoming birthday. Joanna's boss had a history of being distant and critical, and any seemingly pleasant interactions between them over the years had felt forced.

In addition, on Joanna's last birthday, her boss had given her an unwrapped cashmere blanket. Afterwards it came out in conversation with her boss's assistant that the regifted blanket had been rejected by his wife due to its excessive shedding. While she was offended by the lack of thoughtfulness, she still felt like she 'should' get him a present. But she was confused about whether this signal was a 'real' or a 'fake' value.

Here's what we did. We practiced deep listening using a simple Yes/No inquiry; I asked Joanna to think about her boss, drop down past her initial reaction to notice her emotional STUF, and ask a simple question: *Do I want to give my boss a birthday gift?*

Not surprisingly, her first gut response was a clear *no!*

She felt overlooked and taken for granted, even insulted by the obvious regift that was now shedding all over her desk chair. But her fast and automatic reaction was suspect. So we inquired further.

Joanna was able to drop down beyond her 'no' to learn that, while she felt upset by her boss's behavior, in this context, she wasn't actually threatened by it. And as she sat with the hurt and disappointment, she was able to connect to a deeper signal: her value of Consideration. When we did the Yes/No inquiry again, this time she noticed a soft but firm 'yes.' She told me it mattered more to express consideration for his birthday than to deny him the gesture of a modest thoughtful gift.

In this way, being clear about your values not only helps you see when you're moving toward what you care about, it will also make it more obvious when you're choosing what you *don't* actually want. With practice you'll be able to harness your moments of choice as opportunities to tune in, hang out, drop down, and value on.

VALUES DECODING EXERCISES

These next few exercises will help you develop a master list of core values for practice. Keep in mind, sometimes your values are crystal clear. You will either recognize them because they feel like familiar songs you love and that resonate with a deep part of you. Other times, it may be confusing to see a value you think you 'should' choose but that may not actually be as meaningful to you. And other times, they may not speak to you at all.

As a way to increase your fluency with values, review the following list and write down the 10 values that most resonate with you. This will become your 'master' list that you'll reference throughout the rest of the book. Don't worry about picking the 'perfect' values; you can always change and edit your list. You can also add your own if you don't see some of your values listed here.

LIST OF **VALUES**

Abundance	Enjoyment	Order
Accountability	Equality	Originality
Achievement	Excellence	Peace
Acceptance	Expertise	Possibility
Adventure	Exploration	Practicality
Ambition	Expression	Purpose
Audacity	Fairness	Reliability
Authenticity	Family	Resourcefulness
Autonomy	Fitness	Respect
Balance	Freedom	Security
Beauty	Friends	Self-actualization
Belonging	Fulfillment	Self-control
Celebration	Fun	Self-reliance
Challenge	Generosity	Sensitivity
Civility	Growth	Serenity
Community	Health	Service
Compassion	Helping	Simplicity
Contribution	Honesty	Spirituality
Cooperation	Honor	Spontaneity
Courage	Humility	Stability
Creativity	Independence	Strength
Curiosity	Innovation	Support
Dependability	Insight	Teamwork
Determination	Integrity	Temperance
Devotion	Intelligence	Thoughtfulness
Diligence	Intuition	Tolerance
Discipline	Justice	Trust
Diversity	Leadership	Understanding
Effectiveness	Learning	Unity
Efficiency	Loyalty	Usefulness
Empathy	Mastery	Vitality

Another way to clarify your values is to reflect on moments of heightened pleasure and moments of intense pain. For example, I can briefly reflect and recognize that one of my life's peak moments was doing physical stunts on water skis, pointing to my core value of Adventure. Alternatively, some of the most painful moments in my life were seeing

KEEP CALM AND VALUE ON

high school friends who are Black struggling with socioeconomic structural inequalities, highlighting my value of Fairness.

Or you could try clarifying core values by projecting yourself into the future, all the way to your memorial service, and list what you hope people would say about you, and identify the values that go with those tributes.

Use the reflection exercises that follow to search for any values you may want to add to your master list.

REFLECTION: BUILD YOUR MASTER LIST OF VALUES

Take a moment here to reflect on your own peak experiences or painful moments. Think of situations that have created the most joy or vitality, or, the most pain or disappointment for you. Write down what values they reflect and add these to your master list.

To complete your values list, try the following exercise. Imagine yourself at the memorial service for your own funeral. Write down what you'd like to hear people say about you at the end of your life. For example, if I imagined my own funeral service, here's what I'd hope people might say about me, and the underlying values:

- She listened to and understood others deeply. (Empathy)
- She was insatiably curious and always learning. (Possibility, Learning, Growth)
- She played at the edges and didn't just accept the status quo. (Creativity, Curiosity, Possibility)
- She didn't shy away from taking risks. (Adventure, Autonomy)
- She knew how to have fun. (Play)
- She created art and music and poetry that inspired me. (Play, Creativity, Self-expression)
- She didn't take herself too seriously, knew how to amuse herself, and sometimes also the rest of us. (Humor, Play)

> - She was always willing to share resources and time. (Generosity)
> - She didn't shy away from difficulty and was willing to grapple with painful issues of life. (Courage, Commitment)
> - She believed everyone mattered and advocated for justice. (Fairness)

Once you've finished your imaginary eulogy, see if you can identify the underlying value in each one. It's okay if the same values keep showing up. That just means it's clear how much they matter to you. (If it's helpful, refer to the list of values.) Next, add any new values you identify to complete your master list. They will help you figure out what might matter most to you in a given situation. You'll use this master list as a reference to help you do the experiential exercises in each of the chapters to come.

THE YES/NO INQUIRY

It's great when you know that Connection is what matters most when you and your partner are grieving a loss, or that Leadership is what matters most when your team is not performing. But in certain situations you may struggle to clarify what matters most.

In this case, you could also try a simple Yes/No inquiry with listening more deeply to your emotional STUF for the signals. For example, let's assume that you've listed Family as a core value, and that your parents invited you for dinner on the weekend. But let's also say you get easily triggered whenever you're around them. And on top of that, you've been working 15-hour days the past week, and you've been looking forward to a downshift (making Self-Care a contender).

What do you do? You might be conflicted, and be unsure whether Family is what matters most in this context. On one hand, you love your parents and care about your relationship with them. On the other hand, they are predictably hypercritical and they love to complain about politics (which you find annoying and exhausting). Also, your lack of sleep is likely to make you even more vulnerable to being triggered and acting on the familiar and unhelpful urge to criticize them, ending up in a tit for tat and leaving early, like you've done in the past.

It's time to drop down and do the deeper listening. To clarify what matters most in this context you need to learn to hear the resonance of your values. As with any emotion triggers, just thinking about a question will trigger your emotional STUF. And you can use it as a guide.

Start by asking yourself a yes/no question: *do I want to spend Saturday night with my parents?*:

- Notice what happens in your body. Are there sensations of tension or relaxation? Opening up or closing down?
- Notice your thoughts – that it would be energizing, depleting, or on balance worth it to spend time with them?
- Notice if you have an urge to call and accept the invitation, or to text and ask if you can do it the following weekend. Does the urge seem like a fast and automatic reaction, or like it comes from a deeper signal?
- Notice your feelings. Interest? Overwhelm? Guilt? Excitement? Meh? Drop in as deep as you can to see if you're getting default feedback or a values-based signal to decode what matters most.

If by chance you discover equal resonance with both values (Family and Self-Care), don't despair. When there doesn't seem to be a clear intention or direction it either means you need to do more inquiry, or that the stakes are lower, meaning you'd be #winning no matter which one you choose. Or you may need to experiment by choosing one or the other, and then seeing what you learn. Try not to overthink it. Either way you'll be doing something that matters.

PUTTING YOUR VALUES INTO ACTION

Now that you've created a working master list of values, you'll practice designing your values-based actions in real time. Once you can decode which value matters most in a given situation, the next step is to identify specific actions you could take to express or embody the value.

For example, if you choose to prioritize Family, your values-based action(s) might look like:

- agreeing to meet for dinner
- silencing your phone during the visit to give your parents undivided attention
- hanging out an extra 30 minutes after dessert, even though you're tired
- listening patiently to your father's filibuster about the abuse of the earned income tax credit.

Or, if you choose Self-Care, your VBAs might include:

- staying home
- making your favorite meal
- taking a hot bath
- reading, or getting lost listening to your favorite music.

And if you want to prioritize both Family and Self-Care, you might suggest meeting for brunch the next day instead of dinner so you can have quality time with you parents and get plenty of downtime and sleep the night before.

In any case, you'll benefit from preparing specific values-based actions you want to take in advance of any predictable trigger situations.

PRIORITIZING WHAT MATTERS MOST

A client of mine, 'Dave,' was struggling with how to respond when he would get regularly triggered in interactions with his ex-wife, 'Rebecca'. He usually prioritized his value of Harmony – a sense of peacefulness and ease – in their coparenting relationship. Other times, a desire for Collaboration with his ex-wife seemed to matter more. And, when he was in a triggering situation with her, it would sometimes become less clear which value mattered most to him.

His values seemed to conflict. At first he thought he was prioritizing Harmony, and later realized he was just avoiding the discomfort of asking her to collaborate about the coparenting schedule. And, in the past when Dave had asked her to compromise, his ex-wife had expressed disapproval, which triggered all kinds of unwanted STUF. And because he had developed an unhelpful default pattern of trying to avoid discomfort, he would often act on the urge to stay quiet.

After learning how to clarify what matters most and take VBA when he gets triggered, here's what he did. Over a weekend exchange of their two young children, Dave and Rebecca were discussing logistics for the upcoming holiday. They had already agreed they would each have the kids for part of Thanksgiving so they could both enjoy a meal with their children and their respective families. Rebecca suggested she bring the kids to Dave's parents' house at 5 p.m. because her family had a tradition of eating at 2 p.m. on Thanksgiving. However, Dave knew that his kids would be exhausted by then, and would not be able to enjoy visiting with his family, much less another meal.

While Dave had empathy for Rebecca's love of ritual and tradition, he also wanted equal consideration. When he did an inquiry and asked himself whether Harmony or Collaboration was more important in this situation, he was able to drop down and clarify that what mattered most was Collaboration. The values-based action he identified was requesting that Rebecca set an earlier mealtime with her family so he could see his kids by 3 p.m. and they could both have quality time.

Dave also committed to experiential skills practice to help him prepare to execute this VBA for the five days leading up to seeing Rebecca. By surfing his wave of discomfort and overriding the urge to stay quiet, when it came time to ask, Dave was ready and able to execute his VBA. Even though Rebecca initially balked at his request which was a secondary trigger, Dave kept surfing. And after waiting patiently for a response, this time Rebecca said yes. Dave learned he could take his unwanted STUF with him, while acting on his value of Collaboration. In our next session Dave told me that even if Rebecca had said no, he would still have been proud of himself.

It's safe to say that taking VBA won't always go this well. But when you do VBAs, at least you're taking action that is meaningful to you. You're intentionally choosing how you'll show up. No matter what the outcome is.

And that's all you ever have control over.

WTF? INQUIRY

So what else can you do when you're struggling to differentiate unhelpful default urges from values-based signals? You can do a WTF? (What's The Function?) inquiry. Since the goal of emotional efficacy is to maximize what matters most in context, this tracking tool will help you figure out which direction your actions are taking you.

The WTF? inquiry will help you level up in moments of choice and guard against unwittingly taking VBAs that may be unhelpful default behaviors in disguise. You can use it to track your actions, away or toward what matters in the moment.

For example, let's say that after emotion surfing you feel overwhelmed and suspect your actions are less about what matters, and more about avoiding discomfort and distress? You can just ask yourself, *what's the function of doing this here and now? Am I choosing this action to express my value, or am I choosing this action to avoid yucky emotional STUF?* When you're in rough waters, a WTF? inquiry will help you figure out if you are moving toward or away from what matters – and help you course correct as needed.

> ... A WTF? INQUIRY WILL HELP YOU FIGURE OUT
> IF YOU ARE MOVING TOWARD OR AWAY
> FROM WHAT MATTERS - AND HELP YOU
> COURSE CORRECT AS NEEDED.

TUNING IN AND TRACKING

My coaching client 'Kent' was very bright, had high expectations bordering on perfectionism, and often had the experience of indignation about why other people didn't do things the way he did, or how he thought they should. While he was pleasant and friendly 80% of the time, in the other 20% when he would get upset; he had a pattern of exploding in meetings and hurling acerbic and condescending criticisms at his team, as well as clients. It was common for him to become verbally aggressive and express discontent with phrases and such as: 'This is pathetic; do I seem stupid?', and, 'Why does anyone think this is acceptable?'

In those moments he described feeling personally attacked, intolerably disappointed, and even lonely – as if other people didn't care as much as he did or just couldn't play at his level.

While Kent thought he had made efforts to be less critical and more composed, his 360 assessment and interview with his team and several board members suggested otherwise. And, with two senior people recently leaving, the leadership team was understandably concerned about being able to retain and attract employees. The assessment helped Kent see that his actions were moving him away from his values in context. He came face to face with the lack of safety his staff experienced and the resulting decrease in collaboration, creative problem solving, and risk-taking among his coworkers. And it was an opportunity to clarify what really mattered to him: to become a more effective leader.

To help Kent increase his Effectiveness, we started with the core skills of emotion awareness and emotion surfing. He quickly got the hang of tuning in when he was triggered, and surfing through any unwanted STUF that showed up. But for Kent to be more effective, he would need to shift from his pattern of being critical, arrogant, and distant when he was triggered to aligning his actions with his value. For that, he needed to make sure he prepared VBAs that would get the job done. We used the WTF? inquiry (on the following page) to track what actions moving toward and away from the value of Effectiveness would look like.

WTF? **INQUIRY**

 **EFFECTIVENESS**

AWAY TOWARDS

AWAY	TOWARDS
Being overly critical, e.g. *this is pathetic or stupid*	Pausing as soon as you realize you are triggered to tune into STUF
Using aggressive language, e.g. *I'm going on a search and destroy mission*	Surfing through all your emotional STUF instead of reacting
Raising your voice or talking in a sharp tone	Taking VBA:
Body language that shows you're unimpressed:	- don't assume you know what someone is thinking or doing
- head in hands	- asking questions. e.g. *help me understand how you're thinking about this?*
- eyes looking down or away	- problem solving inquiries, e.g. *what can we do to better address this problem?*
- slumped over	
Taking action without consulting or seeking input from team members	- ask exec team for support, e.g. send emojis when they notice they are getting triggered

This tracking helped Kent see more clearly what direction each of his actions would move him related to his value of Effectiveness. As an additional VBA, Kent asked several of his team members to send him silly emojis during meetings if they saw him falling back into unhelpful defaulting. And he agreed to respond to them with emojis of appreciation.

Well done, Kent. 👍☺

CREATING A VALUES-BASED ACTION PLAN

Here's how executing VBA will look from the moment you first notice your emotion trigger to taking action. Say you get triggered, and you surf through all your emotional STUF. Most likely the intensity of the painful emotion wave becomes tolerable enough to override the urge that comes with it. And you can bring any remaining discomfort and distress with you. Here and now is the moment of choice where you'll drop down, decode what matters and take values-based action.

To practice VBA, you'll want to plan ahead using predictable and recurring triggers (from your list of trigger scenes from chapter 3). A plan of action will help you know exactly what you'll do when an emotion wave hits. Once you've used them in the VBA experiential practice, you'll be better at it in real time.

If you're not clear what your value is for your chosen trigger scene, you can use your master list of values (Relationships, Work, Health, and so on). Using the values-based action plan on the next page, work through the following steps:

- Pick a recurring trigger or challenge in your life that you know will activate a wave of unwanted emotional STUF at a medium level of intensity (between 4 and 6 on a 10-point scale).

- Identify the value you want to prioritize in this situation. What matters most to you? (Using the values clarification exercises is helpful.)

- Come up with at least two possible VBAs you could take that would help you express or embody your value in the trigger situation. Be as flexible, intentional, and creative as possible.

- Anticipate what kind of emotional STUF could get in the way of executing VBA: unwanted sensations, thoughts, urges, and feelings.

- List why it's worth taking VBA anyway.

Here's an example:

COMMUNITY

Recurring trigger: when I go out with friends I get socially anxious.

Value: Connection

Values-based actions (VBAs) I want to take: create some pre-planned conversation starters; have a conversation with at least one new person; share something appropriately vulnerable if the opportunity presents.

Emotional STUF I predict will show up before and/or while I'm doing VBA: racing heart, sweaty palms, tension in shoulders (sensations); *get me out of here*, and *no one here would be interested in me* (thoughts); impulse to leave; impulse to find a corner to hang out in and watch other people instead of talking to them (urges); nervous, worried (feelings).

Now it's your turn.

REFLECTION: CREATING A VALUES-BASED ACTION PLAN

Use your notebook to complete this values-based action plan. You'll reference this plan in your future experiential practice.

RELATIONSHIPS

Recurring trigger:

Value:

Values-based actions (VBAs) I want to take:

Emotional STUF I predict will show up before and/or while I'm doing VBA:

Why I want to take VBA anyway:

WORK

Recurring trigger/challenge:

Value:

Values-based actions (VBAs) I want to take:

Emotional STUF I predict will show up before and/or while I'm doing VBA:

Why I want to take VBA anyway:

HEALTH

Recurring trigger/challenge:

Value:

Values-based actions (VBAs) I want to take:

Emotional STUF I predict will show up before and/or while I'm doing VBA:

Why I want to take VBA anyway:

COMMUNITY

Recurring trigger/challenge:

Value:

Values-based actions (VBAs) I want to take:

Emotional STUF I predict will show up before and/or while I'm doing VBA:

Why I want to take VBA anyway:

RECREATION

Recurring trigger/challenge:

Value:

Values-based actions (VBAs) I want to take:

Emotional STUF I predict will show up before and/or while I'm doing VBA:

Why I want to take VBA anyway:

OTHER

Recurring trigger/challenge:

Value:

Values-based actions (VBAs) I want to take:

Emotional STUF I predict will show up before and/or while I'm doing VBA:

Why I want to take VBA anyway:

If you try all these exercises and the experiential practice and you're still struggling with values-based action, more help is on the way. In the next three chapters you'll learn new skills to regulate your emotions so you can pivot to what matters – even when your emotion wave is a giant bomb.

THE VBA OBSTACLE COURSE

Here are some common obstacles that may come up as you practice values-based action:

- *In the moment you might not be clear about what VBA will move you toward your value(s).* Even when you surf your emotion wave and even when you see you have a choice to do something other than act on the unhelpful default urge, you may struggle to find your values-based action. If you get stuck, you can pause and ask yourself, *how do I want to show up in this moment?* and see what comes to mind. You could also pause and accept being stuck momentarily, and voice it to yourself or to someone else. For instance, if you're practicing Compassion with your child, when you are feeling frustrated you could pause when you get triggered and then say, 'I'm really trying to figure out how to respond to you compassionately, but I'm just drawing a blank and I need a moment.' This is still a move in the right direction versus, for example, losing it over the Legos you've stepped on for umpteenth time that day. Or, maybe the VBA of validating someone else's feelings when you're triggered is too much of a stretch for you at first. Try something less ambitious to start (for example, not saying anything at all) to see what works.

- *You might be thrown by the outcome or another person's reaction to your VBA.* Remember, all you can control is how *you* show up in any given situation. Sometimes you'll make valiant efforts to do what matters, but it might not give you the results you expected. For instance, let's say when you get triggered by your child's behavior and your value is Compassion, your VBA is to validate how frustrated your child is feeling. Maybe you even ask questions to better show empathy for why she is upset. But let's say your child responds to you by getting even more frustrated. Now you have another moment of choice in front of you. You can recalibrate and look for another way to embody or express Compassion. Maybe it's just listening, or suggesting you both take some time to settle your feelings and talk afterward. Whatever the case, when things don't go as you hope, you can remind yourself that you can't control the outcome, only how you're showing up in the actions you take.

- *Some triggers are like an Achilles' heel.* Sometimes triggers are intensely painful. And if you've practiced the same response to them, breaking the unhelpful default pattern feels that much harder. Maybe you've responded to anticipatory anxiety by taking fast-acting anxiety medication before big presentations at work for so many years, you can't imagine trying to taper it or trying to perform without it. Or maybe you're caught in an intense dynamic with a family member that is so well-rehearsed it seems impossible to shift. If this happens, be gentle with yourself and remember, overriding unhelpful default urges is no small feat. Keep surfing until you can act on your values. You may benefit from your experiential practice before you'll be able to better harness your moments of choice.

- *You might lack the willingness to tolerate the unwanted STUF that comes with doing hard things.* Doing VBA can temporarily intensify your unwanted STUF, so it's understandable if you get sidetracked. So even if you love the idea of taking values-based action, it may mean you'll encounter increased discomfort and distress. You might have every intention to do values-based action but your well-worn patterns are going to be easier to follow. Or you might unwittingly choose a favorite avoidance strategy from your unhelpful defaulting repertoire. The reality is that acting on your values will often require you to sacrifice some sense of safety, certainty, coherence, comfort, or pleasure. To strengthen your willingness, try validating how hard it feels. You might even say to yourself something like, *it makes sense this is hard; if it was easy I would have already done it.* Then you can also reconnect to willingness by reminding yourself why VBA is meaningful – more meaningful than avoiding the unwanted STUF. And then try again. If you're still stuck, you can list the costs and benefits of doing VBA versus not doing VBA in the situation. Finally, experiential practice, experiential practice, experiential practice.

VALUES-BASED ACTION EXPERIENTIAL PRACTICE

You'll want to practice values-based action in an activated state so it will be easier to use when you need it. Like the skills of emotion awareness and emotion surfing, practicing the pivot to VBA in an activated state will increase the likelihood that you can do it IRL. Looking at the examples you identified for your VBA plan, choose one VBA to rehearse.

To rehearse the skill of values-based action, you can use the following script, and you can also access a guided experiential practice at www.draprilia west.com/practice.

SET UP

Find a private, quiet place and get into a comfortable position where you're likely to stay alert. Close your eyes or find a single spot in front of you to focus on by just softening your gaze.

SELECT A TRIGGER

Choose a trigger based on a memory or recurring event to activate medium intensity of discomfort and distress. (Keep in mind, in the low range you can struggle to access your emotional STUF, and in the high range you can be easily overwhelmed.)

SELECT VBA

Pick at least one values-based action that will move you toward what matters most in your trigger scene.

ACTIVATE EMOTION

1. Set your trigger scene by imagining it as a movie and describe what you notice as if it's happening in real time, including:
   - where you are
   - what time it is
   - who you are with.
2. Go to the exact 'frame' where you anticipate you'll get emotionally activated.
3. Describe anything you are seeing, hearing, touching, tasting, and otherwise doing in as much detail as possible, frame by frame until you reach a medium level of activation.
4. Stop the scene and shift to emotion surfing.

EMOTION SURFING

Surf your emotion wave by bringing an intention of curiosity to hanging out with each part of your emotional 'STUF' for two minutes each:

(Sensations) For at least two minutes, scan your body from head to toe for any sensations that stand out to you:

- Notice their size and shape.
- Notice whether they're moving or staying the same.
- Notice any tension in the sensation.
- Notice if there's any temperature.

Bring an intention of allowing the physical experiences that go with sensations. Imagine making space for them, or welcoming them to be there and do whatever they want to do. Be curious about how they behave when you are just watching them.

(Thoughts) Shift your attention from sensations to noticing thoughts for at least two minutes:

- When a thought shows up, say to yourself 'there's a thought' and then let the thought go.
- Refocus on your breath as a way to place a pause between thoughts.
- And then watch for the next thought to show up, and repeat.

(Urges) Shift to watching any urges for two minutes:

- When you notice one, get curious about how intense the urge is: low, medium, high?
- Notice what it's like to just sit with the impulse to do something or not do something.
- Rate the discomfort on a scale of 1 to 10, with 1 being as relaxed as you can imagine, and 10 the most uncomfortable you can imagine.
- Notice if the urge changes in intensity as you sit with it.

(Feelings)

- Label each feeling.
- Validate and welcome the feelings, saying something like: *It makes sense I'm feeling* [insert label]. Or, *it's okay for the feeling of* [insert label] *to be here.*
- Get curious about whether there are any other feelings, underneath the first feelings you noticed.

VALUES-BASED ACTION

Go back to the exact trigger frame where you have a moment of choice – to act on the emotion urge, or to take values-based action.

Visualize in as much detail as possible doing your values-based action(s) while you continue emotion surfing for at least five minutes, describing your actions and experience to yourself frame by frame:

- What would you or an outside observer see you doing?

- How would it be in your body to do this values-based action? Notice and allow any sensations.
- What kinds of thoughts would show up? Practice letting them go.
- What other urge or urges show up as you take values-based action? Notice what it's like just sitting with them.
- Notice any feelings might you have and just allow them, or validate them.

Repeat the VBA sequence twice.

REFLECT

To wrap up the experiential practice, take a few moments to reflect using the following prompts:

- Did anything surprise you?
- What, if anything, was challenging?
- What did you learn?
- Write down anything else you want to remember.

CHAPTER 06 CHALLENGES

· Think back to how you responded to a recent trigger and try to find at least one 'fake' value or an old value that seemed like it was what mattered most in your moment of choice.

· Make a commitment to taking values-based action in one of the domains of your life toward a core value you identified in your master list. Use the WTF? inquiry to track whether your planned VBAs move you toward or away from the value you've chosen.

· Ask a friend how avoidance of discomfort or distress is holding them back in some area of their life. Ask them what they would do differently if they could tolerate the unwanted emotional STUF and act on what matters most.

· Lock in the learning by sharing your commitment to taking specific values-based action this week and why it matters with someone you're comfortable with. Make a plan to tell them how it went afterward.

· Practice using values-based action using the guided experiential practice at least three times before you move forward.

CHAPTER 06 LEARNINGS

- Values are freely chosen intentions or directions that reflect your most authentic interests, desires, and yearnings.

- To thrive, human beings need to be connected to the meaning behind their doing.

- Values-based action adds the intention of dropping down to listen to and act on what matters to the *tuning in* of emotion awareness and *hanging out* of emotion surfing.

- Taking values-based action entails clarifying what matters most to you in context, and then choosing specific behaviors to express or embody that.

- Sometimes 'old' values or 'fake' values can interfere with clarifying what matters most.

- Linking your actions or goals with your values makes them naturally rewarding and increases your willingness to do hard things.

- Your actions always move you toward or away from your values in any situation. You can use a WTF? (What's The Function?) inquiry to track your actions.

- In a moment of choice, doing VBA may intensify unwanted STUF. And/or, you might feel better afterwards.

- You can be distressed and do your VBA anyway.

- To practice values-based action when you're triggered, identify and take specific actions to express or embody what matters most in context.

- Using experiential skills practice with visualization can help you execute VBA when you're triggered in real time.

07

THE
POWER
OF
PERSPECTIVE-
TAKING

Learning how to think really means learning how to
exercise some control over how and what you think.

David Foster Wallace

EMOTION SURFING AND VALUES-BASED ACTION are often all you need to shift from unhelpful defaulting to valuing when you're triggered. Aligning your actions with your values is what helps you unlock the best possible version of yourself in moments of choice.

And while it's great when you can just surf your way to VBA, what about times when a tsunami blindsides you and, despite your best efforts, pulls you under?

It's inevitable that waves will sometimes knock you sideways and have you choking down the emotional equivalent of a mouthful of seawater.

Maybe your mother calling with advice about that job interview is one frustration too many after a long day. Or, while you could cope with your boss asking you to work late four times, five makes your head explode. Sometimes you need extra help finding your way to making values-based moves.

Enter the emotional efficacy skill of mindful coping.

MINDFULLY COPING BACK TO VALUES-BASED ACTION

As its name suggests, mindful coping helps you regulate your emotions while staying connected to the here and now and finding your way to taking values-based action. The skills sequence progresses like this: when you get triggered, you'll tune in and hang out (surfing), but instead of going straight to VBA, you'll use mindful coping to downshift your emotional activation until you can do what matters.

In the next three chapters you'll learn three mindful coping skills:

· perspective-taking

· relaxation

· attention-shifting.

Here's how it works. Say, for instance, even after expert-level surfing, a big wave overtakes you during a work meeting, and you're left still wanting to strangle the colleague who just happily took credit for months of your painstaking work on the successful product launch. So much so that the epic takedown your emotion urge is tempting you toward seems like fair and just punishment.

But, let's also say you can also hear the faint signal from deeper down telling you what matters most: keeping your cool in front of your boss and several investors throughout the rest of the meeting. You may not know how to get there in your current state of emotional activation. This is where using one (or more) mindful coping skills can help dial down the intensity of your emotion wave so you can chill out enough to productively rejoin the conversation.

While mindful coping might sound great, at this point you might also be wondering, if these skills can de-escalate discomfort and distress, why are you just learning about them now? Why not just go straight to regulating whenever you get triggered?

There are several important reasons why you've learned the skills in this order:

- *Mindful coping is not as effective and efficient as surfing your way straight into values-based action.* Regulating your emotions is great, especially when it helps you calm down enough to do what matters. But unless chilling out also happens to be what matters most, by itself mindful coping won't move you toward your values. You won't develop the efficiency and effectiveness that comes from being able to surf your emotion wave and going straight to VBA when you can. For this reason, you'll want to reserve mindful coping skills for times you really need them to get to values-based action.

- *Using mindful coping whenever you're triggered can lead to unhelpful default patterns.* Regularly avoiding discomfort and distress will not only cause all the usual consequences you know about, you'll also miss out on building your tolerance to surf. You're more likely stay in the shallows and you'll never master the tsunamis.

- *Sometimes when you face incredible pain and terrible things happen, the best you can do is surf.* Even when you know how to regulate your emotions, it doesn't always work. Even your best mindful coping may be no match for intense triggers. Sometimes the best you can do is hang out with your experience. In these cases, riding out the wave or distracting yourself is sometimes the best values-based action you can take.

In this chapter, you'll learn how to use perspective-taking skills when you're triggered to help you find your way back to VBA.

YOUR THOUGHTS AS MOMENTARY POINTS OF VIEW

The first mindful coping skill, perspective-taking, can help you regulate by unhooking from unwanted mental content. As you know, thoughts can be formidable emotion triggers. And while you can't ever control, suppress, or stop thoughts from randomly showing up, you can always add perspective – other possible ways of seeing. And now that you have the ability to hang out with your emotions – including unhooking from thoughts by letting them go – this is just one small step further.

> WHILE YOU CAN'T EVER CONTROL, SUPPRESS,
> OR STOP THOUGHTS FROM RANDOMLY
> SHOWING UP, YOU CAN ALWAYS ADD PERSPECTIVE -
> OTHER POSSIBLE WAYS OF SEEING.

Just like having a relationship with each part of your emotional STUF, you also have a way of relating to your thoughts. And, just as the overarching goal of emotional efficacy is more flexible, intentional, and creative choice-making, the goal of perspective-taking is to expand flexible, intentional, and creative thinking, which has the added benefit of helping you regulate your emotions when you're triggered.

Take a moment here to think about your thinking. Consider that your mind is always making up words or images that create the content of your thoughts. This is what gives you a perspective in any moment. And it's just as easy to believe everything your emotions tell you as it is to believe all of your thoughts. It takes no effort at all to believe your thoughts are telling you the capital T truth. Psychologist Daniel Kahneman describes it as believing that *what you see is all there is*.[1] Sound familiar?

If you're one of those people who tends to over-think, or you 'live in your head,' you may find perspective-taking to be particularly life changing. Here's why. As with all your emotional STUF, your thoughts can tell you about both values and (helpful and unhelpful) defaults. As a result, you may relate to your thoughts as facts or commands telling you how to act, without first inquiring as to what matters most.

In other words, you may completely buy into everything you think. And this attachment to your thoughts can cause major unhelpful defaulting and a whole lot of unnecessary suffering. When you see your thoughts as the Truth, you can become rigidly stuck in one way of seeing something. This can also lead to missed opportunities. It doesn't lead to the flexible, intentional, creative choice-making you need to design your best life.

In fact, if you're like most people, you have already spent a lot of your life buying into your thoughts and their stories, which can seem to keep you safely anchored in the world. And while thoughts do tell you about valid experiences you're having, following them blindly can keep you from being curious and doing the inquiry it takes to connect with what really matters, especially when you get triggered. Which, as you know, happens really easily.

In fact, it's likely that …

… even right now …

…… as you slow down …

……… to think about these words you're reading …

………… you're also having thoughts about why …

…………… this sentence is broken up this way.

Maybe you notice you have an opinion about it.

It's a break with convention.

It's weird.

This is just silly.

No, it's manipulative.

Perhaps it's even formatting heresy.

What the heck is going on

way over here

on the right side now?

Regardless, you can see how easy it is for us to come up with opinions – or even beliefs – when we get emotionally activated. And, to believe they are 'right.' Believing everything you think is what Daniel Kahneman has referred to as 'overconfidence.'[2] It is obvious when you become overconfident because you'll be hooked by your thinking. When you get fused with your thoughts, it's like your mind is selling one *incredibly righteous holier-than-thou* perspective, and you are buying it hook, line, and sinker. And when you're convinced that you're right, you'll have a very hard time seeing things any other way. You will be willing to put all your money on red, so to speak. And maybe even double down.

When we believe we're right, it can feel really threatening to even consider changing our mind.[3] So much so that we will outright ignore or deny information that is inconsistent with what we already think. We dig in – even when something else matters more. This can seriously mess with being a boss-level values-based choice-maker.

> WHEN YOU GET FUSED WITH YOUR THOUGHTS, IT'S LIKE YOUR MIND IS SELLING ONE *INCREDIBLY RIGHTEOUS HOLIER-THAN-THOU* PERSPECTIVE, AND YOU ARE BUYING IT HOOK, LINE, AND SINKER. AND WHEN YOU'RE CONVINCED THAT YOU'RE RIGHT, YOU'LL HAVE A VERY HARD TIME SEEING THINGS ANY OTHER WAY. YOU WILL BE WILLING TO PUT ALL YOUR MONEY ON RED, SO TO SPEAK. AND MAYBE EVEN DOUBLE DOWN.

Why would you do this when it's not helpful? You already know the answer: because you're wired to over-index for safety, certainty, coherence, comfort, and pleasure, it can feel imperative to relate to your thinking as the 'whole truth.' Ultimately, believing everything you think will limit what's possible for you in a moment of choice. Fortunately, there is another way of relating to what you think.

Perspective-taking involves relating to your thoughts less as the 'whole truth' and more as valid but momentary points of view. They represent fleeting perspectives based on whatever vantage point you're looking from.

Say you and I are standing on opposite sides of a mountain. You may see lush alpine trees and a snowcapped ridge. But from my side I may see barren rock interspersed with wildflowers. Is either of these perspectives wrong? Nope. It's just how we are both seeing the same mountain from our sides.

> PERSPECTIVE-TAKING INVOLVES RELATING TO YOUR THOUGHTS LESS AS THE 'WHOLE TRUTH' AND MORE AS VALID BUT MOMENTARY POINTS OF VIEW.

You can also have different perspectives all by yourself. Imagine walking around a mountain. You start to appreciate just how many possible views there are. From any POV you can see many different things and make up many different stories and rules about how things are based just on what you're seeing in that moment.

And, in this way, just like all parts of your emotional STUF, your thoughts are never right or wrong. There is always more than what you think in any moment.

WHEN BEING RIGHT IS NOT WHAT MATTERS MOST

As another example, imagine you and I are longtime friends, and we get into a conversation about our shared loved of rock music.

ME: 'Dude. Led Zeppelin is the best rock band of all time.'

YOU: 'No way man, it's Pink Floyd.'

We both have a perspective, yes? But say I'm taken aback – maybe even slightly offended – that you raised my Robert Plant, Jimmy Page, John Paul Jones, and John Bonham power ensemble with your Roger Waters, David Gilmour, Richard Wright, and Nick Mason quartet.

ME: 'Hold up … *Over the Hills and Far Away*, *When the Levee Breaks* and of course the *Rain Song*!?!?!'

YOU: 'Um, hellooooo ... the ENTIRE Wall album, *On The Turning Away* and *Wish You Were Here*!?!?'

(I know, we sound redic – just go with it.)

Our different perspectives may not be problematic, unless our obsession with our respective bands borders on the fanatical, leading one or both of us to take our rigidly attached perspectives too seriously, and the difference in perspectives leads us both to feel threatened. Then, we might both be so committed to being right that our friendship – or at least the rest of this lively conversation – could suffer a brutal blow. In this way, relating to what we think as the only way of seeing can really muck things up.

Ultimately, being rigidly fused with one perspective becomes a problem when it gets in the way of what matters most. It always depends on the greater context. It's totally workable for me to believe I'm right about Led Zeppelin, or politics, or the meaning of life, so long as that overconfidence doesn't interfere with what matters more to me in a given situation.

While the above example is a less intense perspective clash, it can often feel difficult to shift perspective, even when it's in your best interest, desire, or yearning to do so.

> BEING RIGIDLY FUSED WITH ONE PERSPECTIVE
> BECOMES A PROBLEM WHEN IT GETS IN THE
> WAY OF WHAT MATTERS MOST. IT ALWAYS
> DEPENDS ON THE GREATER CONTEXT.

Let's dive deeper to see how you can relate to your thinking more intentionally, flexibly, and creatively.

'SWIPING LEFT' ON UNHELPFUL THOUGHTS

To recap, thoughts are made up of images or words strung together that represent your valid but momentary experiences. When your biases and beliefs get involved, your thoughts can become rigid, absolute, or black-and-white rules or pervasive stories, such as:

- no one who works at the DMV cares how long customers wait
- I have to play 'hard to get' if I want a romantic partner to be interested in me
- whenever things get good, something bad will happen
- Americans are shallow and superficial.

And yet, these rigid, absolute, black-and-white ways of thinking don't always give you accurate, helpful information about the here and now.

Say I am running late for a session – my thought might simply be: *no time for a coffee refill!* But if my rules and stories kick in, I might notice a harsh inner-critic thought like: *you're not living intentionally if you have to rush like this ... you help your clients live better, but you can't even do it yourself!*

In context, my thoughts may or may not be helpful in urging me toward action that is most meaningful. But if I relate to them as directives to obey, my tendency is to blindly buy into them – even in the absence of any supporting evidence. Like a lot of default messages, thoughts are sometimes not actually fires but more like malfunctioning smoke alarms.

This raises an interesting question: what if you didn't take your thoughts quite so seriously all the time? Imagine a dating app for thoughts, where you get to scroll through all the potential thought candidates that show up in your profile. If you think, *ooh, I'd love to hang out with that thought*, you can 'swipe right' to match with it. Then you can chat them up and maybe even hang out if there seems to be value in it. And, if you don't like the thought or don't want to get involved with it you could say: *bye, Felicia!* And swipe left (making it disappear). And, even if the thought keeps showing up in your feed (as they often do), you could keep swiping left.

Just like a dating app, you may find that certain thoughts are much more attractive to you than others. For instance, having the thought *I can't listen to this even a minute longer* could be a really 'attractive' thought if you're FaceTiming with someone who is defending their belief that the earth is flat (assuming you're more comfortable with the thought that the earth is more orb-shaped). On the other hand, if you have that same thought *I can't listen to this even a minute longer* while standing in front of your boss when she is giving you the specs for a new project ... er, not so 'attractive.'

With the flat-earth-FaceTime example, your thought would likely come with an urge to say *see ya!* with your 'swipe left' finger, allowing you to search for more attractive thoughts. But in the second scenario with your boss, getting involved with your thought about not listening is likely to distract you from what really matters in context – your boss's request or your rapport with her. Buying into that thought could even motivate you to tune out or noticeably roll your eyes and miss what she's trying to download to you, leading to negative consequences.

The point is, you can choose which thoughts you want to engage. And just knowing you have this choice can shift how much power they have over you, and your choices.

THE ALWAYS STREAMING CONTENT OF YOUR MIND

The reality is, you don't just get involved with thoughts here and there, like a dating app. Unless you're an extraterrestrial or enlightened being, you're almost always thinking.

Here's another metaphor to illustrate the busy animated life of your mind: your thoughts make up on-demand content streaming powered by your mind. You have a choice to listen in or log out anytime, but there is almost always something streaming.

For example, if you were to tune in to the constant flow of thinking when you're feeling great, you might hear something like this:

WELL HELLO, HELLO, HELLO! You're tuned in to KWX-WINNING and things are looking bright! As expected, the forecast is vitality, connection, gratitude, productivity, and wow, aren't you feeling loved today?! Wait, look over there, aren't those flowers gorgeous?! Ohhhh, hey, would you look at that? I see you, you gorgeous thing in the mirror! Ahhh, it just feels so good to be alive ... so much to look forward to ... life feels like a big game of Choose Your Own Adventure, and every ending seems so enticing!

Or, in moments you're not feeling great, you might hear something more like this:

> Oh … you, again. Nope, it's not a bad dream, you actually sound like Eeyore up in here. This is the inner narrator you're stuck with because you're tuned in to KMZ-YOUAREBROKEN, where you get the very latest in breaking bad news 24/7 about the same old problems with the same old people in the same old situations in the same old life. Nothing new here. Nothing to see. Not even really sure what the point is. People are disappointing you. You're disappointing you. And it's just not worth the energy or risk of trying to do anything about it. Besides, it's not like you could even if you wanted to. Remember last time you reached out when you were this lonely? Nobody called you back! One thing's for certain: everybody else is living their best life so there must be something very wrong with you.

As you can hear, these stations are streaming very different content. You may have even noticed an emotional charge of those different perspectives just from reading them. That charge is what makes it so easy to get fused with one or the other way of thinking. And it can impact all your other emotional STUF and create waves, moods, or even lead to lifelong patterns of thinking known as mindsets.

This is why learning to unhook from a single rigidly held perspective is so powerful. You can relate to any or even multiple content 'stations' for what they are – ever-changing thoughts based on myriad factors and context, rather than some absolute, constant truth. You can choose which thoughts to get involved with, and which ones you let pass by. In this way, your mind is an endless playground of valid but momentary perspectives where you get to choose what you want to listen to.

> YOU CAN CHOOSE WHICH THOUGHTS TO
> GET INVOLVED WITH, AND WHICH ONES
> YOU LET PASS BY. IN THIS WAY, YOUR MIND
> IS AN ENDLESS PLAYGROUND OF VALID BUT
> MOMENTARY PERSPECTIVES WHERE YOU GET
> TO CHOOSE WHAT YOU WANT TO LISTEN TO.

FROM 'LOSER' TO FAILING A TEST

My friend 'Justina's' text read: *I'm a loser.* I knew she'd been scheduled to take the bar exam that week, and I could only assume what had happened. As soon as we got on the phone, she told me, 'I've never prepared for a test so exhaustively in my life ... and I missed by one point. One point!! It's my worst nightmare come true: I prepare to the best of my ability, and I still don't pass.'

I felt terrible for her. I knew how hard she'd worked to go to law school, especially as a single mother of a two-year-old and not a lot of financial stability. I also knew she struggled with patterns of performance anxiety and procrastination. And I knew how hard she studied this time, unlike other times when she would only give 75% effort at the last minute – holding back just enough that she could blame her lack of effort if she didn't succeed. But this time was different. She had thrown herself in 100%.

Meanwhile, she had received stellar feedback from internships and client work about her knack for coming up with creative approaches to complex cases. And she'd been recognized by several veteran attorneys for her contributions to big clients. But her thought *I'm a loser* felt like high-octane capital 'T' truth.

I asked if I could offer another perspective. Happily, she said yes. I reminded her that her thought *I'm a loser* was a very old thought that came from difficult experiences that had shaped a lot of her life. As a child Justina had immigrated from an urban area in South America, landing in the middle of America among white suburban nine-year-olds who found her accent and clothing perfect fodder for teasing.

To compensate, Justina had worked hard to fit in with her peers. And even though she assimilated to life in the mid-West, she was preoccupied with being 'good enough,' and she was easily threatened by anything that could be interpreted as failure. The looming threat of failure followed her all the way through law school, especially when she was expected to perform. Now jumping through the last hoop – passing the bar – she was devastated to learn her worst fear had been realized.

Here's how the conversation went:

ME: How true does the thought *I'm a loser* feel?

JUSTINA: 110%.

ME: Okay. I can understand that. You've spent so much of your life avoiding situations that could lead to failure. No wonder this feels so threatening.

JUSTINA: It's awful. I can't even think about studying more and retaking it now. It feels like I'm never going to pass.

ME: Okay, so, let's see if you can defuse from that thought by adding perspective. Pretend you're on trial for being 'a loser' in this situation ... what would your defense attorney say about the lack of evidence for it?

(She paused and groaned as she could see where I was going, but incredibly, she was willing to play along.)

JUSTINA: Your honor, the bar exam is never completely valid or reliable since it measures the performance of knowledge at a single point in time, which we all know can vary based on anything from a person's mood to the amount of sleep they had the night before to the level of anxiety during test administration, as well as inconsistently normed scores attributed to different versions of the test.

ME: Oh, wow, impressive defense! What happens when you shift perspective like that?

JUSTINA (sighing): I'm more relaxed now. And I can tell that telling myself I'm a loser is the way I punish myself to motivate myself not to fail – and it didn't even work.

ME: Okay, and what if I say, 'but you're a loser'. Does that thought still hook you?

JUSTINA: No ... I'm really *not* a loser. I just failed the frickin' bar.

Justina had been relating to her thought *I'm a loser* as if it were the absolute and only truth of the situation. And it felt completely accurate to her because it's such a well-rehearsed thought. But with just a momentary shift in perspective, she could see other ways of relating to what had happened, and to her thought. Studying for the bar again and the delay in being licensed was painful, but being hooked by her thought was unhelpful and was causing her (unnecessary) suffering on top of the pain. By shifting perspective, she found immediate relief, was able to get on with what mattered most, and a few months later she passed the bar.

Maybe you're already aware that your thoughts are not always telling you the Truth, or that they can be unhelpful. Or maybe this feels like really 'new news' and you're now realizing you've been a more than captive audience for the streaming stations of your mind. Just knowing you don't have to believe everything you think allows you to see thoughts more as movies playing in your mind. And from this POV, you can also zoom out to look at life from other perspectives.

REFLECTION: GETTING CURIOUS ABOUT YOUR THINKING

Take a moment now to get curious about your relationship with your thinking and ask yourself:

- Do you tend to buy in to most of your thoughts as 'right' or 'true'? Are there certain thoughts that you get more hooked by than others? (For example, being right, feeling disrespected, not fitting in, being entitled to certain things, not being good enough.)
- Do you tend to act on whatever your thoughts tell you, or do you pause and get curious about what the thought might be indicating? (For example, *Is this thought signal or noise?*)
- Recall a recent distressing situation. Can you identify being hooked by any particular thoughts that created unnecessary suffering? If so, can you now see those same thoughts, rules, and stories as valid but momentary perspectives?

To add to your knowledge about perspective-taking, you'll learn the skills of *coping thoughts* and *radical acceptance*. Using these skills for perspective-taking will defuse the power your mind gives your thoughts, stories, and rules.

COPING THOUGHTS: EXPANDING YOUR POV

Coping thoughts are pretty much what they sound like: alternative perspectives that help regulate your emotions in moments of discomfort or distress. They don't get rid of painful or unhelpful thoughts, but they connect you to more helpful POVs. Coping thoughts introduce new narratives that help you disentangle from whatever unhelpful storyline happens to be streaming.

> COPING THOUGHTS INTRODUCE NEW
> NARRATIVES THAT HELP YOU DISENTANGLE
> FROM WHATEVER UNHELPFUL STORYLINE
> HAPPENS TO BE STREAMING.

In real time, here's how coping thoughts work. Imagine you have a boss who unexpectedly drops into a meeting for a project you're leading. Halfway through the meeting, she asserts her opinion on how things should proceed. As project lead, you could understandably get triggered and – assuming what matters most is staying present for the meeting – you have some not so helpful, automatic thoughts, such as: *she doesn't trust me*, and, *I look foolish in front of my coworkers because she seems to be overriding my authority.*

And, let's say, as soon as you notice you're triggered, you start surfing the wave, hanging out – even welcoming – sensations; the tension in your chest, heat in your face, and your rapidly pounding heart. You allow the distressing thoughts to come and go. You notice an urge to school your boss on the carefully considered rationale for your plan, but instead you sit with it. Finally, you label your feelings – irritation, disappointment, and embarrassment – and validate how much they make sense in the situation. And now imagine that in doing this, even if the intensity of your emotion wave has levelled off, you still can't focus on what matters most: tracking what's happening in the rest of the meeting.

This is where you could use a coping thought to help you take perspective.

You could start by pausing and getting curious about alternative narratives, like walking around the mountain to see what else there is. You could ask yourself, *Are there times I believe my boss actually does trust me?* And maybe the answer would be, *hmmm, she did invite me to present our quarterly report to investors last month. She also recommended me to lead that project that has been stalled for a few years because she thought I could effectively execute it.* Or even, *sometimes my boss does seem to trust me, even if it's not evident in this meeting.*

Or, let's say all the evidence you can find supports your boss not trusting you. You could still tap into other ways of seeing that. Your coping thought could be, *she really doesn't trust me, but at least I get paid well enough to tolerate being micromanaged.*

Or, for the distressing thought about looking foolish, you could use a coping thought like, *most of my coworkers respect my leadership skills, and they probably see she's misunderstanding the direction we've chosen.*

Or, *even if I feel like I look foolish, it doesn't mean everyone else thinks I look foolish.*

Again, coping thoughts can be any thoughts that expand your perspective. They could remind you of past experiences where you were effective in similar situations, help you see something a little differently, or validate your experience. They could even offer the opposite perspective to the automatic thought. And, they could hold two seemingly differing realities at once, such as *I look foolish and that's okay.*

But the secret sauce is simply that the coping thought works for you – to regulate your emotions so you can refocus on what matters. You don't want to be so Pollyanna that your coping thoughts sound outlandish. Most of us have a bullshit detector that goes off if we exaggerate or become hyperbolic, especially when we're talking to ourselves in a moment of distress. And coping thoughts only work if you can believe them. Your mind has to be able to get on board with them.

Telling yourself you're nicer, cooler, smoother, prettier, more successful, or better looking than Jennifer Lopez or Keanu Reeves probably won't work.

> ... THE SECRET SAUCE IS THAT THE COPING THOUGHT WORKS FOR YOU – TO REGULATE YOUR EMOTIONS SO YOU CAN REFOCUS ON WHAT MATTERS. MOST OF US HAVE A BULLSHIT DETECTOR THAT GOES OFF IF WE EXAGGERATE OR BECOME HYPERBOLIC, ESPECIALLY WHEN WE'RE TALKING TO OURSELVES IN A MOMENT OF DISTRESS.

So, in the previous scenario where your boss overrides your plans, if you were to create a coping thought like, *it doesn't bother me at all for my boss to micromanage me*, that would just be magical thinking. It wouldn't work because it's too far off from how you're experiencing the situation, even as a momentary perspective.

Or, if you come up with a coping thought like, *my boss thinks I'm the best project lead to ever grace these conference rooms*, unless you actually believe that, your mind won't accept it.

You may need practice finding thoughts that resonate as reasonable alternative perspectives. You can start by finding coping thoughts that will work for you in specific situations where you tend to get overwhelmed by big emotion waves. To help you generate some ideas, here are some examples of different kinds of coping thoughts you can use when you're too triggered to act on your values:

- Just because I'm feeling this way doesn't mean it's true.
- This emotion will pass, and I can ride it out just like I have before.
- I can take my time to figure out how to respond.
- I've been here before, and I can do this again.
- I can feel anxious/angry/scared/sad without acting on my emotion urge.
- This emotion is not dangerous; it's just uncomfortable.

· This feeling won't last.

· I know what I'm doing, and I've got this.

· I don't know what I'm doing, and that's okay.

· In the past I've been anxious and scared, and I've been able to keep going.

· I can put up a boundary or leave any time I need to.

· I may not be as [insert quality] as they are, but I'm a pretty great package.

REFLECTION: TAKING PERSPECTIVE WITH 'STICKY' THOUGHTS THAT HOOK YOU

· Start by recalling a recurring trigger scene that predictably comes with thoughts that hook you. You could refer to your list of trigger situations if you need some examples to work with. Write down any thoughts that show up in this scene.

· Now come up with a few coping thoughts you could use in response to those triggering thoughts next time they come up. If it's helpful, you can use the technique from the earlier example with Justina. Imagine you are your own defense attorney and need to present a case that is believable *and also* shifts the perspective of the judge and jury.

RADICAL ACCEPTANCE: ALLOWING WHAT IS

Another powerful perspective-taking skill is *radical acceptance*, defined as the willingness to accept life on life's terms. Practicing radical acceptance can help you stop struggling with what you can't control or resisting painful realities that can't be changed.

Most people struggle to accept certain painful realities, whether they realize it or not. Life doesn't give you a deck of cards to sort through so you can choose the hand you hold. It constantly shuffles the deck. This means you inevitably experience difficulty and disappointment – not just about what you came into the world with, but also with what happens along the way.

Resisting or struggling with the existence of these painful realities is another way of losing perspective.

And not surprisingly, embracing them is a way of gaining it.

But, maybe you're wondering, *what's so wrong with resisting life on life's terms?* Here's why that doesn't work so well: resisting a reality that already exists outside of your control – as much as you might wish it were different – leads to misery and takes your attention and energy away from things you have control over. (And who wants more unnecessary suffering on top of the inevitable pain that already comes with being human?)

Resisting painful realities usually comes from unhelpful emotional avoidance. And by now you know that doesn't work well. Especially with realities you can't change. Alternatively, when you fully accept the things you cannot change, you not only reduce your suffering but you free up energy to change the things you *can* control, and expand what you really want and care about.

To truly understand what radical acceptance is, let's look at what it *isn't*. Radical acceptance is *not* passivity, surrender, approval, forgiveness, compassion, or love. On the contrary: you can be in action to change whatever you can, while also holding the painful realities you can't change. The difference is, you're not putting energy into resisting them.

This may sound logical, but it's amazing how you can still tend to struggle with unchangeable realities that you find painful. Understandably, you won't naturally want to accept the pain that so often goes with reality. (Remember, you're wired to avoid it.) It's easy to end up struggling with what you don't want, even when it's unhelpful and the struggle is futile.

RADICAL ACCEPTANCE IS *NOT* PASSIVITY, SURRENDER, APPROVAL, FORGIVENESS, COMPASSION, OR LOVE.

Radical acceptance can happen on many levels. You may radically accept large-scale harsh realities such as climate change, racism, and everyday violence that you have limited control over. But where radical acceptance can be less obvious is when your day-to-day expectations aren't fulfilled.

Your car breaks down.

Your alarm doesn't go off.

Your partner spills coffee on your pants.

Your kids want a sandwich without the crust when you're running late.

Your spouse wants a sandwich without the crust when you're running late.

… And the list goes on. When you hold expectations about the way the world and people in it 'should' be, you're setting yourself up for a whole 'should-show' of disappointment.

As the adage goes, *resentments are just expectations waiting to happen.*[4] In fact, it's often the case that I help clients to downward adjust their unrealistic expectations as a way to decrease their unnecessary suffering. Expecting things to always go as you want or as planned is a recipe for unhappiness.

Radical acceptance allows you to experience disappointment while at the same time holding your disappointment in perspective.

PRACTICING RADICAL ACCEPTANCE

Resisting life on life's terms can look a lot of different ways. Sometimes you struggle to accept the reality of things simply because you aren't clear about what you can change, and what you can't. Or you may not understand how something could have happened, leading you to challenge whether you're seeing it clearly. Or, you may feel threatened that a certain reality exists at all. Or your life may have changed so suddenly or drastically that you're having a hard time adjusting to the new terms. Regardless of the circumstances, a lack of radical acceptance will always show up in your thinking.

Here are some painful realities I commonly hear clients struggling to accept even when they are out of their control:

- I didn't get the date/promotion/award/house/job/kids/girl or guy/competent parents I wanted.
- My candidate lost the election and now I'm stuck with this dumbass for four years.
- I can never predict how I'm going to feel one day to the next.
- Now that I'm 50, I know I'll never have the biological children I've always wanted.
- Racism/sexism/ableism/[fill in the blank] exists.
- People shouldn't be so selfish/greedy/aggravated/rich/stupid.
- When I get really depressed, I randomly have thoughts about not wanting to live.
- My ex is getting half of my money.
- I spent half my life in a religious cult and I'll never get those years back.
- I didn't set a reminder to pay that bill, so now I owe an extra fee.
- Everybody lets you down eventually.
- If only I had taken steps to stop [fill in the blank] from happening, everything would be different.
- I rushed but still got to the store 30 seconds after it closed.
- I have random thoughts that would offend people if I told them.
- Even though I'm sober now I can never turn back the clock.
- My body has limitations so I can't do the same things as most other people.

Just recognizing your lack of radical acceptance can be all you need to let go of struggling with what you can't change and take perspective. And it will help regulate your emotions.

Or, if you need more help with one of these familiar painful realities, you could come up with a radical acceptance mantra. This is essentially a coping thought that helps you remember what you can't control and what you can; for example, *racism exists, and while I can't wipe it out, I can speak up when I see it.* Like coping thoughts, radical acceptance mantras must be believable to work for you when you're triggered.

ACCEPTING 'WHAT IS'

My client 'Charles' was an exceptionally bright, affable 34-year-old who came to me for help with depression, anxiety, making friends, and dating. Through the initial assessment, we discovered that a lot of his struggles were a result of interpersonal and communication challenges that stemmed from his unique neurodiversity. Charles presented with all the features of high-functioning Autism Spectrum Disorder, but no one had ever formerly assessed him, diagnosed him, or educated him about how his neuroatypicality might be impacting his life.

Charles had graduated from med school several years earlier than most students in his cohort, and had a thriving, successful practice. But like many people who have his type of neurodiversity, he struggled with reading social cues, experienced heightened distress when routines or rules were broken, or if the environment was new and unpredictable. He would regularly miss how some of his interactions landed with other people. Or, he would get the impact, but only in hindsight.

With the intense pace of medical school, Charles hadn't made new friends since high school. His parents were the only people he regularly talked to. He had only one brief romantic relationship, in his mid-20s, which had left him feeling unsure of himself and confused about 'what women want from men.' He reported feeling alienated a lot of the time. And his lack of social connection explained a lot about why he had been suffering from loneliness, depression, and anxiety for so long. Charles initially struggled with the new information about his neurodiversity, especially the idea that there was something biologically hardwired that he couldn't change about himself.

To start practicing radical acceptance, he worked through an inquiry to deepen his understanding about the benefits of accepting painful realities, and how it can also free up space for valuing.

In the example below, Charles was able to explore in more detail all the circumstances around the reality he found painful, and by the time he completed it, he reported that his distress level about his neurodiversity had dropped from a 9 to a 3 after doing it.

RADICAL ACCEPTANCE INQUIRY

Painful reality I find difficult to accept:

My neurodiversity/diagnosis and how it affects my relationships.

What past events led to the parts of the situation that were/are impossible to control?

I can't control my genetic makeup; I can't control the fact that no one helped me see that my struggles came from my neurodiversity before.

What role, if any, did I play in creating the situation?

I could have sought professional help sooner.

What role, if any, did others play in creating the situation?

Maybe if my parents or one of my teachers or professors noticed something was different for me I could have gotten professional help.

What role, if any, did environmental factors play in creating the situation?

The field of psychology didn't have as much information and wasn't as skilled with diagnosing high-functioning people on the spectrum when I was growing up as they are now.

What *do* I have control over in the situation?

I can only control what I'm willing to learn and do now.

What do I *not* have control over in the situation?

That I have this level of neurodiversity. What's happened in the past.

What did or do I do in response to this situation?
At first I resisted it and avoided talking about it with anyone. Now I am open to learning as much as possible to get better at relationships.

How did/does my response affect my emotional experience?
Resisting it made me feel even sadder and more angry.

How did/does my response affect the emotional experience of others?
My parents were really sad that I was upset about it. I was more irritable at work than usual.

Are there ways I would like to have changed my response so that it led to less suffering for me and others?
I would like to have been more open to learning about it and accepting it.

What would have been different if I had radically accepted the unchangeable parts of this situation?
I would have started doing the social skills training sooner, and maybe more activities, like the dating apps, photography club, and volunteer work.

What, if anything, might I change now if I radically accepted the unchangeable parts of this situation?
I would feel more confident about meeting other people.

What kind of radical acceptance mantra would help me to remember not to resist this painful reality?
I can't change the fact that even when I know what to do, I don't always do it well. But I can still work on my skills and it doesn't mean that people aren't going to like me.

REFLECTION: TAKING PERSPECTIVE WITH YOUR PAINFUL REALITIES

Now it's your turn. Identify a painful, unchangeable reality you're struggling with and then respond to the questions below.

Painful reality I find difficult to accept:

- What past events led to the parts of the situation that were/are impossible to control?
- What role, if any, did I play in creating the situation?
- What role, if any, did others play in creating the situation?
- What role, if any, did environmental factors play in creating the situation?
- What *do* I have control over in the situation?
- What do I *not* have control over in the situation?
- What did or do I do in response to this situation?
- How did/does my response affect my emotional experience?
- How did/does my response affect the emotional experience of others?
- Are there ways I would like to have changed my response so that it led to less suffering for me and others?
- What would have been different if I had radically accepted the unchangeable parts of this situation?
- What, if anything, might I change now if I radically accepted the unchangeable parts of this situation?
- What kind of radical acceptance mantra would help me to remember not to resist this painful reality?

Hopefully you can see how walking through this reflection can help you begin to radically accept your difficult or unwanted situation. Once you get the hang of it, you may not need to use this reflection – you'll acknowledge that you're resisting a reality that is unchangeable and know that a coping thought or mantra can help you stop struggling. You'll have an opportunity to use your coping thoughts and a radical acceptance mantra in your experiential practice.

And you can stop hanging out in the zone of unnecessary suffering.

ME: Okay Charles. Take me back to the trigger scene, to the very moment you sensed that something had happened. You could imagine replaying the scene like a movie and stop on the frame where you could tell something was going on and got triggered.

CHARLES: I was sitting at the breakroom table having lunch and I started talking about how understaffed we were that week, and that I didn't think it was fair that the only thing that determines the calendar is seniority. And that's when I noticed everyone's faces getting still, and I'm pretty sure it's because I got so anxious as I was saying it, and was talking too fast and too loud.

ME: And did thinking about that just now activate you?

CHARLES: Yes, I can tell I'm triggered just remembering it. I'm probably around a 5 or 6 on the scale.

ME: Okay, let's shift to surfing through all parts of your emotional STUF, starting by describing any sensations in your body and making space for them; naming any thoughts and letting them go; noticing any urges to do something or not to do something, and just sitting with them; and then naming any feelings and validating them.

CHARLES: Okay. I'm noticing the heat in my face and tension in my chest and I'm letting them be there. I am hanging out with them. Now I notice the tension quickly relaxing, and the heat is spreading out. Now I am having the thought that *they must think I'm a weirdo*, and I'm letting that thought go. And another thought came up that *this is all happening because I have Asperger's*. And I'm trying to let that go. And now the urge is to stop feeling all this, and I am sitting with that. My feelings are: angry, scared, frustrated, and also, embarrassed. And that makes sense because there's a lot of uncertainty and I'm tired of experiencing all this.

ME: That's really great surfing Charles. What other emotional STUF is showing up?

CHARLES: I'm still having that thought that *I'm defective because of my neurodiversity.* It's a very, very sticky thought.

ME: Okay. Let's pause surfing here, and shift to practicing your coping thoughts and radical acceptance mantra.

CHARLES: Well, one coping thought is *I will always have to work harder to figure out what's expected in certain social situations, and I can learn to do that better.*

ME: Great. Did you notice anything about your emotion wave when you said that?

CHARLES: Yes, it went down a little.

ME: Okay, sounds like it works for you. And how about your radical acceptance mantra?

CHARLES: *I can't change the fact that even when I do know what to do, I don't always do it well* – like talking too loud and fast when I'm anxious even though I know that other people find it to be off-putting. But the rest of my mantra is, *that doesn't mean they won't like me. I have control over improving my skills.*

ME: Well done. We don't always do what we know how to do well. And, you can work on your skills. That you have control over. What else?

CHARLES: I have to accept that my face gets red when I have anxiety with meeting new people or doing things for the first time. And my mantra again is that *it's okay and it doesn't mean people are not going to like me.*

ME: Right, even though it's natural to feel anxiety with new experiences, you can't control what happens to your face when you get anxious. And, it doesn't mean people aren't going to like you.

CHARLES: Yeah, and sometimes it's exhausting, and I'd rather stay home.

ME: That feeling is understandable. When you remind yourself of the reality that people can still like you even if your face gets red, what do you notice?

CHARLES: I feel better. My chest relaxes. The emotion wave is going down more.

ME: Good noticing.

CHARLES: Thanks.

ME: I know one of your values is Connecting, and we'll get to that in a moment. What else about this could you radically accept?

CHARLES: I guess my brain is wired in a more unique way?

ME: Yes. Yes. We are all on a spectrum when it comes to neurodiversity. And some of us are more neurodiverse than others.

CHARLES: And I also know I have to socialize if I want to find a partner and get married.

ME: Right. And now that you've used some coping thoughts and radical acceptance mantras, is this a good place to shift to visualizing your values-based action to move you toward your value of Connection?

CHARLES: Yeah, I can do that.

ME: Great. So, take me back to the room that day, and freeze on the frame just before you started talking, walk me through what I would see and hear if you were doing the actions you designed for yourself to connect more effectively with people?

CHARLES: Well, I notice I still feel embarrassed, but I can imagine doing my VBAs of speaking at a lower volume and slowing down.

ME: Great. What else?

CHARLES: And another VBA was just naming when I get worked up, so I'm imagining just saying *I got a little worked up.*

ME: Great. And then what?

CHARLES: I check to see if people's faces seem more relaxed after I say that. And if they don't, I would wait until we are leaving and pull aside the coworker I play video games with sometimes. I would check in with him whether he thought I was doing anything I wasn't aware of.

ME: Great. So you'd speak slowly and at a lower volume. You could name that you got worked up. Check people's reactions by carefully reading their faces or ask your coworker afterwards. Do you remember your other VBA?

CHARLES: What was it?

ME: To use some humor to lighten up the situation.

CHARLES: Oh yes, that's good. I can say *I got a little 'aggro' and I need to not listen to Eminem's Marshall Mathers CD on the way to work.*

ME: Yes, haha. Well done. You surfed your emotion wave, used radical acceptance to regulate your emotions, and then rehearsed your VBAs to move toward your value of Connection. I'm curious, where is your distress level now?

CHARLES: Oh, it's low ... I'm around a 1 now.

ME: Great. Let's go back to the trigger scene and run through it one more time to give you more practice.

After the experiential practice Charles said reflecting on the situation with his coworkers had become 'a little more interesting than distressing.' When I asked him what, if anything, felt helpful about coping thoughts and radical acceptance, he said, 'it's more logical to radically accept things when you can't change them because not accepting something that already exists doesn't change anything – it's illogical. And it makes you feel better.'

THE PERSPECTIVE-TAKING OBSTACLE COURSE

As with all practice, there will always be obstacles that show up. It may be helpful to review some common obstacles that can get in the way of perspective-taking:

- *You might find that some of your thinking is so familiar you don't notice you're hooked.* This is exactly what you're wired to do: figure out what you think and stick to it in order to protect your safety, certainty, coherence, comfort, and pleasure. Becoming aware of all the ways you might get hooked by thoughts takes time and practice. Many thoughts will be both automatic and familiar, making it easy to miss when you are fused with them. Whenever you're triggered, you can test your attachment to a thought by asking yourself how true it seems. You could ask yourself, *how true does this seem?* Or, you could try to imagine another perspective. Just stopping to be curious about how you're relating to the thought will help you defuse and search for more helpful or effective perspectives.

- *You choose a coping thought that is too far out of the 'reality zone' or a radical acceptance mantra that your mind doesn't buy.* It happens. When you are distressed, you naturally want to change the way you feel, so it's understandable you try to cajole your brain into more thinking you believe will make you feel better. Remember, your mind will reject outright any thoughts that seem over the top. You can test your coping thoughts by simply saying them to yourself and seeing if you notice any downshift in your unwanted STUF. If your level of activation eases up, chances are you've got a workable coping thought.

- *You find there are things you're just not willing to accept yet, or ever.* Hey, that's okay. There are no 'shoulds' in emotional efficacy training; there are just choices and what really matters and what works for you. If your lack of radical acceptance is causing suffering or keeping you from acting in alignment with your values, see if you can just get curious about what matters most. It could be that you are grieving a painful reality that you aren't ready to let go of struggling with. It might not even be helpful or timely to radically accept the painful reality during your healing process. Maybe validating your feelings is more helpful. The important thing is that you are able to do what matters most. And often just becoming aware of how you may be resisting what already exists can give you the willingness to stop struggling with it and focus on what matters.

- *You start using perspective-taking to avoid unwanted STUF instead of taking VBA.* First, stop and name the pattern. Give yourself credit for recognizing what's going on; it happens. (Half the challenge is recognizing when you're *not* being powerful.) Acknowledging the difficulty of what you're trying to do can soften any frustration or judgment that can further derail you. Remind yourself how natural it is to want to avoid your unwanted STUF. Also, remind yourself why it's meaningful to move toward your values in the situation, and try practicing again. Remember – you've trained for this. You can use your WTF? inquiry to track whether using your coping thought or radical acceptance mantra is moving you toward or away from what matters most.

PERSPECTIVE-TAKING EXPERIENTIAL PRACTICE

As with your previous skills, you'll want to practice perspective-taking in an activated state so it will be easier to use when you need it. You can use the following script, and you can also access a guided experiential practice at www.draprilliawest.com/practice.

SET UP

Find a private, quiet place and get into a comfortable position where you're likely to stay alert. Close your eyes or find a single spot in front of you to focus on by just softening your gaze.

SELECT A TRIGGER

Choose a trigger based on a memory or recurring event to activate medium intensity of discomfort and distress. (Keep in mind, in the low range you can struggle to access your emotional STUF, and in the high range you can be easily overwhelmed.)

SELECT MINDFUL COPING SKILL

Choose a perspective-taking skill to rehearse after emotion surfing: coping thoughts, or radical acceptance.

SELECT VBA

Pick at least one values-based action that will move you toward what matters most in your trigger scene.

ACTIVATE EMOTION

1. Set your trigger scene by imagining it as a movie and describe what you notice as if it's happening in real time, including:
   - where you are
   - what time it is
   - who you are with.
2. Go to the exact 'frame' where you anticipate you'll get emotionally activated.
3. Describe anything you are seeing, hearing, touching, tasting, and otherwise doing in as much detail as possible, frame by frame until you reach a medium level of activation.
4. Stop the scene and shift to emotion surfing.

EMOTION SURFING

Surf your emotion wave by bringing an intention of curiosity to hanging out with each part of your emotional 'STUF' for two minutes each.

(Sensations) For at least two minutes, scan your body from head to toe for any sensations that stand out to you:

- Notice their size and shape.
- Notice whether they're moving or staying the same.
- Notice any tension in the sensation.
- Notice if there's any temperature.

Bring an intention of allowing the physical experiences that go with sensations. Imagine making space for them, or welcoming them to be there and do whatever they want to do. Be curious about how they behave when you are just watching them.

(Thoughts) Shift your attention from sensations to noticing thoughts for at least two minutes:

- When a thought shows up, say to yourself 'there's a thought' and then let the thought go.
- Refocus on your breath as a way to place a pause between thoughts.
- And then watch for the next thought to show up, and repeat.

(Urges) Shift to watching any urges for two minutes:

- When you notice one, get curious about how intense the urge is: low, medium, high?
- Notice what it's like to just sit with the impulse to do something or not do something.
- Rate the discomfort on a scale of 1 to 10, with 1 being as relaxed as you can imagine and 10 the most uncomfortable you can imagine.
- Notice if the urge changes in intensity as you sit with it.

(Feelings)

- Label each feeling.
- Validate and welcome the feelings, saying something like: *It makes sense I'm feeling* [insert label]. Or, *it's okay for the feeling of* [insert label] *to be here*.
- Get curious about whether there are any other feelings, underneath the first feelings you noticed.

MINDFUL COPING

Practice your perspective-taking skill(s) for two minutes to downshift your activation level by either rehearsing them or visualizing doing them. If helpful, set a timer for one minute if you need a prompt to switch skills.

VALUES-BASED ACTION

Go back to the exact trigger frame where you have a moment of choice – to act on the emotion urge, or to take values-based action.

Visualize in as much detail as possible doing your values-based action(s) while you continue emotion surfing for at least five minutes, describing your actions and experience to yourself frame by frame:

- What would you or an outside observer see you doing?
- How would it be in your body to do this values-based action? Notice and allow any sensations.
- What kinds of thoughts would show up? Practice letting them go.
- What other urge or urges show up as you take values-based action? Notice what it's like just sitting with them.
- Notice any feelings you might have and just allow them or validate them.

Repeat the VBA sequence twice.

REFLECT

To wrap up the experiential practice, take a few moments to reflect using the following prompts:

- Did anything surprise you?
- What, if anything, was challenging?
- What did you learn?
- Write down anything else you want to remember.

CHAPTER 07 CHALLENGES

- Identify at least three thoughts that feel 100% true and then come up with alternative perspectives to practice unhooking from rigid, inflexible thinking. If you get stuck, ask a trusted friend to help you come up with an alternative perspective.

- Pick a recurring situation in your life where you still struggle with taking values-based action even after you surf your emotion wave. Notice the triggering thoughts that go with the situation, and come up with one or two coping thoughts you can use to help you regulate your emotions.

- Pick a recurring situation in your life where you still struggle with accepting a painful reality. Come up with a mantra to help you regulate your emotions.

- Lock in the learning by sharing with a friend your most 'sticky thoughts' and what you have learned about taking perspective.

- Practice perspective-taking using the guided experiential at least three times before you move forward.

CHAPTER 07 LEARNINGS

Mindful coping skills are used after practicing emotion surfing with the intention of being able to regulate emotions enough to take VBA after emotion surfing.

- The three types of mindful coping skills are: perspective-taking, relaxation, and attention-shifting.

- Mindful coping skills are intended to help you connect to your values, not to simply avoid emotional pain.

- You can use your WTF? inquiry to track your actions away or toward what matters most.

- Some thinking is helpful and some thinking is unhelpful, depending on what matters most in context.

- Perspective-taking helps you relate to your thoughts more flexibly, intentionally, and creatively, as valid but momentary experiences.

- Coping thoughts and radical acceptance are two ways of taking perspective and regulating emotions.

- Coping thoughts remind you of past successes, offer alternative perspectives, validate your emotional experience, or help you hold two seemingly conflicting realities at once.

- Radical acceptance is accepting a painful reality you can't change; it is not passivity, surrender, approval, forgiveness, compassion, or love.

- Coping thoughts and radical acceptance mantras must be believable to be effective.

- Practicing mindful coping while emotionally activated can help you learn to use the skills in real-life distressing situations.

08

REGULATING THROUGH RELAXATION

Cognition is embodied; you think with your body,
not only with your brain.

Daniel Kahneman

IN THE PREVIOUS CHAPTER YOU USED thoughts to expand your perspective to help regulate your emotions. With the next mindful coping skill, *relaxation*, you'll learn to use your body as the portal. Using relaxation exercises, you can dial down the intensity of your emotion wave when surfing alone doesn't get you to values-based action.[1]

As a review of mindful coping, the skills sequence goes like this: when you get triggered, you'll tune in and hang out (emotion surfing), but instead of going straight to VBA, you'll use relaxation to regulate your emotions until you can get back to doing what matters.

The somatic component of emotional experience is a relatively more recent topic of interest in the field of psychology. It is becoming more and more widely understood that somatic experience is integrally connected to the emotional network. This also means it can play a significant role in regulating emotion.

Some people even suggest that all emotional experience is shaped by what's happening somatically.[2] It logically follows that relaxing your body when you're triggered can be an effective strategy for regulating your emotions. This makes relaxation a 'natural' for moments when you need some extra help taking values-based action.

IT LOGICALLY FOLLOWS THAT RELAXING YOUR BODY WHEN YOU'RE TRIGGERED CAN BE AN EFFECTIVE STRATEGY FOR REGULATING YOUR EMOTIONS. THIS MAKES RELAXATION A 'NATURAL' FOR MOMENTS WHEN YOU NEED SOME EXTRA HELP TAKING VALUES-BASED ACTION.

THE POWER OF RELAXATION

It may be a revelation to you just how much of your emotional experience is somatic. And if it is, you're not alone. A lot of people go through life without much somatic awareness, except with obvious experiences; for example, the physical pain of a skinned knee as a child, the physical relief of jumping in cold water on a hot day, or the physical pleasure of a backrub in an anxious moment.

I see this all the time in my work. One of my clients told me she had never been aware of any sensations in her body, until we started practicing emotion surfing. Another client compared his realization of what was taking place in his body to having a quiet orchestra that had always been playing, but that he had never learned to listen to.

It's natural to be surprised to learn how much somatic life exists when you first start tuning in to physical sensations. And even more, to learn how these sensations can impact your emotional experience, and vice versa.

While a lot of people think of 'relaxation' as something you do on weekends, vacations, or to indulge yourself, relaxation as a mindful coping skill is intended to help you regulate enough to access values-based action. Because your level of somatic activation is so powerful, relaxation can interrupt intense emotional activation, returning you to the space where you can better choose your next move. This makes relaxation an important skill to have in your toolbelt when you're triggered.

WHILE A LOT OF PEOPLE THINK OF 'RELAXATION' AS SOMETHING YOU DO ON WEEKENDS, VACATIONS, OR TO INDULGE YOURSELF, RELAXATION AS A MINDFUL COPING SKILL IS INTENDED TO HELP YOU REGULATE ENOUGH TO ACCESS VALUES-BASED ACTION.

More specifically, relaxation has many benefits that can help you regulate in a tough moment of choice:

- improved concentration
- boosted confidence in the ability to handle problems
- reduced activity of stress hormones
- reduced muscle tension and chronic pain
- better sleep quality
- less fatigue
- slower heart rate

- lower blood pressure
- slower breathing rate
- improved digestion
- balanced blood sugar levels
- increased blood flow to major muscles.[3]

IT'S ALL CONNECTED

Depending how tuned in you are to sensations, you may or may not be aware of how connected your body is with the rest of your emotional experience. What's happening with your body in any moment – whether you're holding it in certain positions or breathing in a certain way – can have a big impact on what is happening emotionally.

> WHAT'S HAPPENING WITH YOUR BODY IN ANY MOMENT – WHETHER YOU'RE HOLDING IT IN CERTAIN POSITIONS OR BREATHING IN A CERTAIN WAY – CAN HAVE A BIG IMPACT ON WHAT IS HAPPENING EMOTIONALLY.

You've seen this in your practice of emotion surfing, but now let's take it further. Try this cool experiment:

Take a moment and just nod your head as if you're saying yes for 30 seconds.

Next, name any sensations, thoughts, urges, or feelings that show up.

Now, shake your head 'no' for the next 30 seconds.

Name any sensations, thoughts, urges, or feelings that show up.

Most likely you noticed at least a subtle difference in your experience after nodding rather than shaking, depending on the emotional charge you have linked to each movement.

Because the rest of our emotional STUF responds to whatever our bodies are doing by activating somatic events (sensations), making up stories (thoughts), using sensations and thoughts to figure out what to do next (urges), and interpreting all of this to interpret what's going on (feelings), even subtle physical movements can impact your emotional state.

As you know from chapter 4, your emotional network operates as one big organism. Whatever happens in your body has a big influence on the rest of your experience. This means whenever your defaults or your values urge you to navigate a perceived or actual threat, you'll kick into a higher gear of emotional activation. You may sense a shift in energy, up or down, depending on what your body is sensing it needs to help you adapt in a state of threat. This happens in part through somatic messages, such as the release of hormones, to help you meet the demands of the situation, urging you toward some level of fight, flight, or freeze.

> WHENEVER YOUR DEFAULTS OR YOUR VALUES URGE YOU TO NAVIGATE A PERCEIVED OR ACTUAL THREAT, YOU'LL KICK INTO A HIGHER GEAR OF EMOTIONAL ACTIVATION.

As a result, here's what you might then experience on a somatic level: an uptick in your heart rate and blood pressure, shallow and more rapid breathing, and temperature shifts (warmer or colder). Similarly, when you experience any sensations – such as tension in your chest or a rapid heartbeat – it's likely to trigger corresponding thoughts (for example, *what's about to happen?*), urges (for example, scanning your environment for danger), and feelings (for example, anxiety, dread, or anticipation). And in turn these thoughts, urges, and feelings can amplify or even trigger more sensations, and vice versa, in any combination.

As you know, depending on the context, this somatic (and other STUF) activation can be very helpful. But when there's no actual threat, and you're still in this intensely activated state, you're much less likely to respond flexibly, intentionally, and creatively to effectively act on what matters. Instead, your energy will mobilize you to prepare for any threat to your safety, certainty, coherence, comfort, or pleasure. You'll be surviving while what really mattered was responding to your sensitive friend's request for input that you thought the black dress was more flattering on her than the red one.

Because your thoughts, urges, and feelings (TUF) all react to sensations, a higher level of somatic activation can make it easier to get hijacked by unhelpful defaults, making values-based action or even just emotion surfing seem out of reach. And if you're one of those people who has a more 'reactive' relationship with what's happening in their body, it can be even more challenging to surf through distressing sensations. If you have a history of trauma, panic attacks, or chronic pain or other difficult medical conditions you might be reactive to any sensations that feel even remotely distressing. You'll tend to see them as threat messages.

And as you know by now, when you try to avoid sensations, or any other part of emotional STUF, it can make your emotion wave more intense and last longer, making it even harder to take values-based action.

So, you can imagine how suggestible your emotions might be to relaxation. Relaxing creates a 'safe enough space' for you and all your emotional STUF to register that there is little to no actual threat and that it's okay to calm down.

> RELAXING CREATES A 'SAFE ENOUGH SPACE'
> FOR YOU AND ALL YOUR EMOTIONAL STUF TO
> REGISTER THAT THERE IS LITTLE TO NO ACTUAL
> THREAT AND THAT IT'S OKAY TO CALM DOWN.

As an example, I ended up in a situation early in the pandemic where my emotional activation was on high alert. There were also several other vulnerability factors that raised my threat level to critical: I was in terrible pain. I had developed a severe case of frozen shoulder, and it was excruciating to move my right arm. It was difficult to find a way to sit or lay down that didn't hurt. Sleeping became a constant struggle. And because I had recently moved, I had no one nearby to help with basic lifting tasks, shopping, or errands. As you can imagine, I felt miserable and scared. For weeks, my resting heart rate was consistently up around 105. Throughout the day I randomly had tingly, sharp sensations running down both arms (a common sign of anxiety), and my body was constantly tense and sore from holding itself in unnatural ways so that my shoulder wouldn't hurt.

My emotional network interpreted all of this as a constant threat.

I knew if I needed to get to the doctor for the pain I would have to either get a car service (which felt scary due to the high rates of the virus at the time), or I could call 911 (which could take an ambulance from someone potentially dying). That left me with the prospect of driving myself, which didn't feel entirely safe with one arm. Read: more threat.

But to add insult to injury, I ended up having a cortisone injection between the two vaccine shots, which raised my anxiety level further (a common side effect). Unfortunately, I got very sick from the second vaccine, and for 36 hours I felt like I was on death's door. I couldn't even get out of bed. I was as emotionally distraught as I've ever been. What mattered most was somehow getting through it on my own.

I used cue-controlled breathing to relax, surfing through waves of physical discomfort, and focusing on parts of my body where I didn't hurt so bad (an attention-shifting skill you'll learn in the next chapter).

As I slowed my breathing, using my cue word for my favorite place, 'Point Dume,' on the exhale, my body was able to let go of some tension and settle into a still miserable but less threatened state. I settled in enough to allow the pain instead of resisting it and catastrophizing.

To be clear, I didn't ever get comfortable; I mindfully coped with it and focused on using my skills to ride out the pain. And, I did finally come back to my more tolerable previous state of discomfort 36 hours, lots of tears, and one long much-needed sister-phone-call later. But emotion surfing and relaxation skills were the life raft that got me through.

WHEN LEANING INTO DISCOMFORT ISN'T ENOUGH

'Ava' struggles with chronic pain and has a diagnosis of Fibromyalgia. She also has a history of asthma, which was so severe when she was young that she regularly missed school to stay in bed because medications couldn't control her breathing. She was no stranger to feeling helpless and terrified of her own body.

As Ava entered adulthood, her asthma improved significantly, but she began to develop a heightened sensitivity to any uncomfortable sensations. She also had a demanding job and travelled 10 months out of the year, which took a toll on her sleep, her body, and her overall health. As a result, she lived in constant fear of being fired because she couldn't always meet deadlines.

In the month before Ava came to see me, she had started experiencing panic attacks. She wasn't even sure what would trigger them. She'd get blindsided by huge emotion waves and didn't yet know how to surf them.

And even after a few sessions in which she had practiced surfing and was working toward values-based action, she kept getting stuck. We figured out that the way she was relating to the sensations in her body was fueling her distress. She would immediately try to control or suppress the sensations or put them out of her mind (unhelpful avoidance).

AVA: It happened again this week. I was sitting in the conference room, getting ready to run a team stand up, and I had a panic attack. It was crazy. I was sweating profusely, my heart was racing, and I had prickly sensations in my arms and legs.

ME: Oh, that sounds really uncomfortable. Were you able to try surfing through your unwanted STUF?

AVA: I did try, but it didn't allow me to focus on work. This wave was much more intense. In fact, when I started to tune into my sensations I would get scared, and I couldn't lean into the discomfort long enough to register that I wasn't in a threat situation and settle my body.

ME: That's good insight. And, sometimes, when you feel threatened it is really hard to surf. It can help to have some strategies to dial down the intensity.

AVA: Yes … I can deal with being uncomfortable. You know me – I'm no stranger to discomfort. But this was like something else just took over my body. And, even though I've started practicing the VBA experiential, I don't think I've had enough practice yet. When I sense something seems wrong in my body, my distress goes from 0 to 10 in 10 seconds.

ME: That sounds really intense, and totally natural. And it's great you're practicing the experientials on your own. Now I think adding some relaxation exercises to help you regulate your emotions could make a big difference. Eventually you'll build more tolerance to lean into the discomfort, especially triggering sensations, and refocus on what matters. But it's always good to also have emotional regulation strategies for emergencies like that.

AVA: Great. How do I do it?

ME: You'll start by practicing each of the four relaxation exercises in a neutral state to get familiar with them. Then you'll use them in experiential practice to see what works for you. Everyone is different, and especially with your history of asthma and chronic pain, some of these may work better than others.

REFLECTION: NOTICING YOUR SOMATIC PATTERNS

- Take a moment right now to notice your breathing. First, just notice if you're breathing at all. (Many of us hold our breath temporarily even when we are just trying to understand something.) Notice if your breathing is slow and deep, or more shallow and labored. Were you aware of your breathing before this prompt?

- Also, check in and see where you might be holding any tension in your body. See how many places are holding tension that you might not have realized. Were you aware of any tension before this prompt?

- Take a moment to notice your temperature. Are you hot? Cold? Neutral? Were you aware of this before this prompt?
- Finally, notice how what you're experiencing in your body is impacting your other emotional STUF: your thoughts, urges, or feelings.

PRACTICING RELAXATION

Following are four relaxation skills you can use to regulate your emotions:

- *cue-controlled diaphragmatic breathing*
- *progressive muscle relaxation*
- *five senses*
- *self-soothing.*

Try all these relaxation skills to see which ones work best for you. First, practice them in a neutral state, and then as part of your experiential skills practice when you're emotionally activated.

While mindful coping skills are intended to be used after emotion surfing, they can also be used by themselves in a neutral state. Just make sure you don't unwittingly slip into an unhelpful avoidance pattern that keeps you from what matters most. If you get confused, you can always use a WTF? inquiry to clarify what direction you're headed – away or towards what really matters.

CUE-CONTROLLED DIAPHRAGMATIC BREATHING WITH 5-5-7 COUNT

When you are triggered, or even captivated by something, you tend to take more shallow and rapid breaths, or even hold your breath. Learning how to do cue-controlled diaphragmatic breathing can help you intentionally change your pace to promote relaxation.

For this exercise, find a comfortable sitting position, or lie down if you prefer. You can close your eyes, or keep them open if that's more comfortable. To track your relaxation, start by rating your current level of relaxation on a scale from 1 to 10, with 10 being the most relaxed you can imagine. Now use the following instructions to practice cue-controlled diaphragmatic breathing.

Rhythmic controlled breathing is hypothesized to help reduce stress by helping the nervous system to relax.[4] In this exercise, you'll do three things: 1) shift breath past your chest down into the belly to deepen your breathing; 2) hold your breath to pause; and 3) make your exhale longer than your inhale. This deep and longer exhale will help shift shallow, rapid breathing and calm your nervous system.

Place one hand over your belly and the other hand on your chest. Take a slow, deep breath, sending it all the way down into your belly while trying not to move the hand on your chest and count 1, 2, 3, 4, 5. Then pause and count 1, 2, 3, 4, 5 before exhaling, and then count 1, 2, 3, 4, 5, 6, 7 and let all the tension go with the breath. Repeat this cycle for at least two minutes until you begin to notice the relaxing effects.

If for some reason you find it difficult to hold your breath for a full seven counts at first, you could try a different pattern, such as 4–4–6 or 3–3–5.

Next, you can experiment with deeper relaxation by adding a cue word or phrase on your exhale. To find a cue word that works for you, think of something that helps you connect to a state of calm and wellbeing. It could be a color *(purple, turquoise)*, a place you like *(Point Dume, Tulum)*, or a spiritual mantra or word *('May I be free from harm' or 'Peace')*. Whatever you choose, be sure your cue word is associated with pleasurable feelings and not feelings of sadness, melancholy, or regret. (Say, me thinking of my grandmother's house, which brings up both relaxation and the sadness of missing her.) Once you have your cue word, begin your diaphragmatic breathing with your cue word, inhaling into your belly for 1, 2, 3, 4, 5. Then, say your cue word, hold for 1, 2, 3, 4, 5, and then exhale for 1, 2, 3, 4, 5, 6, 7 and let all your tension go with the breath. Then repeat.

Try to practice this for at least 10 minutes. Afterward, rate your level of relaxation again on a scale of 1 to 10 to track its effectiveness for you.

PROGRESSIVE MUSCLE RELAXATION

In this exercise, you will use 'tension and release' to relax each of the major muscles in your body, one muscle group at a time:

- toes/feet
- calves/shins
- thighs/glutes
- chest/back/abdomen
- hands/fingers
- arms
- neck and shoulders
- face (forehead, cheeks, tongue, eyes, and jaw).

One word of caution before you begin: be careful not to tense your muscles to the point of strain. And if you have any injuries or concerns in certain areas, you may want to skip that muscle group.

Start by finding a comfortable sitting position, or you can lie down if you prefer. You can close your eyes, or you can keep them open if that's more comfortable. Start by rating your current level of relaxation on a scale from 1 to 10, with 10 being the most relaxed you can imagine. Now use the following instructions to practice progressive muscle relaxation.

While continuing to breathe at a natural rhythm, shift your focus to your *feet* and start clenching your toes and pulling the tops of your feet up toward your shins. Hold the tension for a count of 1, 2, 3, 4, 5 and then release, noticing the difference between tension and relaxation for a count of 1, 2, 3, 4, 5, 6, 7, 8, 9, 10.

Next, focus on your *lower legs* and tighten the muscles in your calves. Hold the tension for a count of 1, 2, 3, 4, 5 and then release, noticing the difference between tension and relaxation for a count of 1, 2, 3, 4, 5, 6, 7, 8, 9, 10.

Next shift your attention to your upper legs and tighten the muscles in your *thighs*. Hold the tension for a count of 1, 2, 3, 4, 5 and then release, noticing the difference between tension and relaxation for a count of 1, 2, 3, 4, 5, 6, 7, 8, 9, 10.

Next shift your attention to the back of your legs and tighten your *glutes and hamstrings*. Hold the tension for a count of 1, 2, 3, 4, 5 and then release, noticing the difference between tension and relaxation for a count of 1, 2, 3, 4, 5, 6, 7, 8, 9, 10.

Now move your awareness to your *chest, back and abdomen*. Tighten those muscles by pulling your belly button in as far as you can toward your back and pulling your pecs down and away from your shoulders. Hold the tension for a count of 1, 2, 3, 4, 5 and then release, noticing the difference between tension and relaxation for a count of 1, 2, 3, 4, 5, 6, 7, 8, 9, 10.

Now shift your attention to your *hands* by tightening your *fingers* into fists … squeezing as hard as you can … then release and relax, letting any tension or discomfort flow out through your fingertips. Hold the tension for a count of 1, 2, 3, 4, 5 and then release, noticing the difference between tension and relaxation for a count of 1, 2, 3, 4, 5, 6, 7, 8, 9, 10.

Next focus on your *arms* by pulling your arms in as tight as you can into your body. Hold the tension for a count of 1, 2, 3, 4, 5 and then release, noticing the difference between tension and relaxation for a count of 1, 2, 3, 4, 5, 6, 7, 8, 9, 10.

Now move on to your *neck and shoulders* by shrugging your shoulders up into your neck. Hold the tension for a count of 1, 2, 3, 4, 5 and then release, noticing the difference between tension and relaxation for a count of 1, 2, 3, 4, 5, 6, 7, 8, 9, 10.

Now gently focus your attention on all the *muscles in your face*. First scrunch your eyes as tight as you can. Hold the tension for a count of 1, 2, 3, 4, 5 and then release, noticing the difference between tension and relaxation for a count of 1, 2, 3, 4, 5, 6, 7, 8, 9, 10. Next tense all the muscles in your cheeks and forehead. Hold the tension for a count of 1, 2, 3, 4, 5 and then release, noticing the difference between tension and relaxation for a count of 1, 2, 3, 4, 5, 6, 7, 8, 9, 10. Last, press your tongue against the roof of your mouth. Hold the tension for a count of 1, 2, 3, 4, 5 and then release, noticing the difference between tension and relaxation for a count of 1, 2, 3, 4, 5, 6, 7, 8, 9, 10.

Finally, pause for a few more moments to let yourself notice the difference between the tightness of tension and the comfort of relaxation.

Try to practice this exercise for at least 10 minutes. Afterward, rate your level of relaxation again on a scale of 1 to 10 to track its effectiveness for you.

To deepen this exercise, you can add in the cue-controlled diaphragmatic breathing with a silent or audible suggestion on your exhale by simply saying 'Relax' or 'Let go' to each specific muscle group as you exhale and let go of any tension.

FIVE SENSES

This simple exercise will allow you to ground and relax by tapping into each of your five senses: sound, touch, sight, taste, and smell. Since it only takes a couple of minutes it's especially helpful when you're short on time.

Find a comfortable sitting position, or lie down if you prefer. Start by rating your current level of relaxation on a scale from 1 to 10, with 10 being the most relaxed you can imagine. Now use the following instructions to practice the five senses exercise.

For 30 seconds, focus on everything you can hear around you: voices, nature, music, sounds of movement, the sounds your body makes, the hum of machinery, traffic. If you get distracted by thoughts or anything else, gently bring yourself back to paying attention to sounds.

For 30 seconds, focus on what you can smell. Even if there is not an obvious aroma, continue focusing to detect any scent that becomes apparent.

For 30 seconds, focus on what you can sense through your body, including pressure, texture, temperature, and any contact your body is making with a chair, a couch, or the floor.

For 30 seconds, focus on what you can see, observing the shape, size, and color of everything making up the visual world around you in this moment.

For 30 seconds, focus on what you can taste. Is it sweet, salty, sour, or bitter? Or is it some combination of flavors?

While pausing with each sense, notice if your mind wanders and gently bring yourself back to the sense you're working with.

Try to practice this exercise for at least 10 minutes. Afterward, rate your level of relaxation again on a scale of 1 to 10 to track its effectiveness for you.

If you're *really* short on time, for a super-quick grounding and relaxation exercise, close your eyes and focus on everything you can hear for 30 seconds.

SELF-SOOTHING

Self-soothing practice enhances the use of all your senses by creating pleasurable experiences to relax and downshift your emotional activation. Using sight, hearing, taste, smell, and touch, you'll experiment to see which senses and strategies work best for you. As you practice, keep in mind that some might work better in different environments; for example, at work or at home.

Sense of smell. Focusing on your sense of smell activates thoughts, memories, and sensations that can be calming. What smells do you find pleasurable? You can use them when you need to find calm. Here is a list of examples, but try to come up with some of your own as well:

- Burning scented candles or diffusing essential oils.
- Wearing oils, perfume, or cologne that make you feel good.
- Carrying scented oils or perfumed cards in your purse, wallet, or car.
- Going somewhere that has pleasurable scents, such as a bakery or coffee shop.
- Lying down in a park where you can smell grass, flowers, or other outdoor scents.
- Buying flowers or picking flowers in your garden.
- Hugging someone whose smell makes you feel calm.

Sense of sight. A large portion of your brain is devoted to processing what you see, and what you take in with your eyes can have powerful effects on your emotions. This means you can intentionally leverage the use of visual cues to regulate your emotions by identifying images that bring you pleasure. Here is a list of examples, but try to come up with some of your own as well:

- Look online, through magazines and books, or take pictures of images you like. Make a collage of them to hang on your wall, add as a screensaver on your computer, or keep them on your phone.
- Find a place you can go to that's visually soothing, such as a park, lake, or museum. Take a picture of the place and keep it with you.
- Draw or paint a picture that's pleasing to your eye.
- Carry a picture of someone you love, someone you find attractive, or someone you admire.

Sense of hearing. The sounds you hear around you are powerful because your brain is always scanning for threats, and you can use sounds or music you find soothing to calm yourself when you are distressed. Here is a list of examples, but try to come up with some of your own as well:

- Listen to soothing music: classical, opera, oldies, new age, jazz – whatever genre works for you.
- Listen to audiobooks. Try some to see if they help you relax. You don't even have to pay attention to the storyline; sometimes just the rhythm and tone of someone's voice can be soothing.
- Watch TV shows or movies. Select something boring or sedate, instead of activating (the news is probably a no-no). Keep the volume at a low level.
- Listen to a gentle podcast, like a gardening or music show.
- Listen to white noise, a fan, or a sound machine with pre-recorded sounds, such as birds, waterfalls, wind, rain, and waves.
- Listen to a meditation exercise where you can you imagine yourself relaxing in different ways.

Sense of taste. You can take advantage of the distinct regions on your tongue that differentiate flavors and tastes of food. What are the tastes that are soothing to you that you might turn to when you are upset? Here is a list of examples, but try to come up with some of your own as well:

- Eat one of your favorite meals slowly and mindfully so you can savor all of its various flavors.
- Carry gum, mints, mouth spray, or treats with you to taste when you're feeling upset.
- Eat a comfort food you find particularly soothing.
- Drink something you find soothing, like tea, coffee, or hot chocolate.

- Suck on a popsicle or ice cube, especially if you're feeling warm.
- Find a piece of ripe, juicy fruit and eat it slowly.

Sense of touch. Your skin is completely covered with nerves that carry sensations to your brain. This means you have the ability to use touch, texture, and temperature to impact your emotional experience. Here is a list of examples, but come up with some of your own as well:

- Work in the garden and get your hands into the cool earth.
- Carry something soft or smooth in your pocket to touch when you're upset.
- Take a hot or cold shower and observe the sensation of water on your skin.
- Take a warm bath with bubbles or scented oil.
- Get a massage or massage yourself.
- Play with a pet – yours or someone else's – or visit an animal shelter.
- Wear your favorite, most comfortable clothes.

Once you've practiced each of these relaxation exercises you'll want to make a plan to put these strategies in place so that when you need them, you're prepared.

LESS DISTRESSED ABOUT DISTRESS

My client 'Derek' had a terrible fear of public speaking. As a senior manager at his company, he regularly had to present to the CEO and the board, and the anticipation of it would often wreak havoc on his life for the 24 hours preceding. He had tried a lot of different strategies to avoid feeling so anxious, from positive thinking to power posing – and even a shot a tequila before a big investor pitch. But what he found was that over time his anxiety was getting worse.

The first thing we worked on was helping him decode the threat messages his emotions were sending and learning to surf through all parts of his emotion. While that seemed to help, Derek still noticed that about a day before a presentation, his heart would start to pound intermittently and his body would tense up, all of which activated the other parts of his emotions: thoughts, urges, and feelings.

So we added mindful coping in the form of relaxation to Derek's experiential practice. Specifically, he chose the 5–5–7 cue-controlled breathing to do before he would speak, which calmed all his emotional STUF to slow and regularize his breath. For his cue word, he picked the name of a restaurant that he used to go to with his grandparents for pancake breakfasts in Martha's Vineyard – a memory that evoked feelings of safety and relaxation.

To add to his cue-controlled breathing, Derek also chose self-soothing in the form of a smooth, cool, heart-shaped gemstone his grandfather had given him that he could hold in his hand easily without anyone noticing.

Before his next presentation he practiced several times in session with me: setting the scene and activating the emotion; surfing the emotion wave, adding the cue-controlled breathing, saying his cue word and breathing in for 5, holding his breath for 5 and exhaling for 7 while he rubbed the smooth gemstone in his hand. He then visualized himself getting ready for the presentation and delivering it with expertise all the way to the end, even while feeling anxious and scared. Then he ran through the full experiential sequence again.

Derek also practiced several times on his own. His panic didn't totally go away, but he told me it was only about half of what it used to be, and that he was less distressed about his distress because he no longer saw it as such a threat.

FROM TERRIFIED TO SCARED BUT DETERMINED

My client 'Julie's' breast cancer diagnosis had come out of the blue when she went in for a routine mammogram and was asked to come back for a biopsy the same week. She'd received the results just hours before our session. Her diagnosis was stage 1, and while her doctor felt optimistic about treatment options, Julie's anxiety was understandably very high.

JULIE: I keep surfing my emotion waves as they come, but I'm so anxious I can't focus on anything else.

ME: That's totally understandable. There's so much uncertainty here; it makes sense your anxiety is ramped up because your 3Bs are trying to help you face this threat. Do you feel up to some experiential practice using some relaxation to mindfully cope with the stress?

JULIE: Yes, please. If I practice with you, it will make it more likely I can do it between our sessions.

ME: Okay, great. So just start by letting yourself focus on the uncertainty of your situation. See if there is a particular sensation, thought, urge, or feeling that shows up.

JULIE: It's the thought of telling my children I'm going to have surgery that's most distressing.

ME: Okay, let's use that scene for the experiential. Can you already feel the activation?

JULIE: Yes, I'm already a 7.

ME: Okay, so let's cut off that scene and just surf. Tell me what you notice.

JULIE: My mind immediately gives me the thought, *what if I don't survive this?*

ME: Good noticing. See if you can let that go, come back to your breath, and tell me what else you notice.

JULIE: I feel some tingling in my arms and fingers, and my face feels numb.

ME: Okay. And just slowing this down a bit, see what happens when you make space for those sensations and just allow them to be there, and to do whatever they will do.

JULIE: Well, now the tingling is fading some, but now I notice tension in my stomach.

ME: Okay. And if you draw a line around that tension, what size and shape would it be?

JULIE: It's round and about the size of an apple.

ME: Okay, good noticing. See if you can shift your attention there, and just hang out with the tension. Don't try to push it away or resist it. Just let it be.

JULIE: Yeah. It softened a little, but it's still there.

ME: Okay. Can you give it permission to be there?

JULIE: Yes.

ME: What's happening now?

JULIE: I notice myself resisting the tension.

ME: Good noticing. What else?

JULIE: I feel the urge to punch something. And I just suddenly feel angry. I have done everything right. I have been exercising and eating well since I was a kid. And there's no history of breast cancer in our family.

ME: Yes, so there's an urge to punch something, and anger, and is there also some indignation or shock?

JULIE: Yes, all of that. But now I can feel sadness coming in. And the thought, *it's not fair.*

ME: Yes, you're opening yourself to all the experience. Let's try shifting from emotion surfing now to practicing relaxation to downshift your emotional activation. Before we do, just check in with yourself. On a scale of 1 to 10, how high is your distress?

JULIE: It's up to an 8.

ME: Okay. So, just like we've practiced, using your cue word on the exhale, 'Big Sur.' When you're ready, breathe in for 5, hold for 5, and breathe out for 7 saying your cue word. We'll do that for the next two minutes and I'll count with you while you breathe.

JULIE: (does 5–5–7 breathing for the next two minutes with me counting.)

ME: Now, what do you notice?

JULIE: The tension in my stomach is gone and I don't feel the same sadness. I feel very alert.

ME: Okay, and where is the level of distress now?

JULIE: It's around a 6.

ME: Okay, can we do another two minutes?

JULIE: (Nods, and then does 5–5–7 diaphragmatic breathing with her cue word on the exhale for the next two minutes with me counting.)

ME: Okay, so check in and notice what, if anything, has shifted.

JULIE: Well, I actually feel a little tired now. And I notice the urge to go home and tell my kids and get it over with.

ME: Got it. And what are you feeling?

JULIE: More resigned to the reality of it. And scared, but determined to do my best.

ME: Okay, good. Where is your level of distress now?

JULIE: It's around a 4.

ME: Okay. So what did you learn here?

JULIE: Somehow surfing and relaxation works … even when I'm really upset. It doesn't take away all the distress, but it is definitely more manageable even after only about five to six minutes. And I will focus on doing what matters most, which is telling my kids tonight, and then staying as grounded as possible going through treatment.

ME: That's a great intention. And would you be willing to practice relaxation as your VBA whenever the emotion waves come? You could even add in the five senses exercise since I know how much you love your essential oils.

JULIE: Yes, I can do this in my morning meditation, and also when I get triggered again.

During the next nine months, practicing relaxation actually became Julie's sole VBA for moving toward her value of Health. She was able to use the relaxation practices with emotion surfing when the trigger of uncertainty would hit. Whenever Julie noticed it, she would immediately prompt herself to surf her emotion wave and do her breathing with the essential oil until she was able to ground herself and relax. Even though her anxiety never went away, her relaxation practice helped her stay calm enough to keep taking care of her kids and to make it through treatment, including some unexpected bumps along the way.

THE RELAXATION OBSTACLE COURSE

Here are some common obstacles that can get in the way of relaxing your body as a mindful coping skill:

- *You struggle with staying in the practice.* Maybe 10 minutes is too much of a stretch at first. You can start with one minute and gradually work your way up. Or it could be that with diaphragmatic breathing, you find you get 'air hungry,' which keeps you from staying with the slower count. In that case, try a lesser stretch of 3–3–5 breathing as an intermediate step. Then, you can gradually increase as you go.

- *When you try to relax your body, your mind tells you something's wrong.* If this happens, and you have a history of trauma, you should stop the practice and consult a professional before trying again. That said, feeling uncomfortable can be a very natural response to relaxing. You may feel that you are actually safest when you are anxious because it gives you the sense that you are ready for whatever threat may show up. Relaxing can sometimes feel as if you're making yourself vulnerable and exposed, like my client who experienced anxiety when breathing deeply because he felt as if he was opening himself up to being taken by surprise. If this happens, be gentle and compassionate with yourself. Take a moment to validate your experience, perhaps telling yourself, *it makes sense I am afraid to let my guard down.* As you bring more curiosity and compassion to your feelings as being natural responses to changing a practiced pattern you've long thought was keeping you safe, you'll deepen your ability to just hang out with that experience. From there, you can relax and find your way back to your values and the actions you want to take.

- *You have a chronic health condition or a history of medical trauma and focusing attention on your body is difficult or uncomfortable.* Often these conditions and experiences can lead to a belief that being in our bodies and letting ourselves feel what they do is dangerous. As with any of the skills, find what works for you. Sometimes people who experience chronic pain find that focusing on what matters (VBA), or other mindful coping skills other than relaxation, works better for them. If this is you, feel free to put these aside if you've tried them and they aren't helpful. Or you can experiment and see if you find that practicing relaxation actually helps regulate your emotions. It may be that over time your distress will naturally go down as you practice relaxing and hanging out with any unwanted emotional STUF that shows up.

- *When you do the relaxation exercises, you feel floaty or spacey.* Again, if you find relaxation practice to be too distressing at any point, you should stop and seek help from a trained professional. Otherwise, you can start by focusing on where your feet touch the floor to see if that resolves the experience. It may be helpful to know that if this is happening, it could be your brain's way of trying to shield you from experiencing something it predicts will be unpleasant or even distressing. In this case, you can thank your brain for doing its job of helping you survive, and see if you can get curious about what the experience of even trying to relax is like. You might notice yourself feeling the urge to move away from the sensations and then experiment with going away and coming back as you keep noticing what happens when you go in either direction.

- *You start using relaxation as a way to avoid unwanted STUF.* Name the pattern and give yourself credit for recognizing what's going on. Validate how easy it is to use relaxation to avoid unwanted STUF. Then get back on track by using your WTF? inquiry. Validate how natural it is to want to avoid your unwanted STUF. Finally, remind yourself why it's meaningful to move toward your values in the situation, and try practicing again.

RELAXATION EXPERIENTIAL PRACTICE

To rehearse the skill of relaxation, you can use the following script, and you can also access a guided experiential practice at www.drapriliawest.com/practice.

SET UP

Find a private, quiet place and get into a comfortable position where you're likely to stay alert. Close your eyes or find a single spot in front of you to focus on by just softening your gaze.

SELECT A TRIGGER

Choose a trigger based on a memory or recurring event to activate medium intensity of discomfort and distress. (Keep in mind, in the low range you can struggle to access your emotional STUF, and in the high range you can be easily overwhelmed.)

SELECT MINDFUL COPING SKILL

Choose a relaxation skill to rehearse relaxation after emotion surfing: cue-controlled diaphragmatic breathing, progressive muscle relaxation, five senses or self-soothing.

SELECT VBA

Pick at least one values-based action that will move you toward what matters most in your trigger scene.

ACTIVATE EMOTION

Set your trigger scene by imagining it as a movie and describe what you notice as if it's happening in real time, including:

· where you are
· what time it is
· who you are with.

Go to the exact 'frame' where you anticipate you'll get emotionally activated.

Describe anything you are seeing, hearing, touching, tasting, and otherwise doing in as much detail as possible, frame by frame until you reach a medium level of activation.

Stop the scene and shift to emotion surfing.

EMOTION SURFING

Surf your emotion wave by bringing an intention of curiosity to hanging out with each part of your emotional 'STUF' for two minutes each.

(Sensations) For at least two minutes, scan your body from head to toe for any sensations that stand out to you:

· Notice their size and shape.
· Notice whether they're moving or staying the same.
· Notice any tension in the sensation.
· Notice if there's any temperature.

Bring an intention of allowing the physical experiences that go with sensations. Imagine making space for them, or welcoming them to be there and do whatever they want to do. Be curious about how they behave when you are just watching them.

(Thoughts) Shift your attention from sensations to noticing thoughts for at least two minutes:

- When a thought shows up, say to yourself 'there's a thought' and then let the thought go.
- Refocus on your breath as a way to place a pause between thoughts.
- And then watch for the next thought to show up, and repeat.

(Urges) Shift to watching any urges for two minutes:

- When you notice one, get curious about how intense the urge is: low, medium, high?
- Notice what it's like to just sit with the impulse to do something or not do something.
- Rate the discomfort on a scale of 1 to 10, with 1 being as relaxed as you can imagine, and 10 the most uncomfortable you can imagine.
- Notice if the urge changes in intensity as you sit with it.

(Feelings)

- Label each feeling.
- Validate and welcome the feelings, saying something like: *It makes sense I'm feeling* [insert label]. Or, *it's okay for the feeling of* [insert label] *to be here*.
- Get curious about whether there are any other feelings, underneath the first feelings you noticed.

MINDFUL COPING

Practice your relaxation skill(s) for two minutes to downshift your activation level by either rehearsing them or visualizing doing them. If helpful, set a time for one minute if you need a prompt to switch skills.

VALUES-BASED ACTION

Go back to the exact trigger 'frame' where you have a moment of choice – to act on the emotion urge, or to take values-based action.

Visualize in as much detail as possible doing your values-based action(s) while you continue emotion surfing for at least five minutes, describing your actions and experience to yourself frame by frame:

- What would you or an outside observer see you doing?
- How would it be in your body to do this values-based action? Notice and allow any sensations.
- What kinds of thoughts would show up? Practice letting them go.
- What other urge or urges show up as you take values-based action? Notice what it's like just sitting with them.
- Notice any feelings might you have and just allow them, or validate them.

Repeat the VBA sequence twice.

REFLECT

To wrap up the experiential practice, take a few moments to reflect using the following prompts:

- Did anything surprise you?
- What, if anything, was challenging?
- What did you learn?
- Write down anything else you want to remember.

CHAPTER 08 CHALLENGES

- Try practicing each of the relaxation skills using experiential practice at least once so you have a feel for which ones seem to work best for you when you're activated.

- The next time you get triggered, have one of the relaxation practices available to follow. This will help you become familiar with it, and allow you to use it after emotion surfing when needed to get to VBA.

- Pick a triggering scene that you know you will experience, or that you can predict will happen, and practice emotion surfing and a relaxation skill, and then visualize returning to taking VBA. When you encounter the trigger IRL, use the same sequence and see if you can find your way to taking VBA.

- Lock in the learning by sharing with someone you feel comfortable what you've learned about relaxation and the skills you're using and why.

- Practice relaxation using the guided experiential at least three times before you move forward.

CHAPTER 08 LEARNINGS

- Just like all the mindful coping skills, relaxation can help you regulate your emotions and get back to VBA.

- Because your emotional STUF is one big network, intervening on a somatic level can downshift emotional activation.

- The four relaxation skills are: cue-controlled diaphragmatic breathing, progressive muscle relaxation, five senses, and self-soothing.

- There are many mental health and physical health benefits to practicing relaxation in any state.

- If you have untreated or unprocessed trauma, practicing these skills without the support of a professional is not recommended.

- Practicing mindful coping while emotionally activated can help you learn to use the skills in real-life distressing situations.

09

SHIFTING EMOTION BY SHIFTING ATTENTION

My experience is what I agree to attend to.

William James

ATTENTION-SHIFTING IS THE FINAL mindful coping skill you'll learn to help regulate your emotions. Simply put, attention-shifting is a psychological power tool. Because your emotional STUF follows your attention, you can actually influence your experience just by changing what you focus on.[1]

This makes your emotional network of sensations, thoughts, urges and feelings a captive audience for whatever you think about, look at, touch, taste, and hear. Being able to flexibly, intentionally, and creatively shift your attention can help you downregulate your activation level.[2]

For instance, if you were to pay attention to what's negative all the time (as the negativity bias is rooting for), your emotional STUF will stay in a state of elevated threat. The power of your attention also accounts for the benefits that come from focusing on gratitude, which naturally improve your outlook and mood. Paying attention to what you appreciate will downshift your threat level, and your emotional activation with it.

> BECAUSE YOUR EMOTIONAL STUF FOLLOWS YOUR ATTENTION, YOU CAN ACTUALLY INFLUENCE YOUR EXPERIENCE JUST BY CHANGING WHAT YOU FOCUS ON.

You can clearly see the powerful relationship between emotion and attention in familiar behavior between parents and children:

When a baby starts crying because they're hungry, tired, or want to be held, the parent can simply shake a rattle in front of the baby's face, and as soon as their focus changes the baby can shift from crying to smiling and gurgling in a matter of seconds.

Or if a young child skins their knee, they can go from a blood-curdling cry to just sniffles when presented with a sweet colorful popsicle.

As we grow older we may not be this easily distracted, but if you are willing to hold your experience more lightly, shifting attention when you get triggered can disrupt your emotion wave when you're vulnerable to being dragged under.

Consider the example in the previous chapter: I was shifting my attention to parts of my body that didn't hurt when I was sick and in pain. This allowed me to gain perspective and calmed me enough to help me keep surfing until the wave resolved. Because what you focus on is so powerful, it explains why attentional control (the intentional focusing of your attention) is effective for helping people struggling with depression and anxiety.[3]

If you've been doing the experiential practices, this will be no surprise. The power of attention explains why you're able to activate yourself simply by focusing on trigger scenes. And it means you already have a leg up on adding this next skill to your toolbox.

As a review, the skills sequence looks like this: when you get triggered, you'll tune in and hang out (emotion surfing), but instead of going straight to VBA, you'll use mindful coping through attention-shifting to regulate your emotions until you can get back to doing what matters most.

FROM *TIGER KING* TO *TED LASSO*

In emotional efficacy skills training, *attention-shifting* (sometimes also referred to as distraction) entails moving your focus away from an aversive trigger and toward something neutral or pleasurable, when emotion surfing alone isn't cutting it. Like all mindful coping skills, this can help you catch your balance enough to take values-based action.

Most importantly, since shifting your attention can shift your emotional experience, imagine how much more access to VBA it could give you. At any point when you notice you're in emotional distress, and it's not a true threat to your wellbeing, you can practice surfing your emotion wave instead of defaulting to the emotion urge. And if you still can't connect to what matters most in the moment, you can shift attention away from whatever is triggering you and toward something neutral, supportive, or even pleasurable.

Attention-shifting is sort of like changing the channel from *Tiger King* to *Ted Lasso*. (If you're like me, it's pure joy and relief.) It not only shifts your attention; it shifts your emotional activation.

ATTENTION-SHIFTING IS SORT OF LIKE CHANGING THE CHANNEL FROM *TIGER KING* TO *TED LASSO*.

While changing the channel might sound easy, as you well know by now, doing anything other than acting on an urge when you're triggered can be challenging. It may not seem possible to shift your attention in the moment of choice – especially if your 3Bs are telling you something is wrong or there is a looming threat.

This is why practice is so important. If you can remember to try attention-shifting, you might find you can at least disrupt the urge to default and then recover enough to put your values in action.

REFLECTION: EMOTION SHIFTS WITH YOUR ATTENTION

Take a moment right now to experiment with how much your attention can influence your emotions:

- For one minute, think about a peak experience from your life. Describe it to yourself in as much detail as possible. Then, notice all the emotional STUF that shows up just from shifting your attention.

- Next, for one minute, think about a painful moment from your life. Describe it to yourself in as much detail as possible. Then, notice all the emotional STUF that shows up just from shifting your attention.

- Now shift back and forth between the peak experience and the painful moment. Watch how your emotional STUF shifts back and forth, following your attention. Notice where it feels harder or easier to switch between the two.

ATTENTION-SHIFTING CAN BE HELPFUL AND UNHELPFUL: WTF?

While the most effective and efficient way to get to what matters is always to pivot straight from the emotion trigger to valuing, this path isn't always available. When your emotion wave overwhelms your ability to take values-based action (VBA), using attention-shifting can help you recover. In situations where you are at risk of defaulting and you don't have much time to surf, take perspective, or relax, shifting your attention can give you the temporary relief you need to come back to the moment of choice.

> IN SITUATIONS WHERE YOU ARE AT RISK OF DEFAULTING AND YOU DON'T HAVE MUCH TIME TO SURF, TAKE PERSPECTIVE, OR RELAX, SHIFTING YOUR ATTENTION CAN GIVE YOU THE TEMPORARY RELIEF YOU NEED TO COME BACK TO THE MOMENT OF CHOICE.

As a now familiar example, when I was suffering with frozen shoulder and sick after my second vaccination, in the 36 hours that followed, what mattered most to me was getting through without having to seek medical attention. I didn't want to put myself at any more risk of getting sick by taking an Uber or going to the hospital in peak COVID season. I was surfing emotion waves that would have made Kelly Slater proud. But I was still in so much pain that I needed more help to ride them out. So I called on the mindful coping skills of Relaxation and Attention-Shifting.

Not only did I do cue-controlled breathing, I also shifted my attention to focus on parts of my body that didn't hurt. And, I watched hours of *Grey's Anatomy* reruns to avoid focusing on the discomfort.

Avoiding pain *in this way in that situation* was not unhelpful defaulting, but a carefully crafted intentional, flexible, and creative choice intended to help me keep moving toward what I cared about: making it through to the next day without risking my Health. Similarly, in situations where you don't have the ability to surf, take perspective, or relax, shifting your attention can give you the temporary relief you need to come back to the moment of choice.

What works when you're triggered can be a moving target and depends on what matters most in context. Like any skills or actions, attention-shifting can be used to avoid emotional pain in both helpful ways (like when I was sick and needed to focus on something other than the pain) and not-so-helpful ways (like opening a random pinging text in the middle of a Zoom meeting you're leading while screensharing with coworkers). However, because it would be easy to use attention-shifting to fall back into unhelpful defaulting you may need to use your WTF? inquiry to track your actions so you don't end up moving away from what really matters.

For example, as I was preparing for the doctoral licensing exam in clinical psychology, I had a really hard time staying focused. Usually I love learning: I'm insatiably curious, and will happily nerd out on nearly any subject you put in front of me. But by the end of my training, like a lot of doctoral students, I was burned out ... crispy even. Forcing myself to absorb any more information, especially in such dense chunks, felt unusually cruel.

Of course, my 3Bs were really noisy about this threat to my safety, certainty, coherence, comfort, and pleasure. As a result I would often find myself distracted by things that had never before seemed so interesting; for example, closets that suddenly needed color coding, binge-worthy TV reruns, or the endless multitude of tantalizing topics I could Google. My exhaustion was urging me to avoid the unwanted sensations, thoughts, urges, and feelings that would come up when I would try to study. So I took lots and lots (and lots) of breaks.

On one hand, this was problematic since avoiding the emotional distress that came with studying – especially since studying was not an actual threat – was moving me away from what mattered most in context: passing my licensing exam. And that just wasn't workable for me.

On the other hand, I did need study breaks, and I knew research supported taking breaks for better learning and improved focus.

So, I took my own advice. I used a WTF? inquiry to decode the purpose of my many breaks. I asked myself, *what's the function of so much break-taking?* And that's when it became clear. While I could see some value in short breaks to give my mind a chance to rest, I could also see that my organizing, TV binging, and endless Googling were going on longer than needed for me to refresh, and they were starting to move me away from what mattered most. Using the WTF? inquiry I determined

SHIFTING EMOTION BY SHIFTING ATTENTION

that – past 45 minutes of breaking – I was just avoiding the aversive emotional STUF that went with studying. And this was moving me away from passing the exam.

So, I made a deal with myself: I could take four breaks max each day, but after 45 minutes, I had to get back to work – no matter what. I even set a timer. And when the break was over, I used emotion surfing to help me settle back into my VBA of studying. It took all my willingness to experience the discomfort, even distress that came with that exam prep, and it never got easier.

In fact, it sucked the whole way through.

But it was the kind of pain I wanted – the kind that comes with doing what really matters.

BABY SHARK TO THE RESCUE (DO DO DO DO DO DO)

My client 'Claire' was recently separated from her wife and was struggling to adjust to their new coparenting schedule. Every time her wife came for the scheduled pickup, she would complain about the arrangement and blame Claire for their difficulties, in front of the children. Sometimes she would even invite herself in, despite their mutual agreement to talk in private and not to enter each other's homes.

When Claire had tried to remind her wife of their agreement, she would become defensive, refusing to take responsibility for breaking boundaries, or airing their grievances in earshot of their kids. Understandably, Claire would get triggered and try to surf, but instead of staying calm and firm, she would give in to the urge to cry and chastise her ex in front of the kids, which further upset everyone.

Claire and I had already worked on clarifying her values related to her children. She knew what mattered most was Harmony, and she was clear that staying calm and restating the agreement was the action that would move her toward it. But, the trigger was so intense she needed something to help her regulate so she could take VBA in the moment.

We used experiential practice to prepare Claire to use attention-shifting to support her taking values-based action:

ME: What's something you could focus on when your wife's behavior triggers you, so you won't default to confronting her in front of your kids? Is there a fun memory you can recall or a silly song you could sing in your head?

CLAIRE: Well, I do like that kid's song that goes, 'Baby shark do do do do do do.' It's hard to take anything seriously when I think about that.

ME: Haha. And just to check, would singing this move your toward or away from your value of Harmony? I could imagine that you could also get to Harmony in other ways, like talking to your wife about it?

CLAIRE: Good question. If I use the WTF? inquiry, in context, it moves me toward my value of Harmony because we've both agreed not to get into conversations about our relationship outside of counseling right now.

ME: Okay, good tracking. You're clear that you're not just using the song to avoid what would be most helpful in this situation.

CLAIRE: Yes, it's really clear to me that keeping things chill is what matters most.

ME: Great. So could you sing *Baby Shark* in your head to shift your attention away from her complaints, attempts to enter the house, or anything else she does that's upsetting?

CLAIRE: I could try ...

ME: Okay, let's practice. Just close your eyes, and put yourself in the exchange. Take yourself to the very moment when your ex will likely be complaining and freeze on that frame. And describe what you see and hear.

CLAIRE: Yep, I'm there.

ME: Good. What's happening?

CLAIRE: She's telling me I never pack the right stuff in the kids' overnight bags, and how she had to buy them new shoes to go on a hike with her new girlfriend last weekend.

ME: Okay. And does that trigger an emotion wave?

CLAIRE: Oh yeah. It's like a 5 to 6 level intensity already.

ME: Okay, let's shift to surfing all parts of your emotion, starting with any sensations in your body and making space for them; naming any thoughts and letting them go; noticing any urges to do something or not to do something, and just sitting with them, even leaning into the discomfort; and naming any feelings.

CLAIRE: I can sense tension in my throat and jaw, and I'm hot.

ME: Where do you notice the heat?

CLAIRE: It's like a wave of heat from my stomach all the way up to my head.

ME: Good noticing. Can you make space for the tension and the heat? Just imagine hanging out with them, almost like a weird and quirky dinner-party guest that you welcome in even if you wish you could uninvite them.

CLAIRE: Yeah, that's a helpful image.

ME: Good. What else shows up?

CLAIRE: Yeah, I'm having the thought, *who does she think she is to come into my house in front of our kids and make me look like a bad mother?!*

ME: Okay, good. See if you can just let that thought go, come back to your breath, maybe notice if you're inhaling or exhaling. And now see what else shows up.

CLAIRE: Now I have that urge again to cry and tell her she is just being so awful.

ME: Okay … see if you can sit with that urge? Just notice how intense it is, and how hard it is not to act on it.

CLAIRE: It's pretty intense.

ME: Yeah. Can you just let it be intense?

CLAIRE: Yes. But I'm mad. And I'm sad. And I'm hurt.

ME: Yeah. I hear that. Mad, sad, and hurt. Anything else?

CLAIRE: Yes, I also notice I feel helpless.

ME: And, can you validate that it makes sense you'd be feeling mad, sad, hurt, and helpless?

CLAIRE: Yeah, it does make sense, especially when she is doing it in front of the kids.

ME: Right. And are there sensations that go with mad, sad, hurt, and helpless?

CLAIRE: Yes, it's like there's tension again – a lump in my throat.

ME: Okay. Any idea what the lump would say if it could speak?

CLAIRE: Hmmm. I think it would say, *why can't you see me? I'm doing my best*.

ME: Ah, okay. So is there's a thought about not being seen for doing your best?

CLAIRE: Yeah, I'm having the thought that *I get missed and unappreciated by her*.

ME: And just out of curiosity, not because there's a right or wrong about it, how high is your distress now?

CLAIRE: It's still around a 5.5.

ME: Okay. So you know you can often act on your values even at moderate levels of distress, but to practice regulating, let's do some attention-shifting. Can you sing the *Baby Shark* song in your head for the next two minutes, and then we'll check back in?

CLAIRE: (Nods and sings for two minutes.)

ME (after two minutes): Okay, what's happening for you now?

CLAIRE: Well, I'm definitely not as upset. It's hard to stay upset when you're singing 'do do do do do do'!

ME: Yeah, that's what we're going for. Now can you imagine taking one of the VBAs we've worked on, calmly asking your ex to step outside to talk to you, maybe putting your hand gently on her arm, or just requesting that she wait outside and call you later to talk? Walk me through that visualization, step by step.

CLAIRE: Yes, I'm seeing myself be very diplomatic, even while feeling hurt and unappreciated, gently placing my hand on her arm, and asking her to step outside in a slow, quiet voice.

ME: Great. Stay with that visualization a few more moments, walking it through. She steps inside, and what do you do? Just replay it again.

CLAIRE: Okay. She steps inside, and I move between her and the children, gently place my hand on her arm and in a low, slow tone, ask if we can talk outside for a moment.

ME: Great. Now what's happening for you?

CLAIRE: I notice that I feel calmer, and that the idea of doing this makes me feel excited and proud of myself.

ME: That's great. Let's wrap here. Would you be willing to rehearse the attention-shifting experiential with *Baby Shark* at least three more times before your ex comes over?

CLAIRE: Yes – I will definitely need to practice to remember to do that when she's right in front of me.

As a reminder, it's never the goal of emotion surfing and attention-shifting to get rid of unwanted emotional STUF. It's just to give you enough relief to be able to refocus on what matters most. As you saw, Claire still felt hurt and unappreciated when she pivoted to valuing. But she was able to shift her attention and regulate her emotions enough to do what mattered most to her in that situation: keep the peace and hold the boundary to protect her children from being exposed to conflict.

... IT'S NEVER THE GOAL OF EMOTION SURFING AND ATTENTION-SHIFTING TO GET RID OF UNWANTED EMOTIONAL STUF. IT'S JUST TO GIVE YOU ENOUGH RELIEF TO BE ABLE TO REFOCUS ON WHAT MATTERS MOST.

It's always helpful to plan in advance any mindful coping for recurrent predictable triggers. For example, while I'm not at all proud of this, I can reasonably predict that if I have to call the DMV, my internet or phone provider, or any other bureaucratic customer service center, it's likely I will end up triggered. (After all, I have spent a lot of my life figuring out how to optimize human behavior, including the systems they operate in. I value Effectiveness and Efficiency.)

Even when I surf my emotion wave, I can become noticeably annoyed. And if I act on the (usually unhelpful) urge to challenge the rationale for what's going on, I can get even more annoyed, not to mention annoying the person I'm talking to. And it leads me away from my value of Respect.

Knowing this ahead of time, I come prepared with strategies to shift my attention while I'm on hold with the repetitive pre-recorded sales pitch with a voice that sounds overcaffeinated and inappropriately excited.

Or, when I'm being transferred for the fourth time to the wrong department and being given the same wrong number I started with to try again.

Or, when talking to people who sound like they have little interest in helping me and remind me of a painful reality I struggle to accept: lots of people are in situations where they do work that is disconnected from meaning.

To mindfully cope in these predicable trigger situations, I'll shift my attention to any number of neutral or pleasurable stimuli; for example, music I like, making a cup of coffee, or playing with a Google search during the call. And, I'll also link my actions to what matters to me. To move toward my values of Effectiveness, Efficiency and Respect, my VBAs in these situations are to stay calm. I say 'please' and 'thank you' and I wait without complaining. And, I remind myself of a coping thought: *all you have control over is how you show up.*

BEFORE YOU ACT, DISTRACT

To help you prepare, you can use the following list of attention-shifting strategies when you're triggered (adapted from the *Emotion Efficacy Therapy* clinician's guide).[4] As always, you can also come up with your own ideas.

PAY ATTENTION TO SOMETHING ELSE

- Get deeper in nature. Go outside: observe the flowers, trees, sky, and landscape as closely as possible. Observe animals, insects, or other living things around you.
- Listen to all the sounds around you. Observe what you can see and hear in as much detail as possible.
- Keep a copy of a mantra, quote, or favorite prayer with you. When you feel distressed, read it to yourself; reading it out loud might calm you even more.
- Walk around your neighborhood or a park and notice the scenery, the colors, and the textures of your surroundings.
- Get out of your house and go for a drive in your car or ride public transportation.
- Plan a daytrip to somewhere you've always wanted to go.
- Pray or meditate. Say a prayer, keep the Serenity Prayer with you, or check out one of the many meditation apps available online or through your phone.
- Listen to music you like or try a genre that is new or even foreign to you.
- Find a space that is quiet and listen to an engaging audiobook or podcast.

- Watch a TV show or movie you know will hold your attention; think about whether you would have written a different plot or ending and what it would be like.
- Learn a new language. There are so many good programs online – pick one and dive in.
- Sing or play a musical instrument. You can even improvise by using a table as a drum and making up your own beats.
- Write in your journal. Write a poem. Write a letter to your Wise Self, God, or your Higher Power.
- Cook your favorite meal or find something to eat you really like.
- Play video games.
- Join an internet dating site or app.
- Make a movie or video with your phone.
- Go to a flower shop and smell your favorite flowers.
- Learn a new creative skill like knitting, crocheting, or photography.
- Make a scrapbook.
- Write a loving letter to yourself.
- Draw or paint a picture or learn how to paint or draw.
- Make a bucket list of things you want to do before you die.
- Make a list of 10 things you're good at or that you like about yourself.
- Put together a list of favorite quotes or mantras.
- Create a blog or website.
- Make a to-do list.
- Clean out your home and find things you can donate.
- Redecorate a room or space in your house.
- Organize your books, files, drawers, or any other similar space.
- Exercise; set a new physical fitness goal for yourself.

- Make a plan of action for finding a new job or a better job if you already have one.
- Make appointments with various professionals – doctor, dentist, optometrist, accountant – and arrive on time.
- Get or give yourself a new hairstyle, haircut, manicure, pedicure, or massage.
- Plan something: a party, event, your next vacation.
- Plant a garden or do landscaping work in your own space or in a community garden.
- Clean out your closet or garage.
- Do homework or other work.
- Clean out your bathtub and take a bubble bath.
- Go grocery shopping and cook a nice dinner for yourself.
- Pay bills.

PAY ATTENTION TO SOMEONE ELSE

- Call, text, or email a friend.
- Visit a friend or invite a friend to come over.
- Call your friends and ask if they need help doing something, such as a chore, grocery shopping, or housecleaning.
- Ask any family members who live nearby if you can assist them with something: running errands, yard work, babysitting, walking the dog.
- Call your local homeless shelter, volunteer organization, or advocacy group and sign up to help.
- Bake cookies for a neighbor or coworker.
- Send a snail-mail letter or card to someone you haven't talked to in a while.
- Write a thank-you email to someone who did something kind for you.
- Write a note to someone who has changed your life for the better and tell the person why.

- Make a list of people you admire and why.

- Join a club or attend a social meet-up group.

- People-watch. Go to a local store, shopping center, bookstore, or park and notice what other people do and how they dress. Listen to their conversations. Observe as many details about other people as you can.

- Play counting games while people-watching, like counting the number of blue-eyed people versus brown-eyed people you see.

- Think about someone you care about. What do you imagine he or she is doing right now?

- Keep a picture of people you love with you and look at their photo whenever you need comfort.

- Imagine a healing, peaceful conversation with someone you deeply care about or admire ... think about the details of what they would say to you to comfort you.

LEAVING UNWORKABLE SITUATIONS

So often what people struggle with is catching themselves *before* they act on their intense emotion urges, especially if their emotion surfing skills are still developing. It doesn't always occur to people that sometimes the best values-based action you can take when things get out of hand is to leave the situation. In part this is because leaving can feel like the very opposite of what you'll want to do in a threatened state.

> SO OFTEN WHAT PEOPLE STRUGGLE WITH IS CATCHING THEMSELVES *BEFORE* THEY ACT ON THEIR INTENSE EMOTION URGES, ESPECIALLY IF THEIR EMOTION SURFING SKILLS ARE STILL DEVELOPING.

My client 'Matt' had always had a difficult relationship with his dad, but now that he was setting boundaries with his father, they had started to argue more frequently. And while Matt was bigger and stronger than his 70-year-old father, their most recent tiff had led to a shoving match where Matt got a badly bruised rib.

In fact, his father's reaction was so fast, Matt didn't see it coming; there was no time for emotion surfing, much less clarifying what mattered most. In the moment, Matt felt so threatened, he shoved his father back. Fortunately, his father was okay. But Matt was afraid it could happen again, and if it did, that he could really hurt his dad.

In the next session, we used experiential practice for mindful coping where Matt visualized taking a 'time out.' As soon as Matt imagined his father starting to argue he noticed the trigger, and started surfing the initial emotion wave, which helped him pause before reacting. Then, in the service of his value of Safety, Matt saw himself going straight to a time out by leaving his dad's house.

We hoped this practice would help Matt avoid a volatile situation and avoid the possibility of another scuffle, so that he and his father would have time to calm down before talking. Matt also took values-based action in advance of meeting his dad – having a phone conversation to let him know if they started to argue, he would be leaving immediately to protect them both.

Fortunately, the phone call and clear boundary Matt set with his father was all that was needed. The next few times they were together there was less tension and they were able to have conversations without getting into conflict. Matt told me his vulnerability to triggers with his dad had also lessened, knowing that he could leave if he ever needed to.

SHIFT YOUR ATTENTION BY TAKING A TIME OUT

- Excuse yourself from a difficult situation and take time and space away from it.
- Ask for a break from a conversation and schedule a time to come back to it when you're less triggered.
- In recurring difficult situations, prepare a script ahead of time that allows you to set a boundary and take a break so you can re-engage when you're clear on your VBA.

'WHEN THEY COME AT ME, I REACT'

My client, 'Sam,' was a successful performing artist who depended on her team of managers for both logistical and creative support. But she had been stuck in an unhelpful default pattern where she would receive texts from her managers requesting that she do things she had not agreed to. And in return, Sam would get upset and fire back texts accusing them of not respecting her or treating her like an adult. Her managers would then either withdraw from the conversation or fire back with explanations Sam considered insulting. It could take her hours or even days to recover because she would ruminate about it (making her emotion wave more intense), and she would lose valuable time and energy she could have been putting into her music.

SAM: My managers really care about me. But when they come at me, I react. They have so many requests one after another, and I just can't cope.

ME: Sounds like you get overwhelmed, and it makes it hard to focus on what matters most.

SAM: Yes, and it sucks because I don't want to accuse them of not respecting me, but in that moment is feels like they are bossing me around.

ME: And what matters most in those situations to you?

SAM: I want to be more involved in the decision-making, you know? It's my brand. I built this brand by making the decisions that launched my career and got me here. They are supposed to be my partners.

ME: What happens when you accuse them of micromanaging you?

SAM: They stop communicating. And then I really worry we are missing opportunities. Or even worse, I worry they are going to quit. And they really are the best at what they do.

ME: Then what happens?

SAM: I just can't stop thinking about it. And then for the next few days I can't talk to them and I can't focus on my music or whatever else I need to be doing to move my career forward.

ME: What matters most here?

SAM: That we can all work together better.

ME: And what would you need to do toward that goal?

SAM: I think I just get too in my head, and I'm too quick to react, you know?

ME: Yes, and if you weren't in your head about it, what would you be experiencing instead?

SAM: I would feel grateful. And I would feel respected.

ME: So, you remember that all you can control is how you show up, so what would you need to do differently here to move toward Gratitude and Respect?

SAM: Before anything else, I need to not act on my urge to text them back immediately when I get triggered.

ME: Okay. So, would it help to do some emotion surfing using experiential practice with this trigger scene in mind?

SAM: That would be good.

ME: Great. What else?

SAM: I would need to calm myself down. When I'm that triggered, I have a hard time being grateful or respectful, much less asking for the respect I want.

ME: Right. Sometimes you need to do some mindful coping to get to your values-based moves.

SAM: Yes.

ME: Do you have a clear idea of what it would look like to act on your values of Respect and Gratitude?

SAM: I think so. I would remind myself they are trying to help me, and remember that I can't do this without them. Nobody succeeds on this level without a team.

ME: Right. And what would your response look like if you were to move toward more Gratitude and Respect?

SAM: I'd start by thanking them for taking care of the situation. And if I felt like I wanted to be involved in something, I could ask them to talk to me before pulling the trigger.

ME: That sounds great. In addition to emotion surfing, you'd want to do something to help regulate your emotions so you could take those values-based actions?

SAM: Yes, I'd need to shift my attention for a bit to let the wave settle first.

ME: What kinds of things could you do? What's something you find neutral or pleasurable that could distract you temporarily?

SAM: I'm a Words with Friends addict.

ME: Ahh. So you could play for a bit to shift your attention?

SAM: Yes. I usually have at least four games going, so that should give me something to do for at least 10 minutes.

ME: Great. What else is predictably neutral or even pleasurable for you?

SAM: I love looking through old photos of vacations. Sometimes that is what keeps me going when I'm tired.

ME: Okay. And do you have access to those on your phone?

SAM: Yes, they are all right here (points to her phone). I could easily spend 15 minutes doing that if I needed to.

ME: Okay, good. Let's come up with one more option. What else could you do?

SAM: I could write in my gratitude journal. I always feel better after I do that, even just for five minutes.

ME: Great idea. And that moves you toward Gratitude too.

SAM: Yes. Okay, this feels like a good plan.

ME: Yes. So let's do the experiential practice so you'll be more likely to remember the sequence next time you get a triggering text.

Using the experiential skills practice with attention-shifting, Sam used a list of five upsetting texts her managers were likely to send as her trigger scenes. To start, she imagined one of the five texts popping up on her phone, surfing through all parts of her emotional STUF, and then she practiced focusing away from the texts for at least 10 minutes using one or all of her attention-shifting skills: writing in her gratitude journal, looking through photos of her last vacation, or playing Words with Friends. Next, she imagined, play by play, taking VBA by responding to her managers' texts calmly, or politely requesting an opportunity to discuss their requests.

The next time Sam received a triggering text, she was able to pause before responding. She surfed the emotion wave and hung out with all her unwanted STUF. She made space for all the uncomfortable sensations. She watched her thoughts and let them go. She sat with the urge to rapidly fire back complaints. And she labeled and validated her feelings instead of judging them or herself. Then she practiced mindful coping: setting a timer on her phone for 10 minutes, she looked at recent vacation photos. When she would notice her attention returning to the triggering text and the urge to start ruminating, she was able to catch herself and refocus on the photos.

After 10 minutes she was able to respond by taking her VBA, requesting a discussion about her schedule. Sam was surprised by how open her managers were to talking things through, as well as how appreciative they were that she wanted to be more involved in the decisions. And as another bonus, she felt better about herself.

THE ATTENTION-SHIFTING OBSTACLE COURSE

Of course, shifting your attention, like any shift when you're triggered, is easier said than done in the heat of the moment. Here are some common obstacles that can get in the way of attention-shifting:

- *You've practiced and you're still struggling to shift your attention when you encounter unwanted emotional STUF.* Keep in mind, you may have to try several times with different strategies to figure out what will work for you when you're triggered. New skills don't always come easily. While experiential skills practice will help maximize your chances of success, it may take trial and error before you get it right. Go easy on yourself while you figure it out.

- *You shifted your attention, and you're not acting on the emotion urge, but you still can't take values-based action.* You could always try another mindful coping skill, such as perspective-taking or relaxation. But let's also be real. Sometimes the best we can expect when we get triggered is to not give into an unhelpful urge. For many of us, learning not to act on our emotional urges is the biggest challenge to our emotional efficacy. And doing something different than what you feel intensely is no small feat. If shifting your attention in the moment keeps you from doing something impulsive or destructive, and it's the best you can do at the time, *then it is functioning as a values-based action.* And in context, that's powerful.

- *Your WTF? (What's The Function?) inquiry reveals that you're using attention-shifting to avoid unwanted STUF.* If you can tell your attention-shifting is moving you away from what matters, stop and name the pattern. Give yourself credit for recognizing what's going on; it happens. Try validating your emotional experience. Remind yourself how natural it is to want to avoid your unwanted STUF. Finally, remind yourself why it's meaningful to move toward your values in the situation, and try practicing again.

ATTENTION-SHIFTING EXPERIENTIAL PRACTICE

To rehearse the skill of attention-shifting, you can use the following script, and you can also access a guided experiential practice at www.dapriliawest.com/practice.

SET UP

Find a private, quiet place and get into a comfortable position where you're likely to stay alert. Close your eyes or find a single spot in front of you to focus on by just softening your gaze.

SELECT A TRIGGER

Choose a trigger based on a memory or recurring event to activate medium intensity of discomfort and distress. (Keep in mind, in the low range you can struggle to access your emotional STUF, and in the high range you be get easily overwhelmed.)

SELECT MINDFUL COPING SKILL

Choose an attention-shifting skill to rehearse after emotion surfing: paying attention to something else; paying attention to someone else; or taking a time out. Keep in mind, if you can't actually do the skill during this experiential practice, you'll visualize doing it.

SELECT VBA

Pick at least one values-based action that will move you toward what matters most in your trigger scene.

ACTIVATE EMOTION

1. Set your trigger scene by imagining it as a movie and describe what you notice as if it's happening in real time, including:

    *   where you are
    *   what time it is
    *   who you are with.

2. Go to the exact 'frame' where you anticipate you'll get emotionally activated.

3. Describe anything you are seeing, hearing, touching, tasting, and otherwise doing in as much detail as possible, frame by frame until you reach a medium level of activation.

4. Stop the scene and shift to emotion surfing.

EMOTION SURFING

Surf your emotion wave by bringing an intention of curiosity to hanging out with each part of your emotional 'STUF' for two minutes each:

(Sensations) For at least two minutes, scan your body from head to toe for any sensations that stand out to you:

·   Notice their size and shape.

·   Notice whether they're moving or staying the same.

·   Notice any tension in the sensation.

·   Notice if there's any temperature.

Bring an intention of allowing the physical experiences that go with sensations. Imagine making space for them, or welcoming them to be there and do whatever they want to do. Be curious about how they behave when you are just watching them.

(Thoughts) Shift your attention from sensations to noticing thoughts for at least two minutes:

·   When a thought shows up, say to yourself 'there's a thought' and then let the thought go.

·   Refocus on your breath as a way to place a pause between thoughts.

·   And then watch for the next thought to show up, and repeat.

(Urges) Shift to watching any urges for two minutes:

·   When you notice one, get curious about how intense the urge is: low, medium, high?

·   Notice what it's like to just sit with the impulse to do something or not do something.

- Rate the discomfort on a scale of 1 to 10, with 1 being as relaxed as you can imagine, and 10 the most uncomfortable you can imagine.

- Notice if the urge changes in intensity as you sit with it.

(Feelings)

- Label each feeling.

- Validate and welcome the feelings, saying something like: *It makes sense I'm feeling* [insert label]. Or, *it's okay for the feeling of* [insert label] *to be here.*

- Get curious about whether there are any other feelings, underneath the first feelings you noticed.

MINDFUL COPING

Practice your attention-shifting skill(s) for two minutes to downshift your activation level by either rehearsing them or visualizing doing them. If helpful, set a time for one minute if you need a prompt to switch skills.

VALUES-BASED ACTION

Go back to the exact trigger frame where you have a moment of choice – to act on the emotion urge, or to take values-based action.

Visualize in as much detail as possible doing your values-based action(s) while you continue emotion surfing for at least five minutes, describing your actions and experience to yourself frame by frame:

- What would you or an outside observer see you doing?

- How would it be in your body to do this values-based action? Notice and allow any sensations.

- What kinds of thoughts would show up? Practice letting them go.

- What other urge or urges show up as you take values-based action? Notice what it's like just sitting with them.

- Notice any feelings might you have and just allow them, or validate them.

Repeat the VBA sequence twice.

REFLECT

To wrap up the experiential practice, take a few moments to reflect using the following prompts:

- Did anything surprise you?
- What, if anything, was challenging?
- What did you learn?
- Write down anything else you want to remember.

CHAPTER 09 CHALLENGES

- From the list in this chapter, compile your own list of attention-shifting strategies you want to try or that you already know will work for you when you need mindful coping. Store it on your phone or somewhere you can easily find it.

- The next time you are triggered, try using attention-shifting alongside a WTF? inquiry to practice tracking the function of your behavior in the situation. This will help you get better at knowing when your actions move you toward or away from what matters to you.

- Practice attention-shifting using the guided experiential at least three times before you move forward.

CHAPTER 09 LEARNINGS

- Emotions follow your attention; your emotional STUF will reflect whatever you focus on.

- Attention-shifting skills allow you to focus away from a distressing trigger and on something neutral or pleasurable to regulate your emotions.

- Attention-shifting skills can help you recover enough to act on your values.

- When in doubt, use a WTF? (What's The Function?) inquiry to be sure your actions are functioning to move you toward VBA (versus unhelpful avoidance).

- Lock in the learning by sharing with someone what you've learned about how attention impacts emotion. Share one thing from you list of attention-shifting strategies that you know works to help regulate your emotions when you're triggered.

- Practicing mindful coping while emotionally activated can help you learn to use the skills in real-life distressing situations.

10

PLAYING INFINITE GAMES

… games help us imagine and invent the future together.

Jane McGonigal

AS YOU ARRIVE AT THIS final chapter you've covered a lot of ground in not so many pages. Let's briefly recap.

> *One.* Your life is made up of moments of choice. In every moment, you have an opportunity to choose how you'll show up. This gives you many possible futures. What you choose will tell you how the story of your life unfolds.

> *Two.* Your emotions are the primary motivational system for your choices. This means your relationship with your emotions is at the heart of the actions you take, moving you toward or away from what matters most to you in a given moment. Inside the emotional matrix simulation, your choices can get hijacked by unhelpful default reactions because it seems like *what you feel is all there is*. Without a powerful relationship with what you feel, you can unwittingly choose an under-realized, under-fulfilled life fraught with more pain.

> *Three.* You have the technology to unplug. But to completely free your choices and your life, you need the skills to decode your emotions, rewire unhelpful patterns, and act in ways that align with your innermost interests, desires, and yearnings – to unlock the best possible version of yourself and design your best life.

And, if you're up for it, there's still one last level of play available to you …

> *Four.* You can design flexible, intentional, and creative actions to stretch for what's possible *in every moment of choice*.

Until now you've learned skills to optimize your moments of choice when emotion triggers threaten to hijack them. That in itself is a huge upgrade, *but* this alone won't help you tap all of what's possible for you in your life.

STRETCHING FOR WHAT'S POSSIBLE

I once heard a description of hell that went like this: in the afterlife, you meet the person you could have been if you'd become the best possible version of yourself. And, assuming you didn't, ouch.

Most of us want all of what's possible – to become the best possible version of ourselves – even if we're not so skillful with moments of choice. When we optimize moments of choice we are stepping fully into our power. Moments of choice are where we fully express or embody what matters most.

But when you're not aware of this, you can let your emotions choose your life for you. I've never heard anyone look back on their life and regret how they felt. But lots of people retrospectively regret choices that didn't align with what mattered most. Because they got hijacked by their emotions. They regret missed opportunities for what else might have been possible.

That's why this next level of play requires more than just boss-level emotional efficacy to stare straight into the face of a fiery dragon of intense pain when you're triggered to do what matters.

You also need the skills to imagine your many possible futures.

To play bigger games in all your moments of choice.

> I'VE NEVER HEARD ANYONE LOOK BACK ON
> THEIR LIFE AND REGRET HOW THEY FELT.
> BUT LOTS OF PEOPLE RETROSPECTIVELY
> REGRET CHOICES THEY MADE THAT DIDN'T
> ALIGN WITH WHAT MATTERED MOST.

YOU ARE ALWAYS CHOOSING

What's happening when there is *no obvious trigger* to flag a moment of choice? Up until this point you've been focused on choices you make when you're triggered. Yet, whether you realize it or not, you're *always* choosing. In fact, even choosing *not* to optimize a moment of choice is a choice.

For example, right now in this presumably emotionally 'quiet' moment, you are choosing ... to continue reading, or to put the book down. Depending on whether you're listening for a signal or distracted by unhelpful noise, you'll move away from or toward what matters most to you. If you're not listening carefully, you'll respond to whatever urge is the loudest. Even when more is possible.

The first expert-player skill for playing full out depends on noticing all potential moments of choice, and then choosing the ones you want to optimize. You already have the technology to do this in obvious moments of choice, but it's so easy to miss the less palpable moments of choice. In quieter emotional waters you're less likely to notice the siren song of the emotional matrix that makes it that much easier to cruise along in autopilot, preserving maximum safety, certainty, coherence, comfort, and pleasure. In these less noisy moments of choice, it's a feat of even more herculean proportions to hear the signal through the noise.

> THE SIREN SONG OF THE EMOTIONAL MATRIX
> MAKES IT EASIER TO CRUISE ALONG IN AUTOPILOT,
> PRESERVING MAXIMUM SAFETY, CERTAINTY,
> COHERENCE, COMFORT, AND PLEASURE. IN THESE
> LESS NOISY MOMENTS OF CHOICE, IT'S A FEAT
> OF EVEN MORE HERCULEAN PROPORTIONS TO
> HEAR THE SIGNAL THROUGH THE NOISE.

The second expert-level skill is learning to stretch your imagination. To play these bigger infinite games, you need to evolve your capacity for imagining beyond overriding unhelpful defaulting. You need to expand your imagination to include all of what's possible.

You can catch a glimpse of this just by imagining what would shift about your actions if you were to approach each moment with curiosity about what you could create. You might ask yourself, *if there were no limitations, and I could design my fantasy life/day/presentation/interaction/ next five minutes, what would I do differently?*

You won't usually achieve this level of creativity because unless you've already gamified what you are doing or have prompts in your routines as reminders, you don't naturally stretch toward this level of optimization.

This is why you can move through life missing how many opportunities you have to shape all of what's possible and meaningful to you. You'll be distracted by the noise of unhelpful defaults and the patterns you've accepted as Reality.

Why?

Because it *feels* true.

This is how we stay unwittingly trapped in the emotional matrix.

This is not some woo woo mumbo jumbo. Because of the tendency to default, most people are so much more capable than they realize. I am talking next-level choice-making here, where you evolve how you're playing in life to tap into what might *feel* impossible.

You don't need a tsunami of emotion or a triggering sensation, thought, urge, or feeling to cue a moment of choice. You just have to get good at recognizing the choices in front of you and designing your actions in sync with your values. Developing this level of flexibility, intentionality and creativity will jettison you out of amateur-level play.

> ## BECAUSE OF THE TENDENCY TO DEFAULT, MOST PEOPLE ARE SO MUCH MORE CAPABLE THAN THEY REALIZE.

Lest I paint too rosy a picture, let me offer the following disclaimer. Optimizing *every* moment of choice is not realistic. (Trust me, I've attempted this fool's errand.) Not only are your defaults sometimes helpful (you still need to survive), your mind and body will need rest from the constant inquiry it takes. A certain amount of rest and recovery happens when you're able to cruise along in autopilot. You won't be able to thrive if you attempt designing what matters most some 35,000 times a day.

What I am suggesting is that recognizing each moment of choice as an *opportunity* allows you to then discern which ones you want to harness.

To play or not to play, that is the question.

'NOT CHOOSING IS A CHOICE'

'Danielle' sat in the chair across from me looking sad and wistful. 'I know it isn't logical,' she said, 'but it just feels like something is still wrong, and I am pretty sure that what's wrong is *me*.'

Danielle unexpectedly lost her mother when she was a teenager, and the unprocessed trauma she carried for over 20 years had sent all her defaults into overdrive. She was always scanning for evidence that bad things were happening (negativity bias), for evidence of what she already believed (confirmation bias), and feelings of hopelessness and helplessness were having a party with her emotional reasoning bias, offering themselves as proof of just how dire things were.

Through trauma processing and grief work Danielle had softened the way she was relating to her long-standing and automatic thoughts about being 'defective' and a 'failure'. But she still had a well-rehearsed unhelpful default pattern of avoiding the discomfort of taking risks and tackling new challenges. This left her struggling with executing her VBAs of searching for work that would move her toward her value of Helping.

ME: Let's get really curious about what's happening here. It sounds like you are clear on what matters to you – and you've identified the VBAs you want to take to explore a new career path that fulfills on your core value of Helping. And you've broken down how to take VBA into specific steps you know how to take?

DANIELLE: Yes.

ME: So, what do you think is getting in the way?

DANIELLE: Maybe I just don't have the discipline.

ME: Interesting thought. I've seen you be very disciplined in other areas of your life, with exercise and nutrition for example.

DANIELLE: Yes, that's true. I don't know why I'm not motivated with this.

ME: Let's be curious about the context for you. Tell me more about what happens when you think about doing your VBAs.

DANIELLE: I can't make sense of it. Even though I know why it matters, and how to take all the steps that will move me toward a more inspiring job that helps people, and even though I'm not really triggered, I still can't seem to motivate myself.

ME: You're struggling to tap the willingness to do them?

DANIELLE: Right ...

ME: What do you think you're waiting for?

DANIELLE: ... to feel ready?

ME: Ahhh. That's a good set up, isn't it? Can you identify which of the 3Bs is telling you that you need to *feel ready* to do your VBAs?

DANIELLE: That I need to feel like I'm ready would be ... is that emotional reasoning?

ME: Well done. It's as if you're waiting for the job to feel more like your favorite ice cream just as it gets a little melty.

DANIELLE: Haha. Right! Or even just any ice cream.

ME: Haha. Fair enough. So in this case, your avoidance comes from the discomfort of not feeling ready? And a bias that you must feel ready to get started?

DANIELLE: I think so, and I know this is a pattern with me, where I wait to 'feel like' doing these things. I do that all the time, actually. I'm better now when I get really triggered. But day to day, when things are calm, instead of moving toward my values, I'll hang out on the couch, go to the gym, or scroll IG.

ME: And since you've rehearsed this pattern for a while, it feels like the easier and more familiar path. It's like you're buying into the idea that what you feel is all there is, so nothing else seems possible.

DANIELLE: Yes ... So what do I do?

ME: You tell me ... what would you have to do differently to move toward your value of work that helps people?

DANIELLE: I'd have to see the moment of choice?

ME: Okay, and how would you know you have a moment of choice?

DANIELLE: Hmmmm. I think I don't know how to see those moments when it doesn't feel like much is at stake.

ME: Ah. And I understand that's how it feels, but do you realize you're actually already making choices in these moments?

DANIELLE: What do you mean?

ME: It sounds like in these moments when you think you're just not choosing what matters, you're actually already choosing *not* to do what matters.

DANIELLE: Oh wow. I've never thought of it that way. So when I don't choose to do what matters, I'm making a choice. Choosing *not* to do my VBAs is a choice.

ME: Right ... Exactly. And using a WTF? inquiry, this choice is moving you away from what matters.

DANIELLE: Right.

ME: So you have a dilemma. I know you really care about work that helps people. And whatever you choose to do, you're going to have unwanted feelings. But you can choose whether you want the kind of pain that goes with avoiding discomfort in the short term and staying disconnected from what you find meaningful, or the kind of pain that naturally comes from doing the hard things that lead you to what matters.

DANIELLE: Wow. Yeah, I'd rather have the pain that goes with doing what matters.

ME: Okay. What's happening for you emotionally right now?

DANIELLE: I suddenly feel more motivated because I realize I am missing out on all these moments I could actually be in action.

This was a turning point for Danielle. She had been waiting to 'feel ready.' In the absence of unwanted emotional STUF, she hadn't put it together that waiting to feel ready was actually a choice *not* to do what mattered. Recognizing and understanding this ineffective pattern opened up the willingness to make more powerful values-based moves. Over the next few weeks she was able to lean into the discomfort of taking risks and put herself in front of people she could partner with toward her value of Helping.

LIVING BY DESIGN: PLAYING YOUR WAY TO THE BEST VERSION OF YOURSELF

Like Danielle, you can harness all the opportunities to design your actions to maximize what matters most. To bring this to life we'll use the metaphor of *infinite games*, inspired by author James P. Carse's book *Finite and Infinite Games: A vision of life as play and possibility.*[1] There are two kinds of games you can play in any moment of choice:

Finite games:

#1: They are guided by goals.

#2: As long as you're on the field, the game is in play.

#3: You can play with a specific type and number of players on a specific field within a limited timeframe.

#4: You play in predefined ways that move you toward predefined goals.

#5: You play to win (or lose).

Infinite games:

#1: They are guided by values.

#2: As long as you're alive the game is in play.

#3: You can play with anyone, anywhere, anytime.

#4: You play in any way that moves you toward your values (VBA).

#5: If you're playing, you're winning, regardless of the outcome.

To be clear, there's nothing wrong with playing finite games. Winning, and even losing, a game of soccer, a game of Scrabble, or even employee of the month can still be interesting, satisfying, and great fun. But finite games can be limited in scope, they end, and along the way they don't always connect you to greater meaning of infinite games.

When you regularly play smaller, finite games with your life, you can get lost in a sea of goals, wins, and losses. You can suffer the pain that goes with being disconnected from what matters. And you can miss out on becoming the best possible version of yourself.

WHEN YOU REGULARLY PLAY SMALLER, FINITE
GAMES WITH YOUR LIFE, YOU CAN GET LOST
IN A SEA OF GOALS, WINS, AND LOSSES. YOU
CAN SUFFER THE PAIN THAT GOES WITH
BEING DISCONNECTED FROM WHAT MATTERS.
AND YOU CAN MISS OUT ON BECOMING THE
BEST POSSIBLE VERSION OF YOURSELF.

OPERATING AS A HUMAN 'DOING'

Playing smaller than possible is not surprising given the overly goal-oriented cultures so many of us inhabit. It's easy to become disconnected from the bigger meaning beyond your goals. There's a reason the term 'daily grind' exists: because of the way a lot of people tend to see their lives through a finite lens, often working from an endless to-do list as the endgame. And when the goals become ends in themselves or things get hard, you're more likely to give in, give up, and default to playing finite games.

Inside the grind, days are measured by how many tasks we complete within specific timeframes; for example, hours you've logged at work, dishes you've done, steps you've walked, monthly sales targets you've hit. And even when you accomplish your #goals, sometimes checking them off your list is the only thing that's meaningful. When this goes on long enough, it's a perfect storm for life-interfering anxiety, depression, and stress, if not a full-blown existential crisis.

You can especially see this in the workplace. So often employees are rewarded for achieving specific results and outcomes that are wholly devoid of meaning in themselves. Traditional performance reviews (which are increasingly recognized as less than effective) tend to evaluate people using goal-driven metrics that often have little to do with what really matters toward accomplishing the greater mission of the company. As an employee, you'll either 'fail to meet, meet, or exceed expectations', and you'll be considered for raises and benefits based solely on these metrics that only measure *what* you accomplish, not *why* or *how*.

Given how important connecting to meaning is for wellbeing, this makes sense. And it's the reason many of my clients seek help with burnout and overwhelm from what I call 'death by 1000 goals.' They end up feeling like they're drowning under the weight of being expected to do more, better, with less, in the increasingly volatile, uncertain, complex, and ambiguous (VUCA) world we live in.[2]

This creates a crisis of meaninglessness because all this 'doing-ness' isn't enough for humans. Ultimately, you won't thrive when you operate as a human 'doing.' As a human 'being,' you need the meaning that comes from connecting to the 'why' behind the 'doing.' To thrive, you need more meaning than checking boxes.

Over too much time, accomplishing tasks that aren't linked to some greater purpose will leave you exhausted and disconnected from the meaning that makes things worth doing and life worth living.

> AS A HUMAN 'BEING,' YOU NEED THE MEANING THAT COMES FROM CONNECTING TO THE 'WHY' BEHIND THE 'DOING.' TO THRIVE, YOU NEED MORE MEANING THAN CHECKING BOXES.

You may put in your time and count your rotations, but to what end? Disconnected from meaning, you'll feel like a hamster on a wheel.

Being fully human and the best version of yourself includes embracing and being fully in contact with all the interests, desires, and yearnings that come with being.

This is what gives you the meaning to thrive.

FOR THE LOVE OF THE GAME

In light of this, you might be glad to learn that high emotional efficacy is naturally a game changer. When you can put your values into action in any moment of choice, you automatically shift from playing finite games to playing infinite games.

As the name suggests, infinite games give you unlimited players, places, and ways you can play. Because infinite games are driven by values, they are meaningful to play – no matter the outcome.

This makes values one of the most powerful motivational tools you can wield. Playing infinite games not only helps you optimize meaningful values-based moves, it also has the potential to motivate you to perform at your highest level; for example, connecting with other players, testing your limits, expressing what matters, and actualizing your best possible self. Infinite games expand meaning by creating opportunities to play anytime, anywhere.

> PLAYING INFINITE GAMES NOT ONLY HELPS YOU
> OPTIMIZE MEANINGFUL VALUES-BASED MOVES,
> IT ALSO HAS THE POTENTIAL TO MOTIVATE
> YOU TO PERFORM AT YOUR HIGHEST LEVEL.

In addition to motivation, just like gamifying anything in life, there are other benefits to playing infinite games: they create the conditions to play at your highest level:

- *They give you clear ways to play.* The structure of a game creates a clear way to track your actions toward or away from how you want to show up in a given moment. How flexible, intentional, and creative you are is measured by how skillfully you pivot to what matters most in each moment of choice. In other words, infinite games are played through values-based action.

- *They are unpredictable and challenging, which increases motivation.* You're never sure what will happen. Even when you're clear on the values-based plays you want to make, life can throw a whole heap of VUCA onto the field. All you have control over is how you show up when this happens. The ever-changing, challenging nature of infinite games keeps things really interesting.

- *You're #winning if you play.* With infinite games, there is no losing as in a single finite game. If you're playing, you're expanding meaning in your life – even when you're momentarily 'losing' to an unhelpful default urge or an undesirable result in a particular moment of choice. In this way, as long as you're playing you're winning, because infinite games are meaningful just to play – no matter the outcome.

- *They make you more resilient.* Because you will expect a game to be challenging (overriding unhelpful urges and staying focused on what matters), framing your VBA plays this way can help you tap even more willingness to keep going. You'll develop the tolerance to keep playing, even when it's hard.

- *They never end.* Unlike so many things in life, as long as you're breathing, your infinite games are always available. (This makes both pain and infinite games as certain as death and taxes.) At times you may have different levels of constraint or resources, access to different players, or different interests, desires, or yearnings. But even if all you have is your imagination, you can still play.

> ... AS LONG AS YOU'RE PLAYING YOU'RE WINNING,
> BECAUSE INFINITE GAMES ARE MEANINGFUL
> JUST TO PLAY – NO MATTER THE OUTCOME.

People who live their lives stretching for what else is possible already understand this. They play at the edges of discomfort and growth. They are the most vital, fulfilled, flourishing people you'll encounter, even when/if they don't reach all their goals; for example, lots of money, achievements, power, or social standing. The people living their best lives are those who are so connected to what they find meaningful that doing even the most mundane or difficult tasks is imbued with a sense of purpose.

In this way, playing infinite games is akin to values-based action on steroids. You'll have to tune out the emotional static from your 3Bs which will almost never support a purposeful jaunt toward any unknown destination unless it's to avoid a threat. The outcomes are measured in whether you're playing. As you approach each moment of choice with curiosity you can rate your play by asking, are you making expert-level values-based moves toward what matters most in context?

This is the key to unlocking your full potential and the future you want to live into.

EMBRACING THE PAIN OF THE GAME

The example of my physical therapy exercises as a values-based action is taken from the larger infinite game of Health I play. As with all infinite games, you never 'arrive' or finish. I'll never be as strong as when I was younger, and the limits from my structural injuries will probably always prevent the vigorous exercising my 'past self' enjoyed. In time, I'll naturally have less overall health as I make my way to shedding this mortal coil. I have no control over the ultimate ending.

So, you may wonder, why bother with this infinite game of Health, much less *any* infinite games when ideal outcomes are unlikely or limited, and death is the certain end? It would be easier to avoid the uncomfortable STUF that comes up when I am reminded of things I can't do anymore whenever I exercise.

I could instead eat more foods that bring me immediate short-term pleasure. I could end the monotonous torture of PT. I could avoid the negative thoughts that show up when I force-hydrate myself, like:

Blech … is this even going to make a difference?

… aren't you just setting yourself up for disappointment?

… you might as well pack it in: your fitness has been canceled.

I could also avoid getting to bed for my eight hours of sleep and instead get lost in endless other more interesting activities.

Here's why I keep playing: I prefer the pain that comes with the game, rather than the suffering that comes from avoiding what matters most. This is 'winning' in any infinite game: embracing the pain and playing full out in every possible moment of choice. You play your way to the best version of yourself.

> THIS IS 'WINNING' IN ANY INFINITE GAME: EMBRACING THE PAIN AND PLAYING FULL OUT IN EVERY POSSIBLE MOMENT OF CHOICE. YOU PLAY YOUR WAY TO THE BEST VERSION OF YOURSELF.

When I get triggered by the mere thought of PT, I'll tune into the emotional STUF that comes up and surf through each part. Then if I'm still triggered, or even in more neutral moments of choice, I'll increase my willingness to play by linking the aversive PT exercises back to why they matter. To make values-based moves on days I'm sore or lethargic I'll remind myself that *research shows that exercise is important for cognitive health as we age.* And that's meaningful because I prefer to stay lucid as long as possible.

Gamifying these exercises is the only reason I ever hit my target number of bridges and clamshells. They start to symbolize beach days in tropical parts of the world, paddle boarding at the marina, and seeing natural wonders of the world on my bucket list, as well as overall quality of life into my older age. Gamifying my actions also naturally makes me curious to see what happens if I keep playing, in every possible way, at every possible moment I choose.

CURIOSITY CRUSHES THE EMOTIONAL MATRIX

You've already been practicing curiosity to slow down unhelpful default reactions and make values-based moves when you're triggered. Now you can also use it to expand your creativity to play infinite games.

From past practice you know that when you get triggered, being curious can make the difference between harnessing an opportunity and unhelpful defaulting. This is even more true when there doesn't seem to be an obvious moment of choice.

While you know curiosity is the antidote to unhelpful default reactivity, here's what you might not yet know about this superpower. Being curious is not just about asking questions (for example, *how do I want to show up in this moment?*), but also about dropping judgments, challenging preconceived notions, and expanding your perspective.

> BEING CURIOUS IS NOT JUST ABOUT ASKING
> QUESTIONS (FOR EXAMPLE, *HOW DO I WANT TO
> SHOW UP IN THIS MOMENT?*), BUT ALSO ABOUT
> DROPPING JUDGMENTS, CHALLENGING PRECONCEIVED
> NOTIONS, AND EXPANDING YOUR PERSPECTIVE.

This means, instead of defaulting to focusing on avoiding what you don't want, you can learn to focus on what else there could be. Bringing a curious mindset will keep you moving beyond what you feel to what else you can imagine. It makes space for the deeper listening you need to prioritize which infinite games you want to play in any moment.

As a simple example, let's say I want to play an infinite game of Health. And let's say I have my VBAs planned for that day; for example, eating lots of leafy greens, hydrating, and an evening workout of sweating, stretching and, of course, PT.

But then let's also say I get a text from a good friend which says, 'let's take an evening walk to watch the sunset and enjoy some homemade ice cream.' Since I also have an infinite game of Play, I now have another choice. Both Health and Play are compelling options. This is a case for curiosity.

I might first notice that the sunset meet up is immediately more appealing and that my first urge is to accept the invite without even considering my infinite game of Health. But before rejecting it outright, my question might be, is there a way to do both? And I may determine that doing both is not doable if I've been working since 7 a.m. and I only have the energy for one.

Now what? Here's where that deeper listening is helpful. I can drop down and do a Yes/No inquiry. I can ask myself, *do I want to skip the evening workout altogether?* If a 'yes' is what most resonates in my emotional STUF, I might notice a lightness in my body, the thought *I've worked out every night for the past five … I can skip tonight without negative consequences.* I might also notice the urge to finish my work more quickly, and that I feel excited.

Or, if a 'no' is what most resonates in my emotional STUF, I might notice some tension in my forehead and the thought, *you are working so hard to be consistent and you know how hard it is to keep it up if you make exceptions too frequently*, and I might have the urge to stick to the plan – even though it's less appealing – and feel proud of myself.

Or, I could get even more curious and more creative and dig deeper … maybe what's possible is an abbreviated workout as well as the meet up? I could just do a protein shake for dinner to save time, do 15 minutes of cardio and 15 of PT and still make the sunset-ice cream hang.

Again, operating in default mode, I would have just skipped my workout and ended up with the pain of avoiding what mattered most to me that evening. I would have acted to maximize pleasure in the short term. But being a practiced player of infinite games, I'm able to listen deeply to what matters most in context.

This might seem simple, but you'd be surprised how often we miss opportunities to get creative because we think too rigidly and too small. As another example, toward the end of writing this book, I was still really struggling with shoulder pain, and as a result I was overall feeling pretty crappy from not being able to move my body much for the preceding six months.

I knew I still had at least a month of work before the book would be ready for editing and I was eager to complete it and excited to share it. I also knew that until I started moving and exercising again, I wouldn't feel better, and the push to finish could be a miserable slog. Both infinite games – Possibility (the book) and Health – were important to me. I felt stuck because doing either would require all my 'extra' time outside of working with clients. So I did a Yes/No inquiry.

The results surprised me. Most of my life I have been happy to power through, summoning whatever extra time and energy it takes to get a job done well. But when I asked myself, *does it matter most to push through this pain to finish the book?* I noticed a lack of resonance in my emotional STUF. But when I asked myself, *does it matter most to take time off to tend my physical health even if it means delaying the book?* I noticed a resounding 'yes' – my stomach and shoulders relaxed, and I had the thought, *that sounds sooooo good.* I felt relieved and noticed an immediate urge to sit down and make a plan with my physical therapist and to block out times for exercise. With curiosity and deep listening, my most important infinite game had become clear.

While this example is a more straightforward dilemma, there will be times when you're not sure which infinite game to prioritize or where you won't be able to plan your VBAs ahead. Sometimes you'll have to decide in real time what move you want to make based on what matters most. These are opportunities for you to experiment. When you bring a curious mindset to your choices, you'll leverage the full power of intentional, flexible and creative play.

If you get stuck or you just don't see a clear direction, try not to get too precious about it. Flip a coin. If you have time, poll a few friends. Just trying something for a certain period will give you a chance to see if it brings more vitality and meaning to your life. And you can take the learning forward.

REFLECTION: CONSULTING WITH YOUR 'FUTURE SELF'

- Take a moment now to dialogue with a future version of yourself. What games would your future self want you to play now? It might help to pick a specific time in the future to look back from … Imagine what future you would care about one month from now. What about six months? A year? Ten years? Sixty years? Identify at least two infinite games your future self would want you to play now.

- What, if anything, is currently getting in the way of you playing those infinite games? Be specific.

- What specific actions can you take to play as flexibly, intentionally, and creatively as possible? Come up with at least three ideas.

AN INFINITE GAME OF KINDNESS

My client, 'Jerry,' came to me struggling with passive suicidal ideation, binge drinking, and compulsive watching of pornography that helped him avoid unwanted feelings of emptiness. Not surprisingly, these avoidance strategies had not been working for him. He was losing sleep and missing important work deadlines, which led to more feelings of guilt and depression.

On paper his life looked good. He had been to the finest schools, had a supportive, wealthy family, and he had many opportunities to pursue whatever he was interested in, shifting from finance to journalism to finally landing a choice role as a studio executive in the entertainment industry.

Even though Jerry enjoyed his work, he told me that since college, he would hit what he called 'existential shadowlands' where he would begin to question his purpose, as well as the meaning of life more broadly. Often, he would sink into despair that would last for weeks or even months. During these periods, he would isolate, escape into hours of adult website watching, and drink his weight in martinis to try to get rid of his emotional pain.

In the first few months we worked on emotion awareness, emotion surfing, and specific values-based actions he could take in different areas of his life. His thoughts about life not being worth living subsided and he was able to replace binge-drinking and watching pornography with exercise. And, he would use the mindful coping skill of cue-controlled breathing when he needed extra help in moments of choice. Even so, Jerry was still feeling quite a bit of ennui and angst about his future.

ME: So, we could talk more about your symptoms of ennui and angst, or we could go straight to the heart of what's keeping you from connecting to greater meaning and causing these symptoms.

JERRY: I'll choose the latter for 1000. (His sense of humor was charming, and also one of the ways he avoided his unwanted emotional STUF.)

ME: Haha, okay. Let's get even more curious about what matters to you. When you think back over your life, what peak experiences stick out?

JERRY: Hmm. It might sound silly, but the first thing that comes to mind is a card my high school girlfriend made me.

ME: Tell me more ...

JERRY: Well, we broke up the summer before we both went off to college, but even so, the first month of college she sent me a birthday card that was hand-drawn ... (He tears up and pauses.)

ME: Take your time.

JERRY: Okay. She had hand-drawn the sky with the exact position of all the stars at the hour, day, month, and year I was born. And I'll never forget what she had written in the card: 'This will forever be my favorite constellation. I'm lucky the stars aligned so that you were born into the same time as me. Seeing myself through your eyes forever changed me – for the better. I'm eternally grateful you were my first love.'

ME: Wow! She really cared for you. And you really impacted her?

JERRY: Yeah. She was special. That card really meant a lot to me.

ME: Tell me more about why it meant so much.

JERRY: You know, I think growing up, my family was always supportive, but it was always a bit transactional ... my brother and sisters grew up with the sense that we had to live up to certain expectations or else.

ME: Or else, what?

JERRY: The fear was that our parents might withdraw their support, financially and emotionally. And the expectations were often more about our outward image and reputation. Our achievements were more important than anything else.

ME: So you felt they cared more about what you did than who you are?

JERRY: Yes, exactly. And, that card was the first time anyone ever took the time to share what I meant to them, not what I did or who my family was. And it was so unexpected because we had already broken up ... There was no agenda. Just appreciation.

ME: Right, appreciation. And I'm hearing several other things that really mattered to you: generosity, connection, authenticity, spontaneity, intimacy ...

JERRY: And kindness. She was genuinely kind.

ME: Yes. Kindness.

JERRY: And now that I'm thinking about it, I just don't see much kindness in my life, which, let's be honest, is work 24/7 right now. When my business associates and I give each other things it's perfunctory. And the gifts are not usually very thoughtful or personal ... a bottle of champagne or tickets to some concert or show. And the women I've dated and friends I have now seem more interested in what they can get than what they give ... I'm starting to see a pattern here.

ME: What's that?

JERRY: The people in my life now are a lot like my parents.

ME: Yes.

JERRY: And there's just a lack of kindness. I've never received a gift that had as much thoughtfulness since that card.

ME: That really was a peak experience for you. When you put all this together, why do you think kindness is so meaningful to you?

JERRY: Oh I know exactly why. When people are kind, there are no strings attached. It's not a transaction ... you're just showing up a certain way with no expectations about what you'll receive in return.

ME: Got it. That does sound different to any interactions between you and your business associates, friends, or current girlfriend you've described. You often mention your employees obviously ingratiating themselves with you, or you've mentioned your girlfriend buttering you up to get you to buy things she wants or agree to pay for the trips she wants to take.

JERRY: Yeah. When I think about it, I don't really know who in my life is really just kind. Maybe my assistant, but she gets paid to take care of me. Haha.

ME: Right, so it would be harder to experience that as freely chosen rather than transactional. And what you're saying is that what really inspires you is spontaneous, unsolicited, unexpecting, thoughtful interaction, aka kindness?

JERRY: Yeah. I think that's part of the hole I have felt so much of my life. And, why I'm also so bored with people. And why I feel angsty about the future. I don't want to live the rest of my life moving from transaction to transaction.

ME: Yeah, that doesn't sound inspiring at all. I notice your energy drops when you say that.

JERRY: So doc, how do I change this?

ME: You tell me ... how would you play an infinite game of Kindness?

JERRY: Ha, there you go with the trick questions!

ME: Haha ... yeah, I'm totally tricking you into creating a more meaningful life for yourself. How do you think you can bring more kindness into your life?

JERRY: So, based on what we've talked about, all I have control over is what I do and how I show up.

ME: Well done!

JERRY: So, for starters, I might be able to choose people who are naturally kind to be my inner circle.

ME: So you'd pay attention to how people show up, and you'd be more discriminating in your friend choices?

JERRY: Yes. And my girlfriend choices. I've been bored and unhappy in this relationship for over a year now. I think I have a story that there's no one out there who could care more about me than what they can get from me.

ME: Ah, so it hasn't felt possible. It feels like what you have is as good as it gets?

JERRY: Exactly. And I have been feeling like I'm just fundamentally broken.

ME: Ah, that's a formidable narrative. That can cause a lot of suffering.

JERRY: I just had another idea.

ME: Let's hear it.

JERRY: I don't actually bring much Kindness to the people in my life. When I'm generous to other people, it's usually because it's what I believe I need to do to live up to expectations, or to keep people in my life.

ME: Ouch.

JERRY: Yes, and it creates deep disappointment and resentment in me. I think it's why I got so depressed.

ME: Makes sense. When you feel hopeless and helpless, it's a recipe for depression. I'm glad you can see that more clearly.

JERRY: It's does help to understand what's been happening.

ME: Yes. So let me ask you another 'trick' question.

JERRY: Uh oh. (Laughing.)

ME: What are a few specific VBAs you can take to play the infinite game of Kindness in your life?

JERRY: Ahhh. Well, I already mentioned changing up my friend group, and my girlfriend.

ME: That's a great start.

JERRY: And I think I could make an effort with my family and my employees. You know, to just take time to either express something more authentic, supportive, and appreciative, or to give things that aren't expected.

ME: That sounds powerful. And as you know, when we play infinite games, we are playing for the love of the game. So you'd be playing because you care about expanding Kindness in your life, no matter the outcome?

JERRY: Right. That will be a big shift from how I grew up and what I know.

ME: Sounds like it. Let's get even more specific. How would things change if you were making values-based moves with Kindness in just one area of your life?

JERRY: Okay. So, with my family, if I just started doing or saying 'kind' things I think they would be a little shocked at first. It would definitely shake up the way we are used to acting with each other. They will probably think I want something from them! Haha.

ME: Maybe so. And, what would it be like to make a consistent effort to be kind with them, even if they were suspicious?

JERRY: I actually think I'd feel really good. I've been so hurt and angry with them. It might sound weird given how much physical and financial support they gave me when I was younger, but the lack of authentic kindness really makes me want to keep my distance.

ME: That doesn't sound weird to me. It makes sense why you have felt angry and hurt when the people you most depend on and who know you the best aren't showing up for unconditional support and kindness.

JERRY: Yeah. Wow. I'm so curious to see how this will land.

ME: Me too. Can you commit to making a list of ideas for how you can express or embody kindness with each member of your family over the next week?

JERRY: Yeah, but do I need to wait to do the VBAs?

ME: Absolutely not – if you feel inspired, go for it. But let's get even more clear about your commitment to practice. Would you be willing to commit to doing at least one act of kindness for each person before our next session?

JERRY: I can do that.

ME: Okay, great. Now let's also predict what, if any, obstacles might show up and get in the way of you playing the infinite game of Kindness this week.

JERRY: Hmm. I guess if someone just reacts really weird.

ME: What would you do then?

JERRY: The urge would be to pull back.

ME: Yeah. Understandable. And what will you do if that urge shows up?

JERRY: Well, I'm playing this game of Kindness for the love of the game, right?

ME: That's the idea.

JERRY: So, I could just surf through the discomfort. Maybe pause. Maybe try again the next time.

ME: That sounds good. And you won't decide that you lost the game and quit because with infinite games, they never end. You have infinite opportunities to keep playing.

JERRY: Right!

ME: Great. So, check in with yourself and tell me what you notice emotionally in this moment.

JERRY: I notice more energy in my body. And, curiosity. Like I'm genuinely curious about what it will be like to start being kind to my family, even unprompted. Haha. I'm already thinking about what I want to do first.

ME: Great.

JERRY: And I also feel a bit more free.

ME: What do you mean?

JERRY: I just feel relieved that I don't have to plan my actions based on other people's reactions – especially my family.

ME: Oh, wow. That does sound freeing. You sound excited. Much less bored. Much less angsty.

JERRY: Yeah, haha. I actually am. I would have never guessed something as simple as being kind could shake me out of that?!

ME: That's the magic of playing infinite games. They keep things interesting, challenging, and meaningful.

INFINITE GAMES ACTION PLAN

As with values-based action, you'll want to clarify your infinite games ahead of time by creating an action plan and using experiential practice to learn to play at an expert level.

Start by picking one of your infinite games and brainstorm possible VBAs for playing. Don't be discouraged if at first you don't have a clear direction, especially if you're entering unchartered territory for yourself. If it helps you can start with broader VBAs, and then get more specific.

HOW I CAN I PLAY MY INFINITE GAME OF: *Creativity*

- *Morning Pages for 15 minutes each day*
- *Connect with one other creative or artistic person each week to discuss ideas and projects*
- *Identify priority creative projects for the next month, quarter, year*
- *Sign up for a class in creative writing*
- *Share one piece of art I find inspiring with someone once a week*
- *Write a weekly letter to my creative self for motivation, reminding myself why I care about bringing my ideas into the world*
- *Write one poem a week and share it with a friend, even if my mind tells me it's crap*

- *Find one 'out of the box' solution to something our team at work could do differently*
- *Find a blog on creativity to follow*

Use the following template to implement a daily infinite game action plan using your specific VBAs. This template not only steps you through identifying infinite games and values-based actions, but also helps you anticipate what you can do when you encounter unwanted emotional STUF, and remember why you're willing to take VBA anyway.

REFLECTION: CREATING YOUR INFINITE GAMES ACTION PLAN

Take your time to come up with VBAs that are as flexible, intentional, and creative as possible across all the domains of your life. Below are some common life domains to get you started.

Use your notebook to complete this exercise.

RELATIONSHIPS

Infinite game:

Values-based actions (VBAs) I want to take:

Emotional STUF I predict will show up before and/or while I'm doing VBA:

Why I want to play anyway:

WORK

Infinite game:

Values-based actions (VBAs) I want to take:

Emotional STUF I predict will show up before and/or while I'm doing VBA:

Why I want to play anyway:

HEALTH

Infinite game:

Values-based actions (VBAs) I want to take:

Emotional STUF I predict will show up before and/or while I'm doing VBA:

Why I want to play anyway:

COMMUNITY

Infinite game:

Values-based actions (VBAs) I want to take:

Emotional STUF I predict will show up before and/or while I'm doing VBA:

Why I want to play anyway:

RECREATION

Infinite game:

Values-based actions (VBAs) I want to take:

Emotional STUF I predict will show up before and/or while I'm doing VBA:

Why I want to play anyway:

OTHER

Infinite game:

Values-based actions (VBAs) I want to take:

Emotional STUF I predict will show up before and/or while I'm doing VBA:

Why I want to play anyway:

If you want to take your infinite games planning to the next level, you can also set aside a specific time each day to generate specific VBAs, anticipate obstacles, and review the skills you can use to navigate them. Then, at the end of the day, you can set aside time to track your results, what happened with each attempt to take VBA, and carry your learning forward. This practice will give you the regular feedback you need to get to an expert level of play.

INFINITE GAMES DAILY ACTION PLAN
DATE: 11/7/2021

Morning prompts

My infinite game: Adventure

Three specific VBAs I could take today:

Reach out to new neighbor about taking a walk at sunset

Hike the trail near the reservoir

Get on a dating app

When things feel difficult, I'll use the following emotion efficacy skills to stay connected to what matters:

Surf the emotion wave if I'm not able to connect with anyone today

Use the coping thought, 'Just because there's a pandemic doesn't mean adventure is cancelled' if I notice a thought like 'This pandemic will never end'

If I get triggered on the app, I can surf and then practice cue-controlled breathing to come back to doing at least 10 minutes of scrolling

Evening prompts

Triggers or obstacles that showed up when I did my VBAs:

My neighbor wasn't available for a hike, and I felt disappointed

My ankle was so sore that I didn't feel like hiking

I got discouraged looking at profiles on the dating app

How I responded to them:

I practiced surfing the emotion wave of disappointment and then went for a hike by myself

I reminded myself why hiking mattered to me when I noticed the urge to curl up on the couch and scroll social media instead

I added some perspective taking by reminding myself that my feelings aren't necessarily predictive of whether I'll meet someone, and committed to using the dating app for at least 15 minutes

What's one thing I could have done better or one thing I learned today?

I can work on radical acceptance that life is uncertain.
I could also take perspective and see uncertainty as a form of Adventure.

Out of regular infinite games practice, my clients have been able to make all kinds of small and large meaningful moves:

- To play her infinite games of Art and Narratives, my client 'Sara' negotiated with a job title change with her boss to better align with what mattered to her. Her boss agreed and changed it from 'web designer and content writer' to 'visual storyteller.' This led to several new opportunities within the company, as people began to see Sara's talent inside a broader vision.

- Through careful tracking with the daily action plan, my client 'Li' discovered his ennui was a failure to fully play his infinite game of Adventure. Within a few months of realizing this, he sold all his shares in his start-up company to travel around the world. Then, with connections he built traveling, he started an adventure blog, so he could keep traveling and play his infinite game on an even bigger level.

- To expand both of her infinite games of Social Justice and Stability, my client 'Abigail' convinced a university to fund research grants for people willing to work with specific low-income communities after graduation as a way to fund her way through law school, while also supporting her two young children.

- Just after her mother was given four to six months to live, my client 'Lily' created an infinite game in her domain of Family. By playing full out, she was able to continue working while moving home to support and grieve with her family, and to also preserve her mother's memory through structured video interviews and cataloguing old photos.

OPTIMIZING YOUR PERFORMANCE

Playing infinite games can also be enhanced through experiential practice, especially when you've chosen an expert level of challenge. Optimizing your play in this case means executing your values-based actions with as much mastery as possible. It's just one small step further from doing experiential VBA practice.

Experiential practice for infinite games is similar to the performance training used in sports psychology and performance coaching. As you already know, rehearsing visualization in an activated state will create new emotional networks, making it easier for you to stay focused on the task at hand. And, using your imagination to rehearse new values-based moves when you want to perform at a high level will help you stay present and focused under intense stress or distress IRL.

To prepare, you'll want to anticipate any likely obstacles and visualize your actions in advance. This can help you perform at a higher level and play your infinite games as powerfully as possible.[3,4] The only difference from the VBA experiential structure is that instead of practicing with a recurring trigger scene, you're looking for opportunities that you anticipate could be challenging and require a higher level of mastery, even if you're not triggered.

For example, my clients will often use experiential practice to optimize their performance when they're preparing for anything stressful, from a brave conversation with a friend to a high-stakes performance in front of their boss or large groups of people:

- A client who had an infinite game of Autonomy had been taking benzodiazepines (fast-acting anti-anxiety medication) for several years anytime she had to speak in public – at work or in her personal life. In the past, every time she would get up to speak in front of people, she would become overwhelmed by all the unwanted emotional STUF that showed up, and she would have to find a way to excuse herself for fear of looking 'foolish.' Now, after depending on these drugs to perform, she was aware they were moving her away from Autonomy. By doing the experiential practice and using emotion surfing, followed by cue-controlled breathing, to regulate her emotions during a presentation, and a willingness to experiment IRL, she was able to taper off the anxiety medication over just a few weeks and give a presentation with only moderate anxiety.

- A client who was a performer and had an infinite game of Self-expression was very comfortable performing in large stadiums but felt inhibited and shy performing for smaller audiences. He would get overwhelmed by the up close and personal format of these shows. All his emotional STUF would ramp up, and even though he could perform up to others' expectations, he would make mistakes that were noticeable to him, and that would then retrigger him. Sometimes he was so activated, he couldn't enjoy performing in these intimate venues at all. Using emotional activation with experiential practice, visualizing the scene, emotion surfing, and then rehearsing his performance using his imagination for 20 minutes a day for the two weeks before a show, he not only flawlessly executed several shows in smaller private venues, he had fun doing it. He even came up with new ideas about how he wanted to perform during the experiential practice.

- A client who was a member of a professional athletic team and had an infinite game of Excellence was experiencing crippling anxiety after witnessing the death of a close friend, which was interfering with their performance. Since then, when his coach would put him in the game, he became overwhelmed by pressure to perform, sometimes so intensely that he would completely lose focus and get taken out of the game. Very quickly, he became too anxious to play at all and had to sit out. By using experiential practice and visualizing all the unwanted emotional STUF that would come up, and surfing through the waves of anxiety, he became able to tolerate the noise and stimulation. In a few weeks he was back in the game – literally. And, he even took his infinite game of Excellence to the next level by incorporating the experiential practice into all his game prep. To optimize performance, he began using the practice to prepare for a myriad of anticipated triggers and obstacles, using this experiential practice to rehearse the actions he wanted to take in those moments. This led to his best stats in any season, but he told me what mattered more was the meaning that came from knowing that he was playing full out.

WHAT YOU CHOOSE IS WHAT ELSE THERE IS

As you come to the close of this book, you may have a deeper understanding of how you can tap new levels of potential when you're more skillful with your emotions. Throughout the book you've seen what's possible when what you feel is not all there is. When you expand your imagination you develop a higher level of willingness to tolerate pain for the sake of what really matters.

As you come to the end of this book, you can hopefully see your best possible life comes from what you choose. Even more than what you feel, the infinite possibilities come from what you choose. What you choose is what else there is – in any moment and for the future you're living into.

> EVEN MORE THAN WHAT YOU FEEL,
> THE INFINITE POSSIBILITIES COME FROM
> WHAT YOU CHOOSE. WHAT YOU CHOOSE IS
> WHAT ELSE THERE IS - IN ANY MOMENT AND
> FOR THE FUTURE YOU'RE LIVING INTO.

So now what? Take some time *right now* to make some commitments to playing infinite games while you have momentum. Here are some things to keep in mind as you make your future game plan:

- *Bring a curious mindset:* Cultivate this mindset so you're not as vulnerable to unhelpful defaulting. Not assuming you already know everything will naturally open up opportunities to see things differently, be more creative, and harness all of what's possible. When you get curious, you can see any moments of choice as opportunities that can be harnessed for valuing.

- *Take risks:* Do the experiential practices *and* practice IRL. If you don't stretch, you can't expect to grow. Growth requires trying new things, taking chances, getting feedback, falling down, refining, and trying again. Learning that something doesn't work can be just as valuable as learning that it does. Choose the kind of pain you're having wisely.

- *Ask for support:* At times, we all need people to be our thought partners, cheerleaders, and shoulders to cry on. Sometimes we also need the help of professionals to navigate complex and unhelpful patterns we can get stuck in. Get to know the edges of how much you can stretch on your own, and when and where you need someone to lean in to. Remember, even when it doesn't feel like it, we are all in this together.

- *Use your powers for good, and have fun:* By gamifying how you live – especially doing hard things – everything becomes more fun and vastly more meaningful. Applying the technology of flexible, intentional, and creative action, not only can you design a best life, but if we all do this together, we can design a 'best world.' A collective infinite game, where all our moments of choice add up, and we do what matters most for us all. That's a whole lot of values-based action. And a future with prosocial evolution depends on this level of play.

> BY GAMIFYING HOW YOU LIVE - ESPECIALLY DOING HARD THINGS - EVERYTHING BECOMES MORE FUN AND VASTLY MORE MEANINGFUL.

THE INFINITE GAMES OBSTACLE COURSE

Playing infinite games is a lifelong adventure. Here are some common obstacles that can get in the way:

- *You don't want to stretch for what matters in every moment.* At this point it would be understandable if you're wondering, *can I really do this all the time? And do I even want to?* The answer is: whatever works for you. That's the beauty of taking the red pill. You don't have to be an emotional efficacy warrior all the time. You know what's possible, and you get to choose when to harness your moments of choice. Nothing in this book is prescriptive. And you don't have to play infinite games in every moment of every day. In fact, there may be times when what matters most is not stretching for all of what's possible. If you're feeling sick, maybe what you care most about is keeping some food down until you recover.

Or if after a disappointment with a friend you're not ready to spring back into playing your infinite game of Relationships, you can choose to play another game, or no game at all, if it works for you. Or, if you issue a snarky response to a coworker in a moment of irritability when what matters most is being Respectful, you might choose to cut yourself some slack. Sometimes, you might even choose to cruise through your day in reactive emotional default mode and accept not showing up as the best version of yourself. What's important is that you know you have a choice and you know when you're choosing.

- *As with your values, you might find yourself playing an infinite game that just doesn't fit.* Throughout your life, what matters most to you can change significantly, and even more in different contexts. I cared a lot more about Productivity when I was in my 20s, and have cared less about that value with every decade that has passed. That means I prioritize other things now, like my Health and Relationships. If I were still playing the infinite game of Productivity at the same level, I would likely notice that I didn't feel as motivated, and my willingness would be harder to tap. If you are feeling a lack of vitality with any of your infinite games, stop and get curious about whether it's a game that 'present-day you' wants to play. It may be time to shift your efforts – maybe your VBAs aren't effectively moving you in that direction; for example, you are throwing dinner parties toward your game of Connection, but no one is coming and it's time to rethink your VBAs. Or, maybe it could be time to drop that particular game altogether and find infinite games that matter more to you now.

- *You lack the structure and support you need to stay flexible, intentional, and creative.* There's no right or wrong way to approach infinite games. But most people I know benefit from having some sort of regular feedback or accountability. This can come from a variety of places: a therapist, a coach, a mastermind, a regular friend meeting, or an accountability partner. In addition to having some sort of partnership, setting aside regular time to track how you're playing your various infinite games can be helpful. Many times I notice that I 'feel' like I'm playing a certain game, but when I sit down to take stock of my actual moves I'm surprised by how infrequent my VBAs are. Or you might get more curious and look for other creative ways for you to track your play or set up a system of feedback.

INFINITE GAMES EXPERIENTIAL PRACTICE

To practice infinite games, you can use the following script, and you can also access a guided experiential practice at www.drapriliawest.com/practice.

SET UP

Find a private, quiet place and get into a comfortable position where you're likely to stay alert. Close your eyes or find a single spot in front of you to focus on by just softening your gaze.

SELECT AN INFINITE GAME AND AN ANTICIPATED OPPORTUNITY

Choose an opportunity to play your selected infinite game and a specific scene you want to play in.

SELECT VBA(S)

Pick at least one values-based action that will move you toward what matters most in your chosen scene.

ACTIVATE EMOTION

Set your performance scene by imagining it as a movie and describe what you notice as if it's happening in real time, including:

- where you are
- what time it is
- who you are with.

Start at the beginning of the scene, and move through it, frame by frame.

Describe anything you are seeing, hearing, touching, tasting and otherwise doing in as much detail as possible.

EMOTION SURFING

When you encounter any unwanted emotional STUF, surf your emotion wave by bringing an intention of curiosity to hanging out with each part of your emotional 'STUF':

(Sensations) Scan your body from head to toe for any sensations that stand out to you:

- Notice their size and shape.
- Notice whether they're moving or staying the same.
- Notice any tension in the sensation.
- Notice if there's any temperature.

Bring an intention of allowing the physical experiences that go with sensations. Imagine making space for them, or welcoming them to be there and do whatever they want to do. Be curious about how they behave when you are just watching them.

(Thoughts) Shift your attention from sensations to noticing thoughts for at least two minutes:

- When a thought shows up, say to yourself 'there's a thought' and then let the thought go.

- Refocus on your breath as a way to place a pause between thoughts.
- And then watch for the next thought to show up, and repeat.

(Urges) Shift to watching any urges for two minutes:

- When you notice one, get curious about how intense the urge is: low, medium, high?
- Notice what it's like to just sit with the impulse to do something or not do something.
- Rate the discomfort on a scale of 1 to 10, with 1 being as relaxed as you can imagine, and 10 the most uncomfortable you can imagine.
- Notice if the urge changes in intensity as you sit with it.

(Feelings)

- Label each feeling.
- Validate and welcome the feelings, saying something like: *It makes sense I'm feeling* [insert label]. Or, *it's okay for the feeling of* [insert label] *to be here.*
- Get curious about whether there are any other feelings, underneath the first feelings you noticed.

MINDFUL COPING

As needed, practice your relaxation skill(s) for two minutes to downshift your activation level by either rehearsing them or visualizing doing them. If helpful, set a time for one minute if you need a prompt to switch skills.

VALUES-BASED ACTION

Go to the exact 'frames' that are high stakes moments of choice – where you especially want to take values-based action.

Visualize in as much detail as possible doing your values-based action(s) using emotion surfing or mindful coping as needed. Describe your actions and experience to yourself frame by frame:

- What would you or an outside observer see you doing?
- How would it be in your body to do this values-based action? Notice and allow any sensations.
- What kinds of thoughts would show up? Practice letting them go.
- What other urge or urges show up as you take values-based action? Notice what it's like just sitting with them.
- Notice any feelings might you have and just allow them, or validate them.

Repeat the VBA sequence twice.

REFLECT

To wrap up the experiential practice, take a few moments to reflect using the following prompts:

- Did anything surprise you?
- What, if anything, was challenging?
- What did you learn?
- Write down anything else you want to remember.

CHAPTER 10 CHALLENGES

- To further clarify infinite games you'd like to play, imagine if you had no fear or aversion to discomfort; what might you be doing differently in your life right now? (For example, leaving a dead-end job or stopping the use of junk food, drugs, or alcohol to self-soothe.) Then identify what value you'd be moving toward with each change you'd make.

- Using one of your core values, take a moment now to create an infinite game playlist using the prompt: *How can I move toward playing my infinite game of:* _____? Then break it down using the daily infinite games action plan.

- Use the daily intentionality practice to create an infinite games plan for at least one day this week. (If you're struggling to figure out which infinite games to play, use the Yes/No inquiry.)

- Try pivoting to curiosity in a moment of choice that is neutral or pleasant, and notice if it changes what you do next.

- Pick a situation where you care about how you perform; for example, a work task, a social event, or even a personal task. Use the experiential to practice how you want to show up.

- Review the learnings from each of the chapters and make a list of what you want to remember going forward.

- To lock in the learning, share with someone what you've learned about infinite games and about one infinite game you have committed to playing.

CHAPTER 10 LEARNINGS

- You are always choosing; even not choosing is a choice.

- It can be harder to see your moments of choice in quieter moments of choice.

- You can play infinite games in everyday life, not just in moments when you're triggered.

- Infinite games are motivating because they give you clear ways to play, they are unpredictable and challenging, there's no winning or losing, they build resilience, and they never end.

- Finite games are played to win; infinite games are meaningful to play, regardless of the outcome.

- Playing infinite games is the apex of living life by design.

- Bringing curiosity to every moment of choice ignites intentionality, flexibility, and creativity.

- Your daily action plan allows you to expand your infinite games every day, and to incorporate what you learn so you can level up your play.

- Infinite games experiential practice leverages emotional activation and visualization to improve execution in anticipated performance situations.

- So much more is possible when you realize that what you feel is not all there is.

AFTERWORD

Speaking of moments of choice, this book has been a real journey for me. It will probably not surprise you to learn that how much more is possible – for me, for you, for all of us – has always been a huge point of pain in my life. And not surprisingly, this pain reflects my value of Possibility and this book is a values-based action towards that infinite game I play.

I started writing just after the COVID-19 pandemic spread to the US, and shortly before a period of intense civil unrest and new levels of uncertainty and challenge for everyone.

We were all in a painful breakup with life as we knew it.

Understandably I felt sad, anxious, and tired. I struggled with the increase of work demands, living alone, far away from family and most of my close friends, and being connected only through a computer screen. It tested all my emotional efficacy superpowers. It required a ton of focus, clarity about what mattered, and willingness to do hard things. If I had relied on what I was feeling, it's unlikely I would have been able to keep going, much less write this book.

I'm grateful I had the skills to choose the pain of doing what mattered most.

I share all this because I believe it's important to say that I'm also walking the path, and I invite you to keep walking it with me. To embrace the reality that so much more is possible beyond the emotional matrix.

To make even a tiny dent in closing that gap between where we are and what could be.

Where what we feel is not all there is.

Where what we choose is what else there is.

To play for our best possible future …

Join me?

GLOSSARY OF NERDY TERMS

Attention-shifting: intentionally and flexibly changing your focus to downregulate emotion.

Avoidance strategies: a behavior, private or public, you do to move away from unwanted emotional experiences.

Biases: predetermined or prejudiced ways of thinking or feeling.

Confirmation bias: the tendency to search for, interpret, favor, and recall information in a way that confirms pre-existing beliefs, even in the absence of supporting evidence.

Coping thoughts: thoughts you create to expand perspective and help you unhook from unhelpful thoughts.

Defaulting: acting on hardwired or learned automatic reactions, regardless of the context (see also Helpful defaulting and Unhelpful defaulting).

Defaults (aka the 3Bs): automatic processes of biases, biology, and beliefs about emotion oriented to help you maximize safety, certainty, coherence, comfort, and pleasure.

Distress tolerance: the ability to lean into discomfort and distress without reacting in unhelpful ways.

Emotion: energy in motion in the form of sensations, thoughts, urges, and feelings; also, your primary motivational system.

Emotion awareness: the ability to non-reactively observe all parts of an emotion: sensations, thoughts, urges, and feelings (STUF).

Emotion efficacy therapy (EET): a brief protocol to help people develop more flexible, intentional, and creative relationships with their emotions; also known as emotional efficacy training. See also Emotional efficacy.

Emotion regulation: the ability to downshift your emotional STUF when you're triggered without reacting in unhelpful ways.

Emotion surfing: tuning in and hanging out with discomfort or distress when you're emotionally triggered (aka, mindful acceptance).

Emotion trigger: a private or observable stimulus that starts and fuels a wave of emotion.

Emotion wave: a swell of emotional energy prompted by a trigger which has distinct lifespan phases, including trigger, peak, and resolution.

Emotional alchemy: the experience of having your emotions change and shift as a result of watching them non-reactively.

Emotional (or experiential) avoidance: anything you do to alter, control, or move away from unwanted emotional STUF; also known as experiential avoidance.

Emotional beliefs: stories and rules a person has about their emotions.

Emotional coping style: a pattern of responding inflexibly to emotion triggers, ranging from over-regulation to under-regulation.

Emotional efficacy: flexibly, intentionally, and creatively maximizing what matters most in context.

Emotional intelligence: skillfulness in navigating personal and interpersonal interactions.

Emotional network: all parts of experience (sensations, thoughts, urges, and feelings) that interact and influence each other.

Emotional reactive default mode: the built-in programming humans have to react to emotion triggers in ways that keep them safe by increasing coherence and reducing uncertainty.

Emotional reasoning: a bias that whatever you feel is true, even in the absence of supporting evidence.

Experiential practice: a skills training technique taken from exposure research that combines emotional activation with imaginal or actual skills practice to accelerate learning, retention, and recall.

Goals: specific markers that help you measure your progress toward a measurable outcome; also, finite games.

Helpful defaulting: acting on hardwired or learned automatic reactions to survive a threat.

Infinite games: metaphor adapted from the work of James Carse; a way of approaching choices and actions involving life as ongoing limitless games you play (not to win) because they are meaningful to you.

Learning history: individual, social, cultural, or environmental events that shape a person's beliefs and behavior.

Mindful coping: coping strategies used following mindful acceptance practice to downshift your emotions when you are triggered to help reconnect with VBA; includes: perspective-taking (coping thoughts and radical acceptance); relaxation (cue-controlled diaphragmatic breathing, progressive muscle relaxation, five senses exercise, and self-soothing); and attention-shifting.

Moment of choice: the space or time between an emotional trigger and how you respond to it, privately or observably.

Negativity bias: the tendency to scan for or focus on potential threats.

Neurodiversity: the unique combination of genetic loading, biological predispositions, and vulnerabilities each human has from birth.

Neuroplasticity: the ability of the brain to reorganize and restructure itself as a result of learning.

Performance optimization: rehearsing specific behaviors using visualization and experiential practice to support skillful execution.

Perspective-taking: flexibly relating to your thoughts as momentary ways of seeing.

Psychological flexibility: the ability to adapt your behavior to your values in context.

Radical acceptance: allowing painful realities you can't control to be what they are; accepting life on life's terms.

Relaxation: strategies for downshifting your emotional activation, including cue-controlled diaphragmatic breathing, progressive muscle relaxation, five senses exercise and self-soothing.

Resilience: the ability to recover effectively from distress or difficulty.

Shoulds: beliefs that are not freely chosen; aka 'old' or 'fake' values.

Unhelpful defaulting: acting on hardwired or learned automatic reactions that move you away from what matters most in context.

Universal hardwiring: the neural architecture and predispositions all humans have from birth.

Values (also Valuing): freely chosen intentions that give you direction and motivation based on your innermost interests, desires, or yearnings.

Values-based action (VBA): specific behaviors that move you in the direction of what matters to you in a given context.

Visualization: rehearsing behaviors using your imagination for anticipated situations; sometimes used in experiential skills practice.

Willingness: how motivated you are to take VBA to play your infinite games while simultaneously experiencing unwanted STUF.

ACRONYMS

3Bs: hardwired and learned processes which influence your relationship with your emotions: biases, biology, beliefs.

STUF: the four ways we experience emotion: sensations, thoughts, urges, and feelings.

WTF? or What's The Function?: an inquiry to help you track whether your behavior is helping you regulate your emotions so you can take VBA, or helping you avoid unwanted emotional STUF.

ENDNOTES

01. YOUR LIFE AS MOMENTS OF CHOICE

1 Kahneman, D. (2011). *Thinking, fast and slow*. Farrar, Straus, and Giroux, p. 20

2 Daum, K. (2012, October 16). 'How to make great decisions (most of the time).' Retrieved from https://www.inc.com/kevin-daum/how-to-make-great-decisions-most-of-the-time.html

3 Kahneman, D. (2011). *Thinking, fast and slow*. Farrar, Straus, and Giroux, p. 20

4 Ibid.

5 Todd, R. M., Cunningham, W. A., Anderson, A. K., & Thompson, E. (2012). 'Affect-biased attention as emotion regulation.' *Trends in Cognitive Sciences*, 16(7), 365–372. https://doi.org/10.1016/j.tics.2012.06.003

6 Gutnik, L. A., Hakimzada, A. F., Yoskowitz, N. A., & Patel V. L. (2006, December). 'The role of emotion in decision-making: a cognitive neuroeconomic approach towards understanding sexual risk behavior.' *J Biomed Inform*. 2006 Dec;39(6):720-36. doi: 10.1016/j.jbi.2006.03.002. Epub 2006 Apr 7. PMID: 16759915.

7 Barrett, L. F. (2017). *How emotions are made: The secret life of the brain*. Houghton Mifflin Harcourt.

8 McKay, M., & West, A. (2016). *Emotion efficacy therapy: A brief, exposure-based treatment for emotion regulation integrating ACT and DBT*. Context Press/New Harbinger Publications.

9 Ibid.

10 Kring, A. M., & Sloan, A. M., (2010). *Emotion Regulation and Psychopathology*. New York, N.Y.: The Guilford Press.

11 Grant, A. M., Curtayne, L., & Burton, G. (2009). 'Executive coaching enhances goal attainment, resilience and workplace well-being: A randomised controlled study.' *The Journal of Positive Psychology*, 4(5), 396–407. https://doi.org/10.1080/17439760902992456

12   Garnefski, N., & Kraaij, V. (2007). 'The Cognitive Emotion Regulation Questionnaire: Psychometric features and prospective relationships with depression and anxiety in adults'. *European Journal of Psychological Assessment*, 23(3), 141–149. https://doi.org/10.1027/1015-5759.23.3.141

13   Carver, C. S., Johnson, S. L. & Joormann, J. (2008). 'Serotonergic function, two-mode models of self-regulation, and vulnerability to depression: What depression has in common with impulsive aggression.' *Psychological Bulletin*, 134(6), 912-943.

14   Kleiman, E. M., Riskind, J. H., Schaefer, K. E., & Weingarden, H. (2012). 'The moderating role of social support on the relationship between impulsivity and suicide risk.' *Crisis: The Journal of Crisis Intervention and Suicide Prevention*, 33(5), 273-279. doi:http://dx.doi.org/10.1027/0227-5910/a000136

15   Eisenberg, N., Fabes, R.A., Guthrie, I. K., & Reiser, M. (2000). 'Dispositional emotionality and regulation: Their role in predicting quality of social functioning.' *Journal of Personality and Social Psychology*, 78(1), 136-157.

16   Richards, J. M., Daughters, S. B., Bornovalova, M. A., Brown, R. A., & Lejuez, C. W. (2011). Substance use disorders. In A. Bernstein, M. J. Zvolensky, & A. A. Vujanovic (Eds.), *Distress tolerance: Theory, research, and clinical applications*. New York, NY: Guilford Press.

17   Caprara, G. V., Di Giunta, L., Eisenberg, N., Gerbino, M., Pastorelli, C., & Tramontano, C. (2008). 'Assessing regulatory emotional self-efficacy in three countries.' *Psychological Assessment*, 20(3), 227.

18   Gratz, K. L., & Roemer, L. 'The relationship between emotion dysregulation and deliberate self-harm among female undergraduate students at an urban commuter university.' *Cogn Behav Ther.* 2008;37(1):14-25. doi: 10.1080/16506070701819524. PMID: 18365795.

19   Berking, M., Wupperman, P., Reichardt, A., Pejic, T., Dippel, A., & Znoj, H. (2008). 'Emotion-regulation skills as a treatment target in psychotherapy.' *Behaviour Research and Therapy*, 46(11), 1230-1237.

20   Richards, J. M., & Gross, J. J. (2000). Emotion regulation and memory: 'The cognitive costs of keeping one's cool.' *Journal of Personality and Social Psychology: Personality Processes and Individual Differences*, 79(3), 410-424. doi: http://dx.doi.org/10.1037/0022-3514.79.3.410

21   McCracken, L. M., Spertus, I. L., Janeck, A. S., Sinclair, D., & Wetzel, F. T. (1999). 'Behavioral dimensions of adjustment in persons with chronic pain: Pain-related anxiety and acceptance.' *Pain*, 80(1-2), 283-289. doi: http://dx.doi.org/10.1016/S0304-3959(98)00219-X

22 Marx, B. P., & Sloan, D. M. (2002). 'The role of emotion in the psychological functioning of adult survivors of childhood sexual abuse.' *Behavior Therapy*, 33(4), 563–577. https://doi.org/10.1016/S0005-7894(02)80017-X

23 Stafford-Brown J., & Pakenham K. I. 'The effectiveness of an ACT informed intervention for managing stress and improving therapist qualities in clinical psychology trainees.' *J Clin Psychol.* 2012 Jun;68(6):592-13. doi: 10.1002/jclp.21844. Epub 2012 May 4. PMID: 22566279.

24 Ibid.

25 Bond, F. W., & Bunce, D. (2000). 'Mediators of change in emotion-focused and problem-focused worksite stress management interventions.' *Journal of Occupational Health Psychology*, 5(1), 156–163. https://doi.org/10.1037/1076-8998.5.1.156

26 McKay, M., & West, A. (2016). *Emotional efficacy therapy: A brief, exposure-based treatment for emotion regulation integrating ACT and DBT.* Context Press/New Harbinger Publications.

27 Jeffcoat T., & Hayes S. C. 'A randomized trial of ACT bibliotherapy on the mental health of K-12 teachers and staff.' *Behav Res Ther.* 2012 Sep;50(9):571-9. doi: 10.1016/j.brat.2012.05.008. Epub 2012 Jun 9. PMID: 22750188.

28 Noone, S. J., & Hastings, R. P. 'Building psychological resilience in support staff caring for people with intellectual disabilities: pilot evaluation of an acceptance-based intervention.' *J Intellect Disabil.* 2009 Mar;13(1):43-53. doi: 10.1177/1744629509103519. PMID: 19332508.

29 Kashdan, T. B., Barrios, V., Forsyth, J. P., & Steger, M. F. 'Experiential avoidance as a generalized psychological vulnerability: comparisons with coping and emotion regulation strategies.' *Behav Res Ther.* 2006 Sep;44(9):1301-20. doi: 10.1016/j.brat.2005.10.003. PMID: 16321362.

30 Bayrami, M., Nosratabad, T., Esmaeilpour, K. & Shiri, A. (2021). 'Effectiveness of emotion efficacy therapy on internet dependency and negative cognitive emotion regulation strategies among students addicted to internet: a quasi-experimental design.' *Urmia Medical Journal.* 31, 927.

31 Bond, F. W., Lloyd, J., Flaxman, P. E., & Archer, R. (2016). Psychological flexibility and ACT at work. In R. D. Zettle, S. C. Hayes, D. Barnes-Holmes, & A. Biglan (Eds.), *The Wiley handbook of contextual behavioral science* (p. 459–482). Wiley Blackwell.

32   Gloster, A. T., Meyer, A. H., & Lieb, R. (2017). 'Psychological flexibility as a malleable public health target: Evidence from a representative sample.' *Journal of Contextual Behavioral Science, 6*(2), 166-171. https://doi.org/10.1016/j.jcbs.2017.02.003

33   Biglan A., Layton G. L., Jones L. B., Hankins M., Rusby J. C. 'The value of workshops on psychological flexibility for early childhood special education staff.' *Topics Early Child Spec Educ.* 2013 Feb 1;32(4):10.1177/0271121411425191. doi: 10.1177/0271121411425191. PMID: 24223451; PMCID: PMC3820423.

34   Ruiz, F. J., & Odriozola-González, P. (2017). 'The predictive and moderating role of psychological flexibility in the development of job burnout.' *Universitas Psychologica, 16*(4), 1–8. https://doi.org/10.11144/Javeriana.upsy16-4.pmrp

35   Bond, F. W., & Bunce, D. (2000). 'Mediators of change in emotion-focused and problem-focused worksite stress management interventions.' *Journal of Occupational Health Psychology, 5,* 156-163.

36   Jeffcoat, T., & Hayes, S. C. 'A randomized trial of ACT bibliotherapy on the mental health of K-12 teachers and staff.' *Behav Res Ther.* 2012 Sep;50(9):571-9. doi: 10.1016/j.brat.2012.05.008. Epub 2012 Jun 9. PMID: 22750188.

37   Bond, F. W., & Bunce, D. 'Mediators of change in emotion-focused and problem-focused worksite stress management interventions.' *J Occup Health Psychol.* 2000 Jan;5(1):156-63. doi: 10.1037//1076-8998.5.1.156. PMID: 10658893.

38   Kashdan, T. B., & Rottenberg, J. (2010). 'Psychological flexibility as a fundamental aspect of health.' *Clinical Psychology Review, 30*(7), 865–878. https://doi.org/10.1016/j.cpr.2010.03.001

39   Nicola W. Burton, Ken I. Pakenham & Wendy J. Brown (2010). 'Feasibility and effectiveness of psychosocial resilience training: A pilot study of the READY program.' *Psychology, Health & Medicine,* 15:3, 266-277, DOI: 10.1080/13548501003758710

40   Lee, F. K., Sheldon, K. M., & Turban, D. B. (2003). 'Personality and the goal-striving process: The influence of achievement goal patterns, goal level, and mental focus on performance and enjoyment.' *Journal of Applied Psychology, 88*(2), 256–265. https://doi.org/10.1037/0021-9010.88.2.256

02. INSIDE THE EMOTIONAL MATRIX

1   Hanson, R., & Mendius, R. (2009). *Buddha's brain: The practical neuroscience of happiness, love & wisdom*. Oakland, CA: New Harbinger Publications.

2   Kashdan, T. B., Barrios, V., Forsyth, J. P., & Steger, M. F. 'Experiential avoidance as a generalized psychological vulnerability: comparisons with coping and emotion regulation strategies.' *Behav Res Ther.* 2006 Sep;44(9):1301-20. doi: 10.1016/j.brat.2005.10.003. PMID: 16321362.

3   Goleman, D. (1995). *Emotional intelligence: Why it can matter more than IQ*. New York: Bantam Books.

4   https://en.wikipedia.org/wiki/List_of_cognitive_biases

5   Baumeister, R., Bratslavsky, E. & Finkenauer, C., & Vohs, K. (2001). 'Bad is stronger than good.' *Review of General Psychology* 5. 10.1037/1089-2680.5.4.323.

6   Bergeison, M. (Producer). (2010, September 22). 'The Science of Happiness' [Greater Good podcast]. Retrieved from https://greatergood.berkeley.edu/podcasts

7   Stanovich, K. & West, R. (2007). 'Natural myside bias is independent of cognitive ability.' *Thinking & Reasoning*, 13(3), 225-247, DOI: 10.1080/13546780600780796

8   Kahneman, D. (2011). *Thinking, fast and slow*. Farrar, Straus and Giroux, p. 86

9   Summers, J. (2017). 'Post hoc ergo propter hoc: some benefits of rationalization.' *Philosophical Explorations*, 20(sup1), 21–36. https://doi.org/10.1080/13869795.2017.1287292

10 Rimes, K. A., & Chalder, T. 'The Beliefs about Emotions Scale: validity, reliability and sensitivity to change.' *J Psychosom Res.* 2010 Mar;68(3):285-92. doi: 10.1016/j.jpsychores.2009.09.014. Epub 2009 Dec 9. PMID: 20159215.

11 De Castella, K., Platow, M. J., Tamir, M, & Gross, J. J. (2018) 'Beliefs about emotion: implications for avoidance-based emotion regulation and psychological health.' *Cognition and Emotion*, 32(4), 773-795, doi: 10.1080/02699931.2017.1353485.

12 Kashdan, T. B., & Biswas-Diener, R. (2014). *The Upside of Your Dark Side: Why being your whole self – not just your "good" self – drives success and fulfillment*. Plume.

13 Ibid.

03. DISRUPTING YOUR UNHELPFUL DEFAULT PATTERNS

1 Ibid.

2 Ibid.

3 Kleiman, E. M., & Riskind, J. H. (2012). 'Cognitive vulnerability to comorbidity: Looming cognitive style and depressive cognitive style as synergistic predictors of anxiety and depression symptoms.' *Journal of Behavior Therapy and Experimental Psychiatry,* 43(4), 1109–1114. https://doi.org/10.1016/j.jbtep.2012.05.008

4 Marx, B. P., & Sloan, D. M. (2002). 'The role of emotion in the psychological functioning of adult survivors of childhood sexual abuse.' *Behavior Therapy,* 33(4), 563–577. https://doi.org/10.1016/S0005-7894(02)80017-X

5 McCracken, L. M., Spertus, I. L., Janeck, A. S., Sinclair, D., & Wetzel, F. T. (1999). 'Behavioral dimensions of adjustment in persons with chronic pain: Pain-related anxiety and acceptance.' *Pain,* 80(1-2), 283–289. https://doi.org/10.1016/S0304-3959(98)00219-X

6 Richards, J. M., & Gross, J. J. (2000). 'Emotion regulation and memory: The cognitive costs of keeping one's cool.' *Journal of Personality and Social Psychology,* 79(3), 410–424. https://doi.org/10.1037/0022-3514.79.3.410

7 Schloss, H. M., & Haaga, D. A. (2011). 'Interrelating behavioral measures of distress tolerance with self-reported experiential avoidance.' *Journal of Rational-Emotive and Cognitive-Behavior Therapy: RET,* 29(1), 53–63. https://doi.org/10.1007/s10942-011-0127-3

8 Machell, K. A., Goodman, F. R., & Kashdan T. B. 'Experiential avoidance and well-being: a daily diary analysis.' *Cognition & Emotion.* 2015;29(2):351-359. doi: 10.1080/02699931.2014.911143.

9 Wersebe, H., Lieb, R., Meyer, A. H., Hofer, P., & Gloster, A. T. (2018). 'The link between stress, well-being, and psychological flexibility during an Acceptance and Commitment Therapy self-help intervention.' *International Journal of Clinical and Health Psychology: IJCHP,* 18(1), 60–68. https://doi.org/10.1016/j.ijchp.2017.09.002

10 McKay, M., & West, A. (2016). *Emotion efficacy therapy: A brief, exposure-based treatment for emotion regulation integrating ACT and DBT.* Context Press/New Harbinger Publications.

11 Shi, R., Zhang, S., Zhang, Q., Fu, S., & Wang, Z. (2016). 'Experiential avoidance mediates the association between emotion regulation abilities and loneliness.' *PloS One*, 11(12), e0168536. https://doi.org/10.1371/journal.pone.0168536

12 Ciarrochi, J., Kashdan, T. B., & Harris, R. (2013). 'The foundations of flourishing. In T. B. Kashdan & J. Ciarrochi (Eds.).' The Context Press mindfulness and acceptance practica series. *Mindfulness, acceptance, and positive psychology: The seven foundations of well-being* (p. 1–29). New Harbinger Publications, Inc.

13 Tryon, W. W. (2005). 'Possible mechanisms for why desensitization and exposure therapy work.' *Clinical Psychology Review*, 25(1), 67-95.

14 Hayes, S. C. (2004). Acceptance and Commitment Therapy and the new behavior therapies: Mindfulness, acceptance and relationship. In S. C. Hayes, V. M. Follette, & M. Linehan (Eds.), *Mindfulness and acceptance: Expanding the cognitive behavioral tradition* (pp. 1-29). New York: Guilford.

15 Persons, J. B., & Miranda, J. 'Cognitive theories of vulnerability to depression: Reconciling negative evidence.' *Cogn Ther Res* 16, 485–502 (1992). https://doi.org/10.1007/BF01183170

16 Ibid.

17 Szymanski, J., & O'Donohue, W. (1995). Fear of Spiders Questionnaire. *Journal of Behavior Therapy and Experimental Psychiatry*, 26(1), 31–34. https://doi.org/10.1016/0005-7916(94)00072-t

18 Kolb, B., & Gibb, R. (2008). Principles of neuroplasticity and behavior. In D. T. Stuss, G. Winocur, & I. H. Robertson (Eds.), *Cognitive neurorehabilitation: Evidence and application* (p. 6–21). Cambridge University Press. https://doi.org/10.1017/CBO9781316529898.003

19 Craske, M. G., Treanor, M., Conway, C. C., Zbozinek, T., & Vervliet, B. (2014). 'Maximizing exposure therapy: an inhibitory learning approach.' *Behaviour Research and Therapy*, 58, 10–23. https://doi.org/10.1016/j.brat.2014.04.006

04. GETTING EMOTIONALLY 'WOKE'

1 Kircanski, K., Lieberman, M. D., & Craske, M. G. (2012). 'Feelings into words: contributions of language to exposure therapy.' *Psychological Science*, 20(10) 1-6.

2   Bechara, A., Damasio, H, & Damasio, A. R., 'Emotion, decision making and the orbitofrontal cortex.' *Cerebral Cortex*, 10(3), 295–307, https://doi.org/10.1093/cercor/10.3.295.

3   Kahneman, D. (2011). *Thinking, fast and slow.* Farrar, Straus and Giroux, p. 51

05. THE ART OF EMOTION SURFING

1   Craske, M. G., Treanor, M., Conway, C. C., Zbozinek, T., & Vervliet, B. (2014). 'Maximizing exposure therapy: an inhibitory learning approach.' *Behaviour Research and Therapy*, 58, 10–23. https://doi.org/10.1016/j.brat.2014.04.006

2   Kashdan, T. (2009). *Curious? Discover the missing ingredient to a fulfilling life.* William Morrow & Co.

3   Kashdan, T. B., & Silvia, P. J. (2009). Curiosity and interest: The benefits of thriving on novelty and challenge. In S. J. Lopez & C. R. Snyder (Eds.), Oxford library of psychology. *Oxford handbook of positive psychology* (p. 367–374). Oxford University Press.

4   Kashdan, T. (2009). *Curious? Discover the missing ingredient to a fulfilling life.* William Morrow & Co.

5   K. Baclawski, The observer effect, 2018 IEEE Conference on Cognitive and Computational Aspects of Situation Management (CogSIMA), Boston, MA, 2018, pp. 83-89, doi: 10.1109/COGSIMA.2018.8423983.

6   Galante, J., Dufour, G., Vainre, M., Wagner, A. P., Stochl, J., Benton, A., Lathia, N., Howarth, E., & Jones, P. B. (2018). 'A mindfulness-based intervention to increase resilience to stress in university students (the Mindful Student Study): a pragmatic randomised controlled trial.' *The Lancet.* Public health, 3(2), e72–e81. https://doi.org/10.1016/S2468-2667(17)30231-1.

7   Bolte-Taylor, J. (2021, May 26). The 90 second life cycle of an emotion. Interview by WUSA9.com.

06. KEEP CALM AND VALUE ON

1   Adler, A. & Seligman, M. E. P. (2016). 'Using wellbeing for public policy: Theory, measurement, and recommendations.' *International Journal of Wellbeing*, 6(1), 1–35. doi:10.5502/ijw.v6i1.1.

2   Cohen, K., & Cairns, D. (2012). 'Is searching for meaning in life associated with reduced subjective well-being? Confirmation and possible moderators.' *Journal of Happiness Studies*, 13(2), 313-331. https://doi.org/10.1007/s10902-011-9265-7.

3   Steger, M., & Kashdan, T. (2013), 'The unbearable lightness of meaning: Well-being and unstable meaning in life.' *The Journal of Positive Psychology*, 8:2, 103-115, DOI: 10.1080/17439760.2013.771208.

4   Ibid.

07. THE POWER OF PERSPECTIVE-TAKING

1   Kahneman, D. (2011). *Thinking, fast and slow*. Farrar, Straus and Giroux, p. 86.

2   Dahl, M (2015, July 21). 'If Daniel Kahneman had a magic wand he'd rid the human race of overconfidence.' *New York Magazine*.

3   Elliot, A., & Devine, P. (1994). 'On the motivational nature of cognitive dissonance: Dissonance as psychological discomfort.' *Journal of Personality and Social Psychology*. 67. 382-394. 10.1037/0022-3514.67.3.382.

4   Taken from https://www.goodreads.com/ quotes/7344287-expectations-are-resentments-waiting-to-happen.

08. REGULATING THROUGH RELAXATION

1   Manzoni, G. M., Pagnini, F., Castelnuovo, G. et al. 'Relaxation training for anxiety: a ten-years systematic review with meta-analysis.' *BMC Psychiatry*. 8, 41 (2008). https://doi.org/10.1186/1471-244X-8-41

2   Barrett, L. F. (2017). *How emotions are made: The secret life of the brain*. Houghton Mifflin Harcourt, p. 30.

3   Taken from https://www.mayoclinic.org/healthy-lifestyle/ stress-management/in-depth/relaxation-technique/art-20045368.

4   Ma, X., Yue, Z. Q., Gong, Z. Q., Zhang, H., Duan, N. Y., Shi, Y. T., Wei, G. X., & Li, Y. F. (2017). 'The effect of diaphragmatic breathing on attention, negative affect and stress in healthy adults.' *Frontiers in Psychology*, 8, 874. https://doi.org/10.3389/fpsyg.2017.00874.

09. SHIFTING EMOTION THROUGH ATTENTION-SHIFTING

1   Ibid.

2   Johnson, D. R. (2009). 'Emotional attention set-shifting and its relationship to anxiety and emotion regulation.' *Emotion*, 9(5), 681–690. https://doi.org/10.1037/a0017095.

3   Ibid.

4   McKay, M., & West, A. (2016). *Emotion efficacy therapy: A brief, exposure-based treatment for emotion regulation integrating ACT and DBT.* Context Press/New Harbinger Publications.

10. PLAYING INFINITE GAMES

1   Carse, J. (1986). *Finite and infinite games: A vision of life as play and possibility.* Free Press.

2   Bennis, W. G., & Nanus, B. (1985). *Leaders: The strategies for taking charge.* New York: Harper & Row.

3   Cumming, J., & Williams, S. E. (2012). The role of imagery in performance. In S. M. Murphy (Ed.), Oxford library of psychology. *The Oxford Handbook of Sport and Performance Psychology* (p. 213–232). Oxford University Press. https://doi.org/10.1093/oxfor dhb/9780199731763.013.0011.

4   Singer, R. N., Cauraugh, J. H., Tennant, L. K., Murphey, M., et al. (1991). 'Attention and distractors: Considerations for enhancing sport performances.' *International Journal of Sport Psychology*, 22(2), 95–114.

Printed in Great Britain
by Amazon